N🚫B. S.
MARKETING TO
THE AFFLUENT

SECOND EDITION

BY

DAN S. KENNEDY

WITH

Nick Nanton, J.W. Dicks and Team,
The Dicks + Nanton Celebrity Branding Agency

FOREWORD BY

Joe Vitale, bestselling author of **The Attractor Factor**

Ep
Entrepreneur
PRESS®

Publisher: Entrepreneur Press
Cover Design: Andrew Welyczko
Production and Composition: Eliot House Productions

This publication is designed to provide accurate and authoritative information in regard to the subject matter covered. It is sold with the understanding that the publisher is not engaged in rendering legal, accounting or other professional services. If legal advice or other expert assistance is required, the services of a competent professional person should be sought.

Library of Congress Cataloging-in-Publication Data
Kennedy, Dan S., 1954–
    No B.S. marketing to the affluent: the ultimate, no holds barred, take no prisoners guide to getting really rich/by Dan S. Kennedy; contributions by Nick Nanton.—[Second edition].
      pages cm
    ISBN-13: 978-1-59918-536-1 (paperback)
    ISBN-10: 1-59918-536-9 (paperback)
    1. Affluent consumers—United States. 2. Marketing—United States.
I. Title.
HF5415.332.A34K46 2015
658.8—dc23   2014044649

Printed in the United States of America

20 19 18 17 16   10 9 8 7 6 5 4 3 2

Contents

BOOK THREE

HOW CAN I GET THEM TO GIVE ME THEIR MONEY?

BOOK FOUR

FIELD TRIPS, DEMONSTRATIONS, AND A CASE HISTORY

How to Easily Attract
the Affluent

By Joe Vitale

I was homeless 30 years ago. No job, no home, no car, no nothing. I struggled in virtual poverty for a decade after that. As I worked on my business and my self, I became an internet celebrity, a movie star, and the author of numerous best-selling books. All of this brought me increased wealth. I'm in the kindergarten category of knowing true affluence, but after paying off my debt, here's some of what I've done with my money:

- bought two exotic handmade limited edition, luxury sports cars, including one previously owned by a rock star (Steven Tyler of Aerosmith) who autographed the engine;

- bought two of the rarest guitars ever known, including one hand carved out of Hawaiian koa wood by one of the greatest luthiers on the planet (Robert Taylor);
- paid for professional auto racing instruction, which allowed me to roar around the Atlanta-Sebring racetrack in a fire suit and a helmet (and paid for a friend to attend with me); and
- given a staggering amount of money to the mother of a little boy who needed a special machine to help him recover from a pediatric stroke (a boy and a mother I've yet to meet in person).

I'm not bragging or showing how frivolous I am. I can easily justify my expenses and even deduct them from my taxes. The truly affluent do far more than this, of course. They have private jets, more than one mansion, and servants to cook for them and their pets, and they spend money on diamond-enhanced cell phones.

But I'm making a point here. I'm declaring that the affluent spend money on two things. Two things that you can provide.

What are they?

Experience and Exclusivity.

As I wrote in my book on circus promoter P.T. Barnum, *There's a Customer Born Every Minute,* people will spend almost any amount of money on something, anything, that will change their internal state. They want to feel something. Provide it, and get rich.

People also want to feel they are unique. If they can buy that uniqueness, they will. Owning something you've made—say, a collectible version of whatever you sell that few others have—is one way to accomplish this sense of individuality.

There's more, of course. That's where Dan Kennedy comes in.

Dan's book is the first one to reveal the direct route to the affluent's bank vault. He shows you how to open it and withdraw bags of loot, legally and joyfully. He talks about Experience and Exclusivity and a whole lot more. His branded No B.S. approach is a simple paint-by-the-number system for getting more than your fair share of the wealth the affluent are willing and even eager to spend.

Dan is a genius at marketing, a copywriting legend, my all-time favorite marketing author, and glaringly brilliant at teaching you to think differently about your marketing efforts. He shows you how to get one thing: results.

To begin, stop thinking there are any limitations to becoming affluent yourself, and start reading this book. You'll then start to attract the affluent—and their money.

Go for it!

JOE VITALE, star of the movie *The Secret* and outrageous internet marketing celebrity, is the author of way too many books to list here but include *Buying Trances, Hypnotic Writing, The Attractor Factor,* and *The Key.* His main website is www.JoeVitale.com.

BOOK ONE

Who Are These People
Who Have All the Money?

Understanding
Mass-Affluent, Affluent, and
Ultra-Affluent Buyers

BOOK ONE

CHAPTER 1

Why You MUST Move—Now

"*Middle class—we thought we should keep one.*"

P rophecy fulfilled.

It wasn't a difficult prophecy. In 2007, I first showed, publicly, the "new economy pyramid," in the first edition of *No B.S. Ruthless Management of People and Profits* (now in a new second edition). A few years before then, I began describing it to private clients and talking about it in closed-door mastermind meetings and seminars. I forecast a literal genocide of the American middle class. And I meant genocide, for I view a lot of it as intentional, deliberate, and orchestrated by political and certain corporate interests. But with or without that, the evolutionary disappearance of the middle class was certain. This was not difficult to foresee. The writing was on the wall, in big letters and numbers, in blood red ink. Many refused, and refuse, to see it. There are denialists—in government, in media, on Wall Street. There are the ignorant, eyes wide shut. But I saw everything there was to see and made my dire prediction. Here it is, in the same visual:

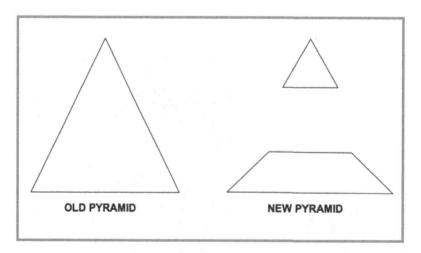

OLD PYRAMID   NEW PYRAMID

This prophecy has come to pass, but it is not yet done. There is a lot more carnage to come.

This book offers a solution. A plan to rescue your business from this disaster. A pathway out of the disaster zone.

To move you from curiosity and from half-hearted, tentative action on the advice and strategies in this book to whole-hearted, passionate, courageous, aggressive, and urgent action, I want to take a few minutes and summarize the facts of this genocide, provide some evidence of its impact so far, and try to paint a vivid picture in your mind of this as a present and accelerating reality.

We can begin with a few statistics. These are compiled from various authoritative sources. I have not footnoted each fact separately, but I have listed many of the sources at the end of this chapter.

How Bad Is It? How Bad Will It Get?

Beginning in the recession triggered in 2007–2008, through 2013, with the damage accelerating and peaking during the Obama years, median U.S. household net worth plummeted by 43%. This manifested in many ways. Upside-down home mortgages the most visible. Declining 401(k) and other retirement savings accounts clearest to many. In these and many other ways, wealth—and with it the ability to buy things for years, even decades to come—*erased*. This damage at the top of the economic pyramid, while harsh, was and is far from devastating. If you have $10 million and lose 43% of it, you still have $5.7 million. It didn't and doesn't matter much to the bottom of the pyramid. If you have zero and lose 43%, you still have zero. But in the middle, it murdered and is a murderer. There it forcibly moves a middle class consumer to a low class consumer. There it changes a frequent discretionary spender into a buyer only of essential commodities. As it slaughters those in the middle, it sucks the very life right out of the economy.

More important, these lost years of lost wealth and spending capability will never be recovered from by these slaughtered middle income consumers, so, in your own business lifetime, you will *not* see a rebound of their spending. To add insult to injury, generational replacement spending by millennials is defying historic trends, is at a minimum, and is concentrated into few categories. Where are the first-time home buyers, home furnishings buyers, new insurance customers, etc., etc.? Buried under college debt, in their parents' basements.

In these years, there has been a drop in net worth in almost all income categories, from the top 5% to the near bottom. Only the bottom 25th percentile saw an increase—but that is deceptive because in calculating, the government counts the earned income tax credit and food stamps as income, and Mr. Obama has been the food stamp president. But there are profound differences in how people in different income categories react and can react to net worth losses.

Toward the top, most high earners have options for amping up their earnings to replace net worth losses. The high six-figure income professional can raise fees, take on more clients or patients, maybe cut overhead or staff. He has a great deal of control. My own earning capability has a dial like a thermostat on it, that I can adjust by my own hand. I always have options: writing three books in a year instead of two, accepting a few more speaking engagements I now turn down, promoting more and attracting more clients. Some top income earners have reacted that way. Others have not—but don't need to—and their discretionary spending capability and willingness still remains intact. They have ample money.

Toward the bottom, they trade down in price. There's been a bleed from Walmart to "dollar stores," for example, handing Walmart consecutive quarters of declines in revenue and profit, and pushing dollar stores' revenues and profits up, as I write this. These consumers cut where they can. They may add a low-wage job to the household. They file bankruptcy in large numbers, expunge accumulated debt, and start over with some restored spending ability. But by and large, their total spending contribution to us marketers and to the economy as a whole varies only a little, because in bad or good times, they are still spending nearly all their income on essentials, holding nothing back, neither saving or investing.

It is in the middle where stagnated and falling wages, loss of one of two jobs in the household, and very recently, cutting of hours—in part, result of Obamacare threats, uncertainties and realities—have its most savage effects. The median income, in the 50th percentile, went from $98,872.00 in 2007 to $70,801.00 in 2009 to $56,335.00 in 2013. Take $40,000.00 out of a $90,000.00 household income and watch everything that happens. That has to happen.

No surprise that home ownership has dropped to a two-decade low, real estate values have not recovered, the real estate market is poor in all but a handful of places, real estate agents' incomes have dropped, the population of active agents shrunk, and the mortgage broker and agent industry a sad shadow of its former self. No surprise that roughly one-third of middle-class households have fallen out of that category and can't get up.

The tricky combination in play of simultaneous, categorized deflation and inflation wreaks greatest havoc right here in the middle, too. Health insurance premiums are rising from 2014 to 2015 by 15% to 35%. Anecdotally, I just heard from a middle class friend of the arrival of his 30% increase letter. At the top, it gets a shrug. At the bottom, they can't pay for it anyway. In the middle though, where the income has plummeted from $90,000.00 to $40,000.00, an increase in a mandatory expense of $900.00 to $1,500.00 a year puts a hurt on them and on anyone but an insurer marketing to them.

In short, not only is the middle class consumer population shrinking, with far more falling down than climbing up, but the remaining population there has shrinking buying power and must use more and more of its buying power in fewer and fewer categories. Probably excluding you and what you sell.

The middle class' economic activity has always been what makes and keeps the rich folks rich and growing ever richer and what creates uplifting opportunity for the bottom levels to move up. Small business provides most jobs and most low-skill, entry-level jobs, but most small businesses are started, grown, and owned by middle-class people, now severely retarded in their ability to start or grow such businesses. The year 2013 was the first in two decades with a decline in the number of new businesses started. Middle-class consumer spending is what created and sustains suburbs, shopping malls, and the huge and wide middle of every business category: retail, restaurants, service providers. Temporarily, some of these categories can appear as healthy as ever by simply raising prices on fewer numbers of die-hard middle class consumers. Movie industry revenues are up even as movie theater attendance has fallen and is falling. But this is the "failing condominium tower strategy": five move out, raise monthly dues on the remaining 50. Five more leave, raise dues again. Eventually, there's one sod left with a monthly service fee of $50,000.00.

The September 17, 2014, issue of *The Wall Street Journal* included a report headlined: "Incomes End a 6-Year Decline, Just Barely." Any good news is welcome. But popping champagne corks or even beer can tabs is *not* called for!

There is a different statistic, far more telling than incomes or unemployment numbers, and far more predictive of future calamity: workforce participation. As of late 2014, fewer than 50% of adults capable of working were working full time. In *The Wall Street Journal*, the astute Mort Zuckerman called "the lack of breadwinners working full time a burgeoning disaster." This is a *trend*, not an incidental fact. Further, this too is concentrated in the shrinking middle class. The question is, of course, *will this trend reverse? If so, when?*

No. It won't. Probably ever, but certainly not soon enough for you to bank on it for your business' prosperity. You have to forget it. There are many underlying facts and trends guaranteeing this I won't take time for here. Automation, technology, the Amazon factor, a political determination to "transform" America into a socialist republic, deliberate retardation of blue-collar job-creating industries for ideological reasons, and many more. I predict workforce participation to find its way from just below 50%, where it is late 2014, to below 40% by 2018. Maybe to 35% by 2025. People are going to get all the leisure time they can handle—but most won't be able to afford to do anything with it!

Now, a few canary-in-the-coal mine demonstrations of the damage done by the damaged and diminished middle class:

- In September, 2014, the TGIF restaurant chain announced it was getting out of the restaurant business! It seeks to sell all 260+ of its company-owned and -operated locations to independent franchisees, some of whom will make it, some of whom will not. Why? The company stated several strategic reasons, dancing around the fact that the mid-level, casual dining restaurant business chain linked to middle-class consumers has become a terrible business and can only be forecast to become an even less profitable, more price competitive, and more difficult business in the future. This mirrors the severe, widely reported troubles at Darden Restaurants, sparking their bargain-priced sale, i.e., dumping of Red Lobster. There are many other mid-tier chains in trouble, in Chapter 11 bankruptcy.

- Quoting from *The Kiplinger Letter: Forecasts for Executives and Investors*, mid-2014, this succinct summary: "Troubles mount for mid-tier retail chains . . . . Sears®, Penney's®, etc. Their core customer base is deserting them. As retirement looms and households shrink for middle-income baby boomers, that group is cutting back on spending, and younger shoppers are opting to buy from discounters or from upscale stores. Many stores WILL disappear and some chains aren't likely to survive. That also spells bad news for both mall owners and other tenants in malls. About 15% of malls will disappear within the decade. In others, rents will drop . . . "

- Finally, the direct-selling industry has long been a favored canary-in-the-coal-mine scenario I watch carefully. The successful and established direct-selling companies like Tupperware® and the established MLM's like Shaklee® and Amway® are evermore investing overseas and growing in countries with growing middle classes, and evermore avoiding investment and seeing shrinkage in the United States.

I could cite a number of additional facts and trends and canary-in-coal-mine examples, all supporting the same very gloomy forecast for a long, cold winter for our middle class and its consumerism.

What Does All this COMMAND YOU to Do?

There are two considerations that should govern your strategy, dictate where you sell, who you sell to. One is Comparative ABILITY to Buy. The other is Comparative WILLINGNESS to Buy. Nothing else matters more.

Consider three households—the Joneses, with low-wage jobs, combined putting just $30,000.00 a year into the coffers; the Smiths, with one at a good paying job, the other at a low-wage job, combined $65,000.00 a year; and the Barons, who own a very profitable business from which they each draw a good salary and bonuses, and who have significant investment income, totaling $300,000.00 a year. All three households include two kids.

What is the same about all three?

The *amount of* money they have to spend on necessities. It goes up a little from Jones to Smith to Baron by choice. Ground beef, steak from the grocery store, premium steak ordered from and delivered by Omaha Steaks. But basically, all three families' necessities are virtually identical. The Joneses and the Barons need the same amount of toilet paper, use the same amount of water and electricity, have to insure their cars, feed themselves and their kids, pay doctor bills, and so on. Again, by choice of premium quality, or by having three cars instead of one, the amount spent may vary, but it won't vary proportionately. The Baron household won't spend ten times what the Jones household spends on necessities.

That means that the *percentage of* income spent on necessities varies a whole lot. Allow for the increase in amount spent for premium choices, more, and bigger, and say that the household's basic and essential needs can be met for $25,000.00 a year, so that's what the Joneses spend, the Smiths spend 50% more—$37,500.00, and the Barons splurge, spending twice that—$75,000.00. Some do, some don't, by the way. Look at this in percentage of income terms . . .

The Joneses spend 85% of their income on basic and essential necessities. There are few choices in this spending. The grocery cart will feature low-cost "fill 'em up" food. Brand loyalty supplanted by coupons and sales. The trip to Walmart, pretty predictable. They have only 15% of income left free to spend flexibly on home improvements, on entertainment, on recreation, on elective health care, etc., and to save or invest, as long as nothing goes wrong. They have only $4,500.00 for all these choices for the entire year. $375.00 a month. One car water pump blown, one furnace repair, one kid toppled out of tree and taken to the emergency room, and a month's, maybe two months', discretionary spending ability is erased. The Joneses that I've described are actually in better shape than most at the low wage bottom of our economic pyramid. Most spend 100%, 110%, 120% of their income just on necessities. They are in debt, stay in debt, get deeper in debt. This is why the payday loan business exists.

The Smiths spend less of their income on the same necessities. The Jones spend 85% of income, the Smiths 58% of income. The Smiths have a wider margin for error and for extra choice spending. They can be sold an expensive night out at the ballgame, a Disney® vacation, new school clothes for both kids. With financing, a new car, even a kitchen remodel. In dollars, they have $27,500.00 a year to use this way. Nearly as much in discretionary spending ability as the Jones' entire income—$2,291.00 a month of flexible spending, saving, and investing power. A blown water pump, a broken furnace, an emergency room bill for Tommy may take a bite, but there's quite a bit left afterward. Also, should the Smiths choose to live beyond their income—a blessed thing for us marketers—they can get a lot more credit than the Joneses, and they can service a lot more consumer debt.

Now, the Barons. They only spend 25% of their income covering the same basic and essential necessities that take 58% of the Smiths' income and 85% of the Joneses' income. Just 25%—75 cents of every dollar stays loose. No locked-in commitments. In dollars, the Barons have $225,000.00 to spend, save, or invest flexibly. If they wisely split that in half, they can plow $112,000.00 a year into tax-deferred retirement savings plans like 401(k)s, into stocks and bonds, into real estate. So that in less than ten years; about seven years, and every seven years, they accumulate $1 million. By comparison, the Smiths can save or invest very little. The Joneses, zero. And even if the Barons act that responsibly, they still have $112,000.00 left over to buy all sorts of unnecessary goods and services and gifts and trips. A big, fat $9,333.00 a month. Should the Barons choose to throw all sane behavior to the wind and live beyond their means—a blessed thing for us marketers—they have the ability to get a whale of a lot more credit and service it than the Smiths.

In big-thumb terms, the Joneses can handle almost no debt service, and are likely maxed out with their debt. The Smiths can handle about $200,000.00 of consumer debt, tops. But the Barons can handle $1 million of debt.

Simply put, if your customers are low-wage or middle-wage earners, the Joneses or the Smiths, you are in very serious trouble—and it's going to get a lot worse before it gets better, if it ever gets better. Think of these customer populations as a place. You live or have your business in this place. Once, it was a nice neighborhood with well-kept homes, safe streets, salt-of-the-earth people. Gradually, it changed. Homes declined in value, got bought up by landlords, more renters, fewer homeowners. Soon drug dealers on corners. Unsafe streets. Such decay rarely reverses.

You *have to* get out.

You can.

Where to go?

While the middle class collapse has been picking up speed, the affluent population has steadied, proved resilient and reliable, and even grown. From 2011 to 2013, the number of U.S. households with incomes exceeding $100,000.00 grew by 6%. Better, the average household income among these affluents also grew by 5%. Net worth also increased by 2%, to an average $1.1 million. The RBC's big, annual Wealth Report, released in June 2014, stated that the number of high-net-worth households with multimillion-dollar net worth rose by 11% from 2011 to 2012, and rose again by another 16% from 2012 to 2013. The wealth of those households rose as well, maybe only nominally, but a 2% boost to $5 million is not chump change. Throughout the top 5% of the pyramid, there is a growing number of customers to sell to, and they have growing spending capability.

Comparative Willingness to Buy

Now, consider Comparative WILLINGNESS to Buy. Obviously, ability links to willingness. But there is a broader optimism vs. pessimism. A Gallup Poll in late 2014 showed 56% of Americans saying the economy is continuing to get worse—only 39% said it is getting better. An NBC News poll had a whopping 70% saying the economy is headed in the wrong direction. Within these numbers, there are biases by bottom, middle, or top of the pyramid. Polling not widely reported, conducted by both political parties' pollsters, showed that, among low-wage workers, 40% classified themselves as optimistic that the economy and/or their own financial picture was improving or would soon improve. Among the top 5% income earners, over 75% cited optimism about the economy in general and/or their own financial futures. Among middle-class-income earners—ready?—only about 25% spoke of the same optimism.

Optimism about the economy and about one's personal economy favors marketers. Pessimism about these things stands solidly in the way.

Here's a bit of proof that this optimism differential is driving spending. North American luxury purchasing grew by 7% in 2013. Mercedes' sales leapt 13%. Upscale fashion merchant Michael Kors reported 2013 revenues beating 2012's by over 35%, and has 96 new stores planned—half in the United States.

There *is* a very nice neighborhood to move your business into, where you can be welcomed by a growing number of optimistic consumers with fat, open wallets. It is the affluent consumer population.

This book is the road map. It gives you the insight, information, inspiration, and practical how-to directions for moving from selling to Joneses or Smiths to Barons and even Big Barons. For many, this is admittedly far from a simple thing. You don't just flip a switch. Your own thinking and attitudes and self-image may need a lot of recalibration. You'll need vision and courage. Your positioning, your products or services, your price strategies, your marketing and selling process, your salespeople may have to change. But I'm here to argue this is no longer a choice. The luxury of time to procrastinate about this is gone. Death is imminent for huge numbers of businesses refusing to move up the consumer income and net worth pyramid. You must now aggressively adapt. Or die.

My friend, the late, great Zig Ziglar, often told the "cooked in the squat" story: a frog thrown into a pot of boiling hot water will immediately leap right back out. But a frog placed in a pan of pleasingly cool water will stay put. He will continue to stay put as the heat is ever so slowly inched up, until the dumb frog is cooked in the squat. That's what has happened to many small-business operators as well as big retail and restaurant chains and entire categories of business. The fundamental, adverse economic trends have worsened slowly, gradually, and these business owners have sat there, getting cooked in the squat. They are very near the boiling point. On the precipice of death. Some know and are perplexed. Others know and are blundering around trying to cool the water by blowing on it. Others are surrendering. CEOs running out the clock on their own careers, retiring, taking golden parachute treasure, and slinking away into the night.

Don't emulate any of these dumb frogs.

Use your big, long legs.

Now.

Sources for above information include: *RBC Wealth Report 2014*; *Panel Study of Income Dynamics–Sage Foundation*; Gallup; NBC News; *The Wall Street Journal*; *The New Class Conflict* by Joel Kotkin (book); Dent Research.com; *The Kiplinger Letter*–Kiplinger.com; *The New York Times*, "How the Recession Reshaped the Economy (A Shrinking, Shifting Middle Class)," 6–15–14; U.S. Government research from Census and other sources; and GKIC publications: *No B.S. Marketing Letter* and *No B.S. Marketing to the Affluent Letter*, www.GKIC.com.

Special Offer Notice: Next Steps

There is no need to wait until you complete this book to take additional, next steps forward, getting assistance from Dan Kennedy in your upward marketing to the affluent and more effective marketing overall. **Page 393** presents a Free Trial Offer for GKIC™ Membership featuring the business newsletters, online resources, and tools created by Dan Kennedy or based on his methods. You will also be invited to hands-on Implementation Boot Camps.

CHAPTER 2

Who ARE These
People, Anyway?

"With money in your pocket you are wise,
you are handsome, and you
sing well, too."

—YIDDISH PROVERB

I have always wondered about the monkeys on monkey islands in our zoos. As we stand there looking at them, amused at their funny expressions and antics, are they entertained by looking at us in our funny clothes? Are the monkeys asking themselves, *Who* are *these goofy creatures, anyway?* I do know, from numerous conversations with my clients, that the rich are strange and odd and incomprehensible, that figuring out what motivates their behavior is as difficult as figuring out why the monkeys act as they do. While we'll never need to decipher the monkeys' thoughts and acts, we do need to decode the rich.

We can begin by organizing the population itself. Throughout this book, I'm going to subdivide the affluent population many different ways:

- Ultra-Affluent
- Affluent
- Mass-Affluent

. . . and specialty market groups, like

- Affluent Boomers and Mass-Affluent Boomers
- Affluent Gays and Lesbians
- Affluent Entrepreneurs and Business Owners

. . . and then by gender, women and men.

These divided groups meet, converge, and also act separately. It is up to you to ultimately develop your own carefully defined target group within the affluent population that is ideally matched with your products, services, even your own personality.

Let's begin with some basic definitions.

- *Mass-Affluent.* Household incomes of $85,000.00 to $150,000.00 and/or net worth exceeding $250,000.00. When I wrote the first edition of this book in 2009, this was the fastest growth segment of the entire consumer market in the United States. How fast things have changed! As described in Chapter 1, the story of The Middle's mass-affluence was written in disappearing ink. Today, the dynamic, explosive growth of this buyer population is occurring in a number of other countries, even as it is in regression here. Still, there is a remaining sliver, and those moving up into this economic place, and they are younger and more ethnically and demographically diverse than any previous mass-affluent population in history. They include families with young children; single-parent households; blue-collar, not just white-collar employees, as well as small-business owners. Consumers who five or ten years ago would have been J.C. Penney shoppers now make some purchases *down* at

Walmart, some at the middle at Penney's, and Kohls, and many *up* at Saks and Neiman-Marcus. And a lot bypassing the entire traditional shopping tier, instead using Amazon. There is obviously money moving about here, but there is also weakness, fragility, and therefore hazard for merchants and marketers depending on these consumers.

- *Affluent.*Those with household incomes of $150,000.00 to $250,000.00 and/or net worth, including primary and additional residence equity, exceeding $1 million. In short, millionaires. As many millionaires bemoan, being a millionaire ain't what it used to be! The status of millionaire, once rarified, is now mainstream. We've had a two-decade millionaire explosion in America, and a similar explosion is now occurring in a number of other countries. America is definitely not done with this. In fact, 2013 was a record year for swelling of the millionaire population in the U.S., with China in second place.

  It is within the Mass-Affluent in move-up mode and the Affluent categories that we find what some demographers have taken to calling "middle-class millionaires"; they are of a very particular mindset, which we'll be talking about at length.

- *Ultra-Affluent.* Those with household incomes of $250,000.00 up and/or net worth of $3 million to $10 million. Here we find the wealthiest 10% of U.S. households as defined by net worth. Their average net worth is $2.5 million to $3.5 million, and average annual income is $250,000.00. They earn 40% of all U.S. income and control 70% of the U.S. net worth. As a group, these 10 million households hold 90% of the value of all publicly traded stocks and mutual funds in the United States. (Statistics are approximate and rounded, based on Federal Reserve, Census, and privately compiled information.)

- *Ultra-Ultra-Affluent.* Household incomes of $1 million and up and/or net worth starting above $10 million but more commonly in the $20 million to $50 million range. Private jet owners* fit nicely here—they have average yearly incomes of $9 million plus net worth in excess of $50 million. Average age 57, 70% men. Each year they report spending $30,000.00 on wine and alcoholic beverages, $150,000.00 at hotels and resorts, $115,000.00 on clothes and accessories, $250,000.00 on jewelry, and $500,000.00 on home improvements and furnishings, and they have at least two residences. As a practical matter, their spending power is unlimited. Their ranks include Fortune 1000 CEOs, Hollywood celebrities and executives, and professional athletes, but more than half are not famous or in exotic occupations or businesses but are, instead, "the millionaire next door" who has moved up. Many have built up and sold businesses or taken their businesses public, creating lump-sum wealth.

- *Affluent Boomers.* You'll find a chapter devoted exclusively to this, pardon pun, booming group actively exploring and even inventing an entirely new approach to retirement and Act 3 and Act 4 of life—and funding it with an unprecedented amount of spending power. The comprehensive resource on this is a separate book, *No B.S. Guide to Marketing to Leading-Edge Boomers and Seniors.* A related book is *No B.S. Guide to Trust-Based Marketing.*

These groups, and other affluent groups, offer an opportunity to marketers as unprecedented as is their prosperity, spending power, and attitudes about spending. In the chapters to come, you will see this new world of opportunity revealed.

---

*Based on studies reported at www.MarketWatch.com and privately compiled information.

CHAPTER 3

The Ultra-Rich:
Different From You And Me

F. Scott Fitzgerald: "The very rich are different from you and me."

Ernest Hemingway: "Yes, they have more money."

—DOCUMENTED EXCHANGE BETWEEN THE FAMOUS AUTHORS,

FROM *MARK MY WORDS*, COMPILED BY NIGEL REES

We are endlessly fascinated with the strange ultra-rich. Fitzgerald's novel of 1925 *The Great Gatsby* was made into a movie starring Leonardo DiCaprio as the enigmatic Gatsby just a few years ago. For years, a popular TV show was *Lifestyles of the Rich and Famous*. Today's cable networks are well populated with "reality" shows featuring the homes and "cribs," cars and lives of the super-wealthy.

Recently, a client of mine, a niche gun manufacturer, told me about a guy contacting him directly, identifying himself as a huge fan of a particular gun—the Hand Cannon (www. BondArms.com)—which sells for $400.00 to $1,200.00. The fellow bought half a dozen, had them delivered to his engraver, and spent over $5,000.00 having each one custom engraved for family members and friends. The customer has, for years, been a member of the Forbes 400. But there are a whole lot more than 400 of these ultra-rich, price-no-object consumers. More like 3 million, with another 10 million or so just a step or two beneath them, striving to climb up and often spending as if already there.

The Forbes 400 list, compiled and published annually by *Forbes* magazine, is a microcosmic look at the ultra-rich. In 2007, the first year that admission required a net worth of at least a billion dollars, many former multimillionaires dropped from the list. In the book *All the Money in the World,* authors and researchers Peter Bernstein and Annalyn Swan provide a terrific in-depth analysis of the earning and spending of these wealthiest people in the world. I recommend the book for those seriously interested in understanding and marketing to the ultra-rich. Here, I'll give you a thumb-sized overview of what they found, as well as my own observations.

First of all, you should be interested in who is on this list. There are many names you know, like Oprah, Bill Gates, Warren Buffett, and the omnipresent modern-day Barnum, Donald Trump—of whom I am a very big fan. I have appeared as a speaker on programs with the Donald. At some of the past Glazer-Kennedy Insider's Circle™ (GKIC.com) conferences, we've had the first *Apprentice* winner, Bill Rancic, and *Apprentice* competitor Kristi Frank; Trump's attorney and chief negotiator, George Ross. We've also had Gene Simmons of the band KISS, most recently Penn of Penn & Teller, seen on *Celebrity Apprentice,* and Joan Rivers—winner of *Celebrity Apprentice.* I study and recommend study of people like Donald Trump, Gene Simmons, the late Joan Rivers—via the documentary about her, *A Piece of Work.*

You might find a variety of statistics interesting and, in some instances, useful. These are from one year of the 400 list. (I find they don't vary much, year to year.) In the particular year I analyzed for this chapter, 270 of the 400 basically made their

fortunes from scratch, and another 56 made a large portion of their money even if also inheriting some wealth. Translation: 80% of the ultra-rich got there through ambition, initiative, drive, grit, ingenuity, hard work, and entrepreneurship. Their wealth has not separated them from those values. Only 74 of the 400 inherited their fortunes. Thinking of the ultra-rich as a silver-spoon-in-mouth crowd born of the lucky sperm club would be a serious mistake. This is not who they are, and it is definitely not how they think of themselves.

Dan Kennedy's #1 No B.S. Key to the Vault

Make all your marketing to the affluent mirror the way they see and think about themselves.

Forty-one of the 400 attended Harvard; 28, Stanford; 14, Yale; and 10, Princeton—a total of 93 from the top-rated, most prestigious universities. But it is worth noting that a higher percentage of the ultra-rich attended run-of-the-mill universities or did not attend college at all. And, as an aside, here's a very interesting statistic about the presumed link between wealth and college: Those on the Forbes 400 list with a college degree were worth less on average than those without a college degree—$3.1 billion vs. $5.9 billion, to be exact—making the college degree almost a $2 billion handicap. I might mention, in the 2007–2008 presidential primary campaigns, both Hillary Clinton and John Edwards insisted it was, quote, *impossible*, unquote, for *anybody* to get ahead anymore without a college degree as basis for their plans to provide free college to everybody, giving each newborn baby a $5,000.00 college fund, and other, similar foolishness. This mythology persists now, even as a college debt bubble bigger than the mortgage bubble that burst in 2008 grows. Of course, what they stated as fact and actual facts never meet. Further, while college enrollments have climbed from 47% in 1973, the year I graduated from high school and did not go to college, to 69% now, college graduation rates have stayed the same, 66%, according to the National Center for Education Statistics. So, while more are going, more are dropping out. Imagine what that statistic will look like if we make college free for all. *Got lousy grades, no work ethic, no ambition? Here's a free ride at Harvard. Have fun.*

That kind of talk—the criticism of the free-college plans I just provided—really resonates with the ultra-rich, by the way. They deeply resent the popular but erroneous idea that they got theirs through inheritance or luck, and they bear even greater resentment for and disapproval of handouts and freebies provided to others. Many, like Warren Buffett and Bill Gates, severely restrict the inheritances passed on to their children. Fundamentally, the more affluent a person is, the more vehemently opposed he is to handouts to anyone under any circumstances, except severe tragedy, such as Katrina.

A wonderful example of talking to this audience in a way that resonates—what I teach as "marketing by values"—is shown in the little article reprinted at the end of this chapter, by a client of mine, Ted Oakley, owner of Oxbow Advisors (www.OxbowAdvisors.com/Kennedy), a wealth management firm specializing in entrepreneur/business owner and retired entrepreneur clients with assets from $10 million to $50 million. This "article" sometimes appears as the second page of a two-page lead generation advertisement, offering free copies of his book *$20 Million and Broke*, but it is also used as stand-alone item in different information packages sent to clients, and in web media. It perfectly syncs with the thinking of his avatar client, the affluent to ultra-affluent.

The ultra-rich are a marrying bunch. Only 11 of the Forbes 400 list I analyzed have never been married. One hundred eighteen have been divorced at least once, but 271 have stayed married to their first spouses—a significantly better percentage than the general population. Cynics would say that has something to do with the high price of divorce. Golfer Greg Norman's divorce was reported to cost more than $200 million, and he wasn't even on the Forbes list! When asked by fellow actor Arnold Schwarzenegger why Arnold was rich and he was not, Burt Reynolds answered number of wives. Still, as many, including former General Electric captain Jack Welch, have observed the reason divorce is so expensive is it's worth it. My own affluence was wounded significantly by divorce, helped by remarrying the same wife. Finally, I got to marry rich.

The age of the ultra-rich skews mature, as you'd expect, but it does span wide. The oldest 400 member, the year I analyzed the list, John Simplot, was 98; the youngest, John Arbold, 33. Average: 65. If you step away from the top of the pyramid, the Forbes 400, and look at the broader affluent population, you will still see age skews senior, pointing the ambitious marketer to the affluent toward affluent boomers.

There is geographic concentration. Out of 400, 88 have their primary residence in California, 73 in New York state—and 64 of those in New York City. This is changing. As cities and states like New York and California evermore greedily tax-target the rich, more and more leave. Limbaugh famously exited New York for Florida, Glenn Beck for Texas, both low-tax states. Hollywood stars have fled Los Angeles in favor of places like Wyoming. Puerto Rico has been using its special tax situation to attract the rich. More and more, companies are moving or expanding into low-tax states, so its workforce of mass-affluent and affluent can benefit. This a factor in Google's locating a large facility outside Silicon Valley, in *Oklahoma*. As I wrote this book, the Oklahoma Department of Commerce and its economic development arm, led by Secretary of Commerce Larry Parman, was a client of mine.

Still, there may be more ultra-rich per square foot in the Stamford, Connecticut, area (basically NYC suburbs) than anywhere. The very upscale Kennedy's All-American Barber Clubs (KennedysBarberClub.com) discussed elsewhere in this book have been birthed in locales with high concentrations of ultra-affluent consumers. As of this writing, there are six in Stamford, Greenwich, and Darien, Connecticut, five in Florida. A lot of wealth remains and will remain located where it has long been, on the coasts. But a lot is also moving. To learn about that, I recommend the book *The Fate of the States: The New Geography of Prosperity* by Meredith Whitney. If you market nationally, not locally, it is vitally important to stay on top of the relocation, movement, and concentrated "geo-pockets" of wealth, so you can direct your mail, place your print ads, and otherwise focus your marketing there—and omit places wealth has left or is leaving. If you are going to open additional stores, sales offices, clinics, etc., this information is critical to making good choices, so you plant where wealth is growing.

The top ten on the 400 list the year I analyzed: Bill Gates, $59 billion; Warren Buffett, $52 billion. Big drop to Vegas casino entrepreneur Sheldon Adelson*, $28 billion; Oracle Software's Larry Ellison, $26 billion. Another drop to the new kids on the block, Sergey Brin and Larry Page from Google, each at $18.5 billion. Vegas entrepreneur and corporate turnaround guy, Kirk Kerkorian, $18 billion; Michael Dell of Dell Computers at $17.2

---

*In interest of full disclosure, as of the writing of this book, I owned stock in the companies denoted with an asterisk.

billion; Charles Koch, an oil man, $17 billion, and his brother, David Koch, also in oil, at $17 billion, both having had a head start through inheritance. Some trivia: David Koch ran as the vice-presidential candidate on the Libertarian Party's ticket back in 1980. The Koch brothers are now big donors to Republican candidates and conservative political groups, thus favorite targets for the liberal and Democratic political candidates and fundraising.

Gates famously began his business in his garage. Buffett is legendary for his preference of investing in "ordinary" businesses like Dairy Queen®, Borsheims and Helzberg jewelry store chains, and Coca-Cola®. Adelson is the son of a cab driver and a college dropout. Ellison, also a college dropout, started his business in 1977. The Google boys are Stanford dropouts who started their business in a borrowed garage. Kerkorian is the son of an Armenian immigrant fruit farmer. He is an eighth-grade dropout. He built his first business, TWA, the airline, from scratch, sold it for $104 million profit in 1996, and began aggressively investing in Vegas properties. Dell started his business selling computers out of his college dorm room. Eight of the top ten built their fortunes, as I described earlier. This is an important point, as it speaks to the psychology of selling to the ultra-rich.

Following are some of the most interesting Forbes 400 members from the same year's roster:

H. Ross Perot ($4.4 billion), the son of a Texas cotton broker. After his stint in the Navy, he went to work as a salesman for IBM®. The data management company he subsequently created was based on an idea of his that IBM rejected. He sold that company for $2.5 billion. His current company uses offshore labor in 20 countries and has a huge technology center in Mexico, even though Perot rallied against the North American Free Trade Agreement

(NAFTA) during his quixotic campaign for the presidency.

Ronald Lauder ($3.2 billion), son of beauty entrepreneur Estee Lauder, who started her face creams business in 1946, whipping up potions in a kitchen sink. She is widely credited with inventing the gift-with-purchase strategy commonly used in the cosmetic industry but having much wider application, including selling just about anything to the affluent. The leveraging of commodity consumer products to ultra-wealth is not at all unique. Also on the list are: Leonard Stern, who owes his $44.1 billion to his dad's Hartz® Mountain pet products; Don Hall's $2 billion has evolved from his uncle's selling of greeting cards beginning at age 18, which became Hallmark®; Hope Hill van Buren's $1.4 billion comes from inheritance from her grandfather, the inventor of condensed soup leading to Campbell's®; John Simplot's company grows the potatoes for about one-third of all French fries sold in America; Forrest Mars Jr.'s delicious $14 billion comes from Mars® candy bars.

Leslie Wexner ($2.8 billion) is an Ohio State dropout who started his first women's clothing store with $5,000.00 borrowed from his aunt. His retail creations include Bath & Body Works® and Victoria's Secret®. Victoria's Secret is, incidentally, a clever marketing construct, a re-imagination of long-reigning then dethroned leader Frederick's of Hollywood®.

Roy Disney ($1.4 billion) is Walt's nephew, best known recently for leading the fight to oust Michael Eisner as Disney's® CEO. Roy's days on the list may be numbered, as a pending divorce promises to divide the wealth. Still, as Walt said, it all started with a mouse—and look at all that has followed.

Frank and Lorenzo Fertitta ($1.3 billion each) started out dealing cards at the Stardust. Bought a "nothing" casino way off the Strip, and parlayed its winnings to include 15 casinos and resorts. But their product you might be most familiar with, a fan of, or repulsed by is the mixed martial arts fighting sport the Ultimate Fighting League, and its long-running reality TV shows and pay-per-view events, which average $30 million in revenue each.

Ralph Lauren ($4.7 billion) is the son of Russian immigrants who grew up in the Bronx, worked as a salesman in a Brooks Brothers™ store, and launched Polo with a saved-up and borrowed $50,000.00 in 1967. He sold 28% of the company, 27 years later, for $138 million and then developed other brands, expanded from fashions to furniture and brand licensing for everything from leather luggage to house paint sold at Home Depot®. In a sense, Lauren himself is the product. The strategy of a personal brand is also not uncommon in the ultra-rich category. You can arguably place Trump there. While not in this ultra-rich category myself, much of my wealth can be chalked up to my self-created status as a valuable personal brand. This is a strategy just about anyone can emulate, in any business, consumer or B2B.

Jeff Bezos* ($8.7 billion) started out simply selling books from his garage via the internet. He survived the dotcom crash and years without a profitable business model to wind up with an online mall topping $10 billion in yearly sales of everything from books to toys to tools. He is a Princeton grad and worked at a hedge fund before starting Amazon®.

S. Truett Cathy ($1.3 billion) started out selling chicken sandwiches to factory and airport workers. Opened the first

---

*In interest of full disclosure, as of the writing of this book, I owned stock in the companies denoted with an asterisk.

Chick-Fil-A® store in a shopping mall in 1967. That chain sells a whole lot of chicken despite keeping all its restaurants closed on Sundays, honoring Cathy's strict Baptist beliefs.

Fred DeLuca ($1.6 billion) turned one sub sandwich shop into 28,000 Subway® restaurants in 86 countries through aggressive franchising, not without controversy—franchisees have filed class action litigation against him; the medical establishment has ferociously criticized the Subway® diet promoted with the now-famous Jared.

Michael Ilitch ($1.6 billion) opened his Little Caesars® pizza shop in 1959, after an injury ended his pro baseball career, and built up a 40-store chain in ten years, then turned to more aggressive expansion, using Ray Kroc's McDonald's® franchising model, building to yearly sales exceeding $1.5 billion.

Ty Warner ($4.1 billion), a salesman's son who dropped out of college to follow in his father's footsteps as an on-the-road sales rep for a plush toy company. Ty kept his thinking cap on while a road warrior and in 1986 created Beanie Babies® and the collector-item status that fueled the craze. He's leveraged the Beanie Babies® money into ownership of a Four Seasons hotel in New York, three luxury resorts, and the cottage where John and Jackie Kennedy honeymooned, which guests now pay $2,990.00 a night to stay in.

Rich DeVos ($3.6 billion) and his high school buddy created Amway™, after several business failures and a stint in another multilevel marketing company Amway later acquired. The company started bottling its lone product, an all-purpose liquid cleaner, in a garage in 1959. Its system of distributors recruiting distributors has led to more than three million of them worldwide generating over $6 billion in yearly sales of its own household, cosmetic, and nutrition products as well as joint ventures permitting their representation of products from Best Buy™, Amazon, and many other retailers. Rich also owns the National Basketball Association (NBA) team the Orlando Magic. And a whole lot of Amway's hometown, Ada, Michigan. I cut my teeth as a young'un in the Amway business and have both a nostalgic fondness for and deep understanding of the person-to-person selling method as a result. One of our own Glazer-Kennedy Insider's Circle's™ businesses, with local chapters, regular meetings, and mastermind groups for small-business owners, active in more than 50 North American cities, has its meeting formats and many of its person-to-person sales and marketing methods rooted in my Amway experience. This method of distribution remains viable and healthy today, including with mass-affluent customers.

By the way, Rich DeVos' autobiography, *Simply Rich: Life and Lessons from the Cofounder of Amway: A Memoir*, is an extraordinary book well worth reading, for its entrepreneurial and life lessons. It also has an instructive window into the personality, philosophy, and thinking of a made-from-scratch ultra-rich business, family, and civic leader.

What so many of these 400 members share in common is the startup of a small business, expansion of that business, then leveraging the wealth created to that point into diversified investments as well as multiplying the core business or brand through one or more means, such as franchising or licensing. These ultra-rich wind up with a unique mindset also held in common from this experience. Among other things, they are methodical. They view everything through the prism of process. They are also deeply suspicious of anyone or anything not symbolic of hard work and methodical development. If you set out to sell them, for example, an exotic safari or fishing trip, the story of your background and how you made yourself into the reigning expert on such travel and the extent of the research, planning, and preparation invested in designing and delivering the experience is essential, and carries more influence than the most persuasive description of the trip and its amenities. This same principle applies to whatever you might sell to the ultra-rich with this startup background.

Donald Trump ($3 billion) cannot be ignored—even if you try. His retail, office, and hotel businesses are all up, thriving. Signed Gucci® to a record-breaking lease for Trump Tower. His brand-licensing business has skyrocketed in earnings and expanded just from taking "points" off the top of real estate projects bearing his name but built and sold by others to a dizzyingly wide range of products and services, from mortgages to men's clothes and even mail-order steaks sold on QVC® and in the Sharper Image® catalog. His licensing-business boom and his speaking fees from $250,000.00 to $1 million have both been made golden by his TV star status. Of late, Trump is far more in the Trump business than in the real estate business. He annually disputes Forbes' valuation of him as low by half or more. For some combination of practical self-promotion reasons and ego, Trump is representative of a relatively small part of the ultra-rich population eager for attention, publicity, and widespread recognition of his success and wealth. (Many others, if not most others, in this informal league of the extraordinarily wealth shun media and avoid public display of wealth, although most still try to outdo and impress their peers.)

There are only 39 women on the 400 list, and generally speaking, ultra-rich women still tend to amass their wealth through marriage, divorce, and inheritance. One of the exceptions is **Meg Whitman** ($1.4 billion), who earned her MBA from Harvard and held executive positions at several consumer products companies, Disney®, and the big private equity and venture capital fund Bain & Company (led to its prominence by

Mitt Romney) before landing in the CEO chair at eBay. Under her direction, the company weathered the dotcom bust, established itself as a solid leader in e-commerce, and has, of late, been broadening and diversifying through acquisitions and focusing major attention on expansion in China. To a lesser degree than Trump, but still in the same vein, Meg Whitman is the face of eBay, actively offering herself up to financial and mainstream media for interviews and having more of a direct relationship with eBay users than most corporations' CEOs have with their customers. On the current list of women in the 400, only Meg Whitman, Martha Stewart, and Oprah Winfrey have entirely made-from-scratch fortunes, and they all have self-promotion in common. (Just as this book was going to press, Ms. Whitman announced her retirement from her position at eBay.)

In many respects, the ultra-rich have the very same concerns and buying motivations as the more ordinary affluent. They are pressed for time and eager that efficiency, competence, and convenience be provided to them—and they're very willing to pay for it. Other than those intangibles, they have few if any needs. As a matter of fact, even income is pretty much irrelevant to them; they have risen to the point of concern only with net worth. They worry about loss—of money, power, status, or security. They seek approval, recognition, respect—some only from peers, others from the world at large, all from those they conduct business with.

What's Gone Horribly Wrong in Estate Planning?

By Ted Oakley

In the estate planning area, most professionals have spent countless hours in the planning and implementation of various models. With each new set of laws come a different approach and an ongoing dynamic of adjustments to stay current. The professional community has generally done an excellent job of staying abreast of changes—and of implementing and adjusting estate plans. But have many of us overlooked the most important part of the process? In short, it is the transfer of hard-earned wealth to future generations. All the planning in the world is of little value if future generations don't understand wealth and assets or know how to effectively handle them.

Over the years in our role as financial advisors, we have witnessed untold numbers of inheritors who had very little knowledge of or appreciation for wealth. In the course of their being in charge of the new wealth, errors in investment and judgment have frequently devastated, if not destroyed, the inheritance. This inevitably brings questions to the forefront. What are we trying to accomplish with all the sophisticated methods of estate planning? Ostensibly the end result is to transfer wealth in an orderly and tax-efficient way. But there is a huge missing component in this process. That missing piece is the education and nurture of future generations on how to first appreciate, then manage, wealth.

In working with third and fourth-generation families, we find it is often eye-opening to see how few really understand why and how all of this works. But in many cases it is too late for education as the die has been cast. This process of instilling what

Estate Planning, continued

future generations need must be started at a young age and carried through with deliberation. It's not an easy thing to do because wealth itself makes many things easier. But "easier" is seldom the best medicine for future generations.

1. *Start early.* It is never too early to map out what you want to teach your children. But you have to spend the time. Teach them how the value of their life today came about. Teach them how their mother and father and/or grandparents spent 12-hour days and endless nights of hard work to accomplish their goals. Help them understand the history of what it took to make a business successful and what goes into the success mentality. Show them from an early age that all this hasn't come without a price, and we as a family are responsible to be good stewards of the wealth. The hardest part is to train the children as if they didn't have wealth in order for them to eventually appreciate it. There is a natural tendency to want to make life easier for our children, but in many ways that is counterproductive.

2. *Learn to work.* Teaching future generations how to work and how to appreciate the dignity of work are vitally important to the overall objective of estate planning. Learning to work does a great deal for the character of young people. They first of all understand that everything doesn't come on a silver platter. They learn responsibility and, most importantly, they gain self-esteem from knowing within themselves that they can have a sense of accomplishment through work. They and their parents spend too much time, effort and money trying to gain something that, through proper guidance and experience, largely comes from within.

Estate Planning, continued

3. *Be consistent.* If you want future generations to understand and respect your values, you have to be consistent. Telling them one thing and then acting out in a different way (one definition of hypocrisy) is disastrous. If you tell your children about a particular consequence, then stay with it! You are in the process of what normally amounts to a 16- to 18-year training class with each child.

4. *Go slowly with the money.* Lavishing everything on a child at an early age may be tempting, but it goes a long way toward defeating the estate transfer process. When offspring get pretty much everything they want anytime they want it, they tend to develop a mindset—a mindset that is hard to change 30 or 40 years later when the time has come for them to be responsible for inherited wealth. By going slowly and expecting them to understand that wealth is not to be taken for granted, you give them better tools to deal with what you will be passing on.

5. *Teach the legacy.* The most important part of your legacy and your children's legacy is spending many hours teaching them how this all came about. This business, this lifestyle, came about because somebody did something. Instill in the future generation a knowledge of and respect for their forebears who did those things; explain how they did them; infuse a reverence for the sacrifices of those who went before. Teach your children about the risks the previous generations took and how that transformed into what the family has today. Wealth didn't "just happen"—and they need to know the story behind their inheritance, which is a sacred trust.

Estate Planning, continued

No matter how many wills, trusts and transfers you do, they won't go very far or last very long if the inheritors don't appreciate what went into creating them. Instill in your children core values and a sense of responsibility, and you give them a huge advantage. You also greatly enhance the chances of the money being used wisely, even philanthropically.

CHAPTER 4

The Question Freud
Couldn't Answer

"No rich man is ugly."

—Zsa Zsa Gabor

I t is no secret that, as the old saying goes, "women control the purse strings." That once meant that the men brought home the paychecks and their wives spent the money. No longer. Many affluent households are wealthy thanks to both spouses' careers providing excellent incomes. Consequently, women have control over spending and investments based not only on the marriage but on equal—or in some cases, greater—financial contribution to it. This has erased old, traditional divisions and delegation of spending.

Surveys from the financial services industry from the 1970s, for example, showed that the married women in more than 80% of affluent households had nominal or no involvement in the investment decisions. Similar surveys from 2000 and later indicate the 80% has moved all the way down to 40%. In mass-affluent households, women are even more likely to be actively involved in the investment decisions. In the 1960s, husbands picked out the family car. In the 1980s, couples picked out that car together. Today, the woman of the mass-affluent household most likely has her own car and chose it herself. Marketing just about anything to the affluent married household now involves the woman at least as much as the man.

In the TV show *Mad Men*, about the advertising world in the 1950s, we see young women going to work for the express purpose of finding a man and getting married—they were the unlucky ones who weren't able to go directly to marriage without a tour around the game board. That was then. This is now. The institution of marriage itself has fallen on hard times and disrepute. As a career goal, it's out the window. The year 2007 marked the first time there were as many single women as married women in the United States, with no sign of that trend reversing.

Beginning in 2005, single women became the second-largest group of home buyers, right behind married couples. They do not stay in apartments until they find husbands and get married. Single women buy nearly twice as many homes as single men. Yet when have you seen any real estate advertising specifically aimed at single women? Comparable examples can be found in numerous other product and service categories, where marketers and marketing have not caught up with and are ignoring opportunities in current reality.

Some single women are single for the traditional reason—not yet (or ever) finding the right man. But there is a growing population of what demographic analysts call the "willfully unmarried," who consciously and deliberately choose to stay single. Among the willfully unmarried women are two groups of special interest to us: the particularly affluent single women and the affluent boomer single women. In these two groups, and particularly in a group composed of overlap from the two, we find untold spending power, controlled by women who are buying their own homes, doing their own investing, planning and funding their own retirements, planning their own vacations, and so on—for life. These women are permanent heads of households, and can and should be marketed to as such. Hardly anybody is. In fact, my files are lacking any good examples of advertising or marketing specific to this to show you!

Late-in-Life Divorce as a Spending Event

The majority of the divorces that occur after 20 to 25 years of marriage are instigated by the wives, not the husbands. Far from grieving quietly, many of these women quickly re-enter the dating and next-husband-hunting game, find it highly competitive, populated by an insufficient quantity of men, and full of older men seeking younger women. Consequently, a number of self-improvement investments occur within 6 to 12 months of divorce: cosmetic surgery, cosmetic dentistry, weight-loss products, new and younger-looking wardrobe, new and younger-looking car. I have several clients who deliberately market to this timing sweet spot, using information compiled from public records combined with other, commercially available, rented mailing lists (see Chapter 29). In short, affluent women age 45 through 60, divorcing after long marriages, tend to go on personal spending binges and be exceptionally susceptible to certain kinds of product and service offers about four to six months post-divorce. Those identified as affluent or, in a way, newly affluent based on their own income no longer shared, alimony, or having secured the principal residence in the divorce, are the biggest spenders.

That Infamous Population of "Cougars"

The older man with the much younger trophy wife has been reversed. According to AARP statistics, at least one in three women between ages 40 and 70 is dating a younger man. About one-fourth of those men are ten or more years younger. Match. com reported a doubling of older women seeking younger men, and that trend has continued. The proof there's a trend is that the phenomenon is earning its own name. Older women expressing preference for and hunting younger men are now familiarly called Cougars. Celebrities do it: Demi Moore, Susan Sarandon, Madonna. TV shows deal with it. Way back in 2005, Fran Drescher's TV show *Living with Fran* dealt with a mother of two in love with a man half her age. VH1 aired a reality show with 20-year-old men competing to date Mick Jagger's 50-year-old ex-wife. *Sex and the City* had a very predatory Cougar as one of its four characters. Far more recently, former *Friends* star Courteney Cox's TV show *Cougar Town* (airing 2009–2015) is self-explanatory.

A not yet explicitly tracked majority of these Cougars are affluent women. The theory advanced in *MicroTrends* by Mark Penn is that the rise of the affluent Cougar reflects "the natural instinct for people with success to trade that success for sexual attractiveness. And what was once achievable only by older men with money is now within reach of women with power and accomplishment (and money)."

The phrase "the natural instinct for" is, I think, an extremely important one. There is, in fact, a natural instinct to attempt leveraging success and prosperity into youth, sex, longevity, even immortality. Some affluent people are even prepaying to be cryogenically frozen upon death in the hope of being later thawed out and resurrected when a medical cure for what ails them is found—and laugh if you like, but companies in this field are doing quite nicely. Men are catching up to women in terms of willingness to spend money to try to buy youth and attractiveness, but this is certainly a prime area of opportunity when marketing to affluent women.

Stigmas Gone

Cosmetic surgery—derogatively called plastic surgery for years—was once almost exclusively for affluent women, or actresses and models. And it was not openly discussed. Today, its popularity spans age ranges from shockingly young to surprisingly old, from mass-affluent to ultra-affluent. And not only is it openly discussed, but it is something of a status symbol. And discussed in ways that might make many people blush. For example, according to a study published in the *Aesthetic Surgery Journal*, 81% of breast surgery patients and 68% of other body surgery patients reported improvements in sexual satisfaction. More than 50% of these patients said they were able to achieve orgasm more easily following their surgery. And 56% also noted increases in their partners' sexual interest and satisfaction following the surgery. You may rest assured that the profession is using this information in its marketing.

This change in attitudes toward cosmetic surgery is representative of comparable changes in attitudes about just about everything, including but not limited to sexuality. Men, take a stroll through the Self-Help, Psychology, Health, and Relationship aisles at your nearest major bookstore (where most men never tread) or pick up and read copies of *Cosmopolitan* as well as the historically more staid *Redbook*. You'll probably be very surprised to discover the discussions going on.

What's most important about all this, from a marketing standpoint, is the willingness of women to confront every imaginable health, beauty, aging, and lifestyle issue head-on, and the willingness of affluent women to spend almost without limitation on themselves, their physical and emotional well-being.

Legal Discrimination

You cannot design a business to be exclusively for men anymore. But you can design any business you like to be exclusively for women. Because discrimination is one of the most powerful of all marketing strategies, this is an opportunity that shouldn't be overlooked.

The same, incidentally, is true for race. The Black Entertainment Television (BET) network and its awards, *Black Enterprise* magazine, and the NAACP are accepted and respected. Start the White Entertainment Network, *White Enterprise* magazine, or the National Association for Advancement of White Folk, and see how things go. I don't begrudge this, by the way; I merely point it out as double standard and, more importantly, as opportunity.

Smart marketers targeting women are all about discrimination. While women tend to be liberal and socially conscious, and decry discrimination in general, they respond very favorably to for-women-only products, services, media, and messages. Ladies' nights still exist and still work, and that says a lot. It's a 1960s device alive and well 40-plus years later. Designing and presenting businesses, products, and services as "for affluent women only—no men invited"—is one of the great growth opportunities of the coming ten years.

It Isn't Simple

As an example of the complexity required for success in marketing to affluent women, consider the financial services field.

In their book *Marketing to the Mindset of Boomers and Their Elders*, Carol Morgan and Doran Levy accuse financial services and investment firms of "conjuring up differences where none exist" in advertising, marketing, and selling to affluent women (investable assets, $500,000.00+) and mass-affluent women (investable assets, $100,000.00+) making their own investment decisions. Assumptions are made by many investment marketers that echo one enunciated by the head of a Charles Schwab initiative aimed at women that "women feel differently and learn differently about investing," so there's a need to "speak to women in terms relevant to their lives and in language that's appealing to them." But in one of her columns, the popular financial writer Jane Bryant Quinn expressed her distaste for financial advertising treating women as "a breed apart." Quinn describes this advertising as "condescending"—"Who," she asks, "besides women are told they need help because they are emotionally impaired?" Quinn cites market research studies confirming that there is no difference in investment patterns by gender.

So who's right?

I would suggest they are both right and wrong.

First of all, lumping the mass-affluent and affluent women together is a serious mistake. Women with $500,000.00 and up to invest have, for the most part, been more involved with their

Recommended Resource

EPM Communications publishes a research-based newsletter, *Marketing to Women*, as well as an annual *All About Women Consumers* research report. Go to www. EPMcom.com.

wealth for a longer period of time. They also have, as a practical matter, access to a different level of financial advisor and choices of investment-related services. They are less likely to be paying attention to Suze Orman and *Money* magazine and more likely to be reading *The Wall Street Journal*, *Forbes*, and *Worth* than their mass-affluent counterparts. In fact, the affluent women should be separated into experience categories, such as Savvy Investors vs. Financial Uninvolveds, and then talked to quite differently. This is a distinct difference of greater significance than the affluent vs. mass-affluent tag.

Some years back, I did some marketing consulting work for the late Joan Rivers, the sharp-tongued comedienne turned super-successful jewelry, cosmetics, and fashion entrepreneur and on-air pitchperson at QVC. When Joan's husband, Edgar, died, she had the shocking experience many Financial Uninvolved women have: confronting money management for the first time, under duress. She had left it all in his hands and wasn't even sure how to balance a checkbook. Financially Uninvolveds who, for one reason or another—often the death or incapacity of their spouse—have significant investable assets to manage but lack background knowledge and experience and therefore lack confidence are most likely to look for a single source of advice and assistance, be far more interested in safety and security than gain or yield, and be most motivated by trust. They will seek someone they can have confidence in, rather than work to have more confidence in their own judgment in these matters. Savvy Investor Women are more likely to collect and consider information from multiple sources, make at least some investment decisions independently, and have direct relationships with multiple vendors, such as an online brokerage account, a stock broker, a financial planner, and one or more banks.

This means: Savvy Investor Women will respond to *information*. Financially Uninvolved Women will respond to trust.

The best segmentation here would be quad:

1. Financially Uninvolved, Mass-Affluent
2. Financially Uninvolved, Affluent
3. Savvy Investor, Mass-Affluent
4. Savvy Investor, Affluent

Second, Quinn is off base in denying that gender differences affect perception of and responsiveness to advertising and overt marketing. I'm afraid she's projecting her own attitudes onto all women. Georgette Geller-Petro, an executive with the financial services giant AXA Financial®, states, "Through feedback from our advisors who work with women, we have found that women's financial goals, as well as how they articulate them, are different than those of men."

Back in the 2007 presidential primary elections, Hillary Clinton's campaign very successfully courted a market segment defined as "women with needs." The label referred to mostly single, high school-educated women with children and low-wage jobs. This caused a client of mine, a business coach to mortgage brokers who noticed an increasing number of strong-minded women joining his program, and me, to coin the term "women with balls." This refers to women operating predominately via the rational thought rather than the emotional, and acting, at least in business situations, more like men. Quinn's comments on this topic, and much of her other writing, make me put her in this category. But it's error for her to project her woman-with-balls mentality onto a majority of other women. In fact, one telling if politically incorrect way to separate women is to put them into the categories of women who think like men and women who do not.

Gender difference matters. There are words and phrases— like *women with balls*—that instantly set many women's teeth on edge and make them deaf to everything else said or written by that person. I do a lot of advertising copywriting in weight loss, alternative health, and beauty categories, and I have to exercise extreme caution about "sounding male" or using instant-turn-off language. However, Quinn is right when she recoils at ad approaches or language that feels "condescending" to her. Women, especially career women, are hypersensitive to being talked down to, to not being given credit for their intelligence, knowledge, and experience. While the militant feminist of the '60s and '70s seems to be a marginalized minority, there is still a profound difference in the way women respond to language, and the way different women respond to the same language.

Consider the main characters in the *Sex and the City* HBO series and follow-up movies. Some women aspire to be like one or all of these characters. Other women are amused and entertained by them, but do not find them at all inspirational. Other women find them shocking. Ridiculous. Embarrassing. These different reactions link to age, geography, career status and experience, education, and affluence. Of course, a TV series like this has to cast a relatively wide net and try for mass appeal—thus its four different characters, including Samantha, older but also more libertine than the others and, in one long plot line in the series, a Cougar. Marketers, however, need not cast such a broad net, unless lazy. We can segment and isolate different types and groups of affluent and mass-affluent women and approach each segmented group very differently from the others.

CHAPTER 5

Boys Will Be Boys, No Matter Their Age

"Man will do many things to get himself loved. He will do all things to get himself envied."

—MARK TWAIN

N o man buys a Lamborghini to get to work.

There are Lamborghini automobiles priced from $250,000.00 to $1.4 million. Significantly, it is the $1.4 million ones that sell out fastest and for which there is the longest waiting list. But the very fact that such a thing as a Lamborghini exists reveals something very, very important about men and selling to them, which is completely contrary to myth.

Myth is that women are emotional, men are *practical*. Women buy with their hearts, men buy with their heads, with intellect and logic.

The Lamborghini is designed and built to travel at speeds illegal on every road in the United States. How practical is *that*?

Truth is, while women mature, men just get older. Arrested development.

Another myth is that men are confident. It is my experience, from selling to, dealing with, and associating with hundreds and hundreds of millionaires, that successful men are anything but self-secure. Actually, they live with an underlying anxiety that no amount of wealth relieves. As a result, they spend a lot of money on symbolic validation of their success, status, and prosperity. For example, most men aren't really clotheshorses. Symbolism aside, most I know could care less about Brooks Brothers® vs. Walmart® as the source of their khakis, sweaters, or socks. But affluent men actually train themselves to appreciate fashion quality and design distinctions, and choose certain purveyors, as a means of self-validation as well as a concern about judgments others will make about them based on their apparel.

It doesn't begin or end with clothes. This same buying for validation—buying what they are supposed to buy from vendors they are *supposed to* patronize—extends to almost every product and service category.

Status

While status is not male vs. female, men do seek and get it differently than do women. For women, status is often a matter of association. For men, it is more a matter of competition and comparison.

A study quoted in the book *The Paradox of Choice* gave participants hypothetical choices concerning status and asked for their preferences. For example, people were asked to choose between a) earning $50,000.00 a year with others earning $25,000.00 or b) earning twice as much, $100,000.00 a year but being surrounded by people earning $200,000.00. In another example, respondents could choose between a) having an IQ of 110 when the IQ of all the others is 90 or b) having a higher IQ of 130 when the others score 150. A number of other similarly constructed a-or-b scenarios were given. More than half of the respondents chose the options that gave them the better *relative* position. That means preferring $50,000.00 to $100,000.00 because they were, at $50,000.00, earning more than others, while at $100,000.00 they were earning less than others.

This means the guy buying the 60-foot yacht may be doing so only because the others at his marina have 48-foot yachts. And, as a matter of fact, many yacht buyers freely admit their size choice was based on the sizes of their peers' or marina neighbors' yachts. A very expensive My _____ is bigger than your _____. From the locker room to the boardroom.

My highest-level Titanium Business Mastermind Group and my Private Client Group have no members earning less than $1 million a year. Most are in the $4- to $10-million neighborhood, and they are all in the same types of businesses. We have other, mixed-breed coaching groups at GKIC, such as the Peak Performers/Implementation Group led by Lee Milteer (GKIC.com). Almost all are men, not by my design. None of these members has anything to prove, nor do they have an economic need for more money. Many find it difficult to motivate themselves. But they all compete fiercely within this group environment. They compete to bring the best business breakthrough or success report to each meeting. They compete to have the highest-grossing seminar or highest-grossing new product launch. They compete based on who has bought the best new toy, who took the best vacation. They compete against each other for *status within the group.*

Competition for status is nothing new. But the plethora of choices has created more competition than ever before, as affluent people find themselves in more environments. If they own two homes, they are living—and competing for status—in two communities rather than just one, and status is won at the country club community in North Carolina through different choices than in the high-rise condominium community in Boston. If they are in diversified businesses instead of single, narrowly defined businesses, they compete for status in a number of different business and professional associations, professional groups, and industries.

Any marketer who finds ways to convey comparative and competitive status to his affluent male customers and clients has the advantage.

This is why visible tiered pricing and attached privilege is such a powerful price strategy in catering to the affluent in general, and affluent men in particular. Many will choose the higher price option, some the highest price option purely because of its conveyed status, whether they actually want the differential goods or services in those higher level options or not. At the Kennedy's All-American Barber Clubs (KennedysBarberClub. com), there are five monthly membership levels. The Disney Parks are as undemocratic, with tiered pricing for everything, all the way up to Private Guides whisking you to the front of every line—from $315.00 to $500.00 an hour (prices vary by season).

This works best when a customer's "level" is visible and seen by others. As a piece of "inside baseball," if you explore GKIC (GKIC.com), you'll discover different Member levels, and you'll discover two major Member conventions/conferences each year. For the conferences, I created the Diamond Members' Lounge, a glass-walled, very visible lounge area with comfortable seating and always present free beverages and snacks. A refuge from the crowds outside. Lower caste Members see it, but can't enter it. At these same conferences, there is usually one celebrity speaker, and only Diamond Members get a meet 'n greet photo opportunity with that celebrity. Because all this is promoted and visible, it drives a significant number of membership upgrades during conference registration and on-site. The upgrade from the level closest to Diamond (Gold) to Diamond is worth about $2,300.00 to the company the first year alone. So 100 upgraded by this status-seeking is $230,000.00, and 400 is nearly a million dollars. I'd add, Diamond Members tend to take everything provided to them more seriously, apply themselves to it, and apply it in their businesses more assiduously, so the differential value they gain far exceeds their differential cost.

Men and Their Toys

In Chapter 23, I talk at length about spending on personal passions.

A friend of mine had, for several years, a very successful mail-order business selling an $850.00 putter. One golf club. A certain number of its purchasers then cheerfully paid $5,000.00 to fly to Las Vegas for a putting clinic with the club's inventor and a professional golf coach. Avid and affluent golfers are possibly the most rabid and irrational spenders on their passion, willing to part with virtually any sum to shave a stroke or straighten a slice, even while insisting on turning off lights in unused rooms at home to avoid wasting hard-earned money. But golfers are not unique in this. Just about every fisherman, hunter, collector, any man with a true passion and the money to indulge it, will indulge it.

I call such ideal customers "irrational, affluent buyers of the slight edge," meaning they will buy into and pay any amount for anything promising a competitive edge over their friends in a shared activity. It's important to understand that their success in business or career is tied to this philosophical approach—seeking and investing as necessary in obtaining even the slightest of competitive advantages, at every opportunity. To see it carried over into their hobbies and recreational pursuits is no surprise or oddity.

Everything for the accomplished, affluent man is a competition. It's never just about having a toy; it's about having the biggest, best, newest, hottest, coolest toy. It's never about playing a game; it's about playing that game better than his buddies.

CHAPTER 6

Marketing to Affluent
Gay and Lesbian Consumers
Is Out of the Closet

*"When it is a question of money, everyone is
of the same religion."*

—Voltaire

I f you are going to go where the money is, pursue the greatest spending power, then you will be joining an every-increasing number of companies somewhat quietly reaching out specifically to gay and lesbian consumers.

In many cases, you have a two-person household, each of its members with above-average education earning above-average incomes—many with no children to raise. They have a lot more money left over every month than their heterosexual counterparts across the street, who have a tricycle and two bicycles lying in the driveway, signifying the existence of three eating, clothes-growing-out-of, medical-emergencies-having, college-fund-needing little monsters living inside.

I'm willing to say here what hardly anybody else is: The vast majority of readers of this book—and of marketers, period—

are heterosexuals who may profess having no problems with gays, but are, in truth, uncomfortable and squeamish about the very idea of designing advertising and marketing programs to attract them as customers, clients, or patients. This chapter may even be making your skin crawl. You may have religious or morality-based beliefs that interfere with tolerance, let alone acceptance. You may have a false view of gays, a mental picture of, say, disgraced Senator Larry Craig of the "wide stance" defense, arrested for trolling for gay sex in a public restroom. You may simply find "these people" foreign, incomprehensible, and unfamiliar, making you uncomfortable for no other reason than that.

Some of those issues are more easily manageable than others. I am certainly not here to tell you what you should or shouldn't believe or feel. And I happen to be in favor of a business owner managing his business to suit his personal preferences. If, for your own nonbusiness reasons, you have no interest in or willingness to deliberately and specifically market to affluent gays and lesbians, and be of service to them, now would be a good time to skip ahead to the next chapter. Just know it is a bad *business* decision and, if you're running a business in which there are shareholders other than yourself, a fiscally irresponsible decision.

And, whether you like it or not, it is antiquated. In a *New Yorker* cartoon, two obviously gay men are seen in their apartment, one talking on the phone, responding to a question: "No, we're not going to the Gay Pride Parade this year. We're here, we're queer, and frankly, we're tired of making a big deal out of it." Mainstream America includes gays and lesbians. Time to get over it.

In 2014, an enormous media hoopla occurred over the first openly gay player being taken by a team in the NFL draft. It shouldn't have been that big of a deal. We are moving toward a time it *will* be a nonstory.

This does not, however, mean that they are a fully absorbed group unresponsive to targeted marketing and specially directed messages. To the contrary, they consistently reward those marketers who make special point of designing unique advertising to appear in the publications only they read and creating especially gay-friendly sales and business environments. The trick, as it is when appealing to any specific group, is not to be condescending or clumsy.

The Travel Industry Goes into New Territory

Back on November 2, 2007, *The Wall Street Journal* carried an article headlined "Las Vegas Goes All Out to Attract Gay Travelers." It reported on numerous resorts and casino companies' marketing strategies and initiatives directed exclusively at gays as well as products and experiences designed for them. For example, it mentioned that at the trendy Palms Casino, there's a line of mostly straight men, some couples, and a few women waiting for entry to the Playboy Club®'s party, featuring the iconic Playboy Bunnies® in push-up bras costumes. Only steps away, there's another line awaiting entry to another club, with a dance floor filled with gyrating, shirtless men dancing with each other.

Dan Kennedy's #2
No B.S. Key to the Vault

Who you bring through your door matters a lot. Why not deliberately get higher value customers?

There is a very good reason that the casino industry as well as luxury hotels and resorts worldwide, cruise lines, and others in travel are, with increasing openness, catering to gay customers: Harrah's Entertainment started aggressively marketing to gays 18 months after the extensive research it commissioned revealed that gay men spend an average of 30% more than straight men when traveling. To put a bit of money math to that statistic, you could have 1,000 straights at your resort each spending, say, $2,000.00 or 1,000 gays each spending $2,600.00. The net difference is $600,000.00. Multiply that by 52 weekends, and you get $31.2 million. As you can see, whom you bring through your doors matters a lot. This applies to you regardless of your business category—travel, restaurants, clothing store, furniture store, financial planning, whatever—both as a general principle and, specifically, regarding gay and lesbian consumers. In many categories, the gays are worth more than the straights. Marketing to the gay and lesbian population is, in its essence, taking a shortcut to a more affluent, more freely spending clientele.

Consequently, Vegas casinos, hotels, and spas as well as resorts located elsewhere are advertising themselves as gay friendly, including ads in gay publications like *OutTraveler* and *Advocate* and the cable TV channel Logo, with images of same-sex couples holding hands at romantic dinners, checking into hotel rooms together, or doing something a bit more risqué. Commitment ceremonies for gay couples are offered by such properties as the MGM Mirage and the Luxor in their wedding chapels.

Only seven years after that *Wall Street Journal* article, as I'm writing this, legal gay marriage is winning its battle, state after state, and is a fait accompli in final stages. TV dramas and comedies, including the enormously popular *Modern Family*, feature gay married couples. Marketers ignore or resist all this to their detriment.

Just as a growing number of companies are careful to reach out to and make welcome gay clientele without turning their businesses into gay places and alienating their other, larger customer bases, any marketer must walk the same tightrope and create the same degrees of separation, including use of gay-targeted media and direct mail that remains invisible to the straight population.

Any such outreach to a particular group begins with striving to understand the target audience and organizing it into manageable subgroups. One method of dividing and understanding this market is by behavior. One research group (from Real World Lesbians and Gays Research Study) has them divided into five categories:

1. Super Gays, 23% of the gay population;
2. Mainstream Gays, also 23%;
3. Party Gays, 14%;
4. Habitat Gays, 25%; and
5. Closeted, 12%.

One by one . . .

Super Gays are completely out, 65% are in a relationship, 66% read gay publications, and 91% consider being gay a big part of who they are. Financially, they have the highest incomes of any gay group, with 16% of this population at household incomes exceeding $100,000.00. Homeowners weigh in at 56%. There is some urban concentration.

Only 44% of the Mainstream Gays are completely out. They are equally likely to live in urban or rural areas, and they rank lower in income, affluence, home ownership, and education than the super gays.

The Party Gays are the youngest group, with 29% aged 18 to 24, and 77% out. They are the least educated and the most likely to eat out in restaurants and visit gay or lesbian clubs frequently.

Conversely, the Habitat Gays are the oldest group, with 41% of them boomers and older. The most of any gay group—77% are out, 59% live in a committed relationship with a life partner, 65% own their own homes, and 37% live in suburban areas. These are nesters at home, and as a result, they watch considerably more TV than the other groups.

The diminishing Closeted group is next oldest, with 40% at least 50 years old. Those that are single is 52%, the most of any gay group, and 47% live in small towns or rural areas, also the most of any gay group.

To make some simplistic connections, we would find the majority of the mass-affluent gays in the Habitat group and the majority of the affluent and ultra-affluent gays in the Super Gay group.

What should be obvious is that delivering the identical marketing message to this entire population is not likely to be productive. There are too many distinct economic, educational, social, life experience, and interest differences among the groups.

CHAPTER 7

Affluent Boomers'
Spending Boom

"He's living beyond his means but he can afford it."

—Sam Goldwyn, Hollywood Mogul

B oomers represent more than 70% of the U.S. households with incomes exceeding $75,000.00 and investable
assets exceeding $200,000.00. More than 70% of boomers
had their wealth increase by more than half from 1992 to 2003,
and another 20% had increases better than 25%. And, from 2007
through 2012, they inherited an enormous transfer of wealth from
their parents with more to come. In 2014, the boomer population
is nearing its peak growth. Now it is moving onward to senior
population. There are 7 to as many as 15 prime spending years
yet in this group's hands, along with enormous ability to spend.
It is no surprise, then, that everybody from financial services
firms to Disney® can be seen frantically scurrying to build
products, services, language, ad campaigns, and sales practices
that will be welcomed by this population.

The Big Wave

We can argue about the exact ages or the beginning of the boomers' wave of spending and investing, fueled by lifestyle changes. We can't argue that it's here. Back in November 2005, *Newsweek* ran a cover proclaiming "Ready or Not, Boomers Turn 60," featuring photographs of the famous turning 60, including former President Clinton and President Bush, Donald Trump, Sly Stallone, Goldie Hawn, Susan Sarandon, Suzanne Somers (who is making an industry out of being 60 herself), and Cher. In 1946, 3.4 million Americans were born—a million more than in the entire previous decade. This bunch has led the way in social, political, and economic change. And they are the early or leading-edge boomers, now leading a wave of enormous potential prosperity for savvy entrepreneurs, CEOs, and marketers. Starting with 2006, and for the next 19 years, one boomer will turn 60 every 7.5 seconds. Of the entire U.S. population, 27% will hit 60 to 65 over the next two decades. The largest number of births in any one year in U.S. history occurred in 1957: 4.3 million; they turned 50 in 2007. In total, this is a slightly moving target; a leading edge passing 60, a huge population just hitting 50, each evolving from here. Within, all kinds of subsegments.

About one-third of boomers range from financially secure and well prepared for retirement to financially independent. About half of that third qualify as wealthy. But the amount of money they have needs to be put in the context of the very different attitudes they have about it than did the previous retirement generations. **Within the boomer population, there is a historically unprecedented percentage of affluent and ultra-affluent consumers coupled with a historically unprecedented willingness on their part to spend their money on themselves. This is a terrific dynamic for us marketers!**

There is also a huge generational wealth transfer occurring. In addition to their own income and accumulated wealth, boomers will inherit $7.2 TRILLION over the next 35 to 45 years.

The affluent boomer nearing, at, or sliding past 60 is a very, very different creature than was your father or grandfather at age 60.

I was 53 when writing the first edition of this book. I'm 59, a couple months from the big 60, as I'm completing this second edition. My father and his friends at 60 were

- eager for full retirement at age 65,
- considering relocation to one home for the rest of their life (Florida and Arizona were the retirement places),
- set for income shrinkage and fixed incomes,
- shrinking spending,
- accepting of aging, and
- moving into the retirement phase as a group in lockstep.

In her book *Turning Silver into Gold: How to Profit in the New Boomer Marketplace*, Dr. Mary Furlong states: "Today, boomers are RE-INVENTING their lives. They are finding NEW places to work, NEW places to travel to (and NEW ways of traveling), NEW ways to spend their days, NEW ways to spend time with their children and grandchildren, and NEW ways to stay vital and connected as they age. Each choice represents enormous business opportunity." The capital letters are mine, not hers, to emphasize that all your assumptions about boomers and all history of boomer businesses are now suspect, as we are literally re-inventing our third and fourth acts of life's play. In the book *After Fifty: How the Baby Boom Will Redefine the Mature Market*, Leslie M. Harris even says: "Boomers see age as a lifestyle choice rather than a chronological imperative."

Today's boomers are very different from my father's generation.

They are not at all eager for classic retirement. A Merrill Lynch survey cited in the book *MicroTrends* puts three out of four saying they have no interest in retirement. In fact, today's boomers are pegging their full retirement at 80, not 65, and are looking for second, third, or fourth careers or new businesses. Career or business opportunities that do not tie them to fixed schedules or brick-and-mortar locations are gaining in popularity. As example, GKIC Member Susan Berkley, CEO of the Berkley Persuasive Voice Academy in New York, tells me that two-thirds of her new students coming to learn how to make money as voiceover talent for radio and TV commercials and audio products are 55 years of age and up, many from very successful executive or professional backgrounds, and are quick to install complete recording studios in both their homes. Another Member, Brent Fogle at Options Trading University in Florida, is discovering the same sort of thing, somewhat to his surprise—the majority of his students finding him online are not young bucks trying to trade their way to a fast fortune with which to buy Maseratis® and Malibu beach houses but 55-to-60-year-old people looking for an interesting way to make some money, stay relevant and active, and have a sense of accomplishment, without being tied down to a job or conventional business.

At our own Information Marketing Association (www.info-marketing.org), we track this same trend: a rising percentage of those starting writing, publishing, speaking, life, or business coaching and consulting businesses in the 50-to-65 age range, about 50% male and 50% female, for motives other than or more complex than money. This booming boomer population's interest in continuing to work well past 60 but not be tied to desk, corner office, store counter, or daily commute suggest great profit in creating opportunities to fit their preferences and capitalize on their experience and affluence.

While Florida and Arizona remain immensely popular with those in their 60s, the trend is toward split-time residences:

owning two or even three homes or condos in different places and dividing time among then, not necessarily in strict seasonal rotation. Yesterday's snowbird migrating south or west for the winter is being replaced by a less migratory, more flexible splitter, who may be at his Michigan home in a university town for much of the winter, for skiing, for holiday activities with family; at his Last Vegas high-rise condo for New Year's and a number of times during the year; and at his Florida home the majority of the time, making it the primary residence, but barely. Boomers are mobile.

This has all sorts of marketplace effects. For example, the reverse mortgage began as a product of interest only to seniors typically 70 and up of modest means or even absent assets other than their home, in need of income, but is now welcomed by people at the minimum age allowed, 62, as a different means of extracting money from their primary residence without going into debt in order to buy their new, second home, their gigantic RV (recreational vehicle), or their luxury time-share membership. Consequently, many mortgage brokers across the country have begun successfully microtargeting "young seniors," that is, boomers with known interest in second or vacation homes, RVs, and so on, and probably an interest in retaining their primary, current homes for life. I foresee a whole new kind of time-share, linking a cluster of homes and condos in a Midwest hometown with a cluster of homes and condos in Florida, each resident having x number of weeks in each location, and y number of weeks in neither, when on cruises and other vacations—all paid via one ownership fee and monthly service fee, all provided by one company.

Boomers are also making up an increasing percentage of the estimated four million and climbing "commuter couples," who by choice for business, career, or family reasons, live apart a significant percentage of time and commute to be together.

Interestingly, the higher you go in affluence, the more you find this occurring.

The old ideas of shrinking income, fixed incomes, and minimum spending are out the window. My parents at 60 tended to become misers about spending on themselves, feeling obligated to preserve every penny for kids and grandkids. Even reasonably affluent retirees tended to tighten their purse strings and stop buying things for themselves. A 65-year-old couple ripping out their entire kitchen and installing a new $100,000.00 state-of-the-art, designer kitchen—unheard of! Also, the norm was a reduced income combining pension from job, Social Security, and yield from investments or savings, but IRAs and 401(k)s did not yet exist or were not popular. Advertisers and marketers viewed this audience as one of rapidly diminishing value and pressed TV networks not to air programming aimed at it—and when they did, the commercials featured denture adhesives and adult diapers, not investment companies, luxury automobiles, home furnishings, or Disney® vacations. Today's boomers have entirely different financial situations and entirely different attitudes.

What Do they Want? What Will they Buy?

As you'll see, as we progress, it is dangerous and foolhardy to do what I'm about to do—generalize—yet I do believe there are overriding themes that offer us big keys to success with boomers. To quote Ken Gronbach, author of *Common Census: Counterintuitive Guide to Generational Marketing*:

> They know what they want. They've been buying the same oil for their cars for years and they wear tan pants . . . . At this point in their lives they want only three things:
> 1. Life made easy.
> 2. Time saved.
> 3. Not to be ripped off.

I'm not *sure* about the undying loyalty to a brand of oil or color of trousers—although, personally, I've happily gone from 30 to 40 different kinds, colors, and fabrics of pants to only two constituting 90% of my wardrobe (tan khakis and blue jeans)—but I definitely buy his **list of three chief wants.** If you examine most ads aimed at boomers, though, you won't find these basic appeals straightforwardly addressed. *Here's how I'll make your life easy. Here's how I'll save you time. Here are solid proof and guarantees.* And if you'd like a good copywriting checklist for a 4-by-6 card, there it is.

Anybody who has turned 50 can tell you: his attitudes, needs, desires, and priorities DO change literally with that calendar benchmark. At 50, and even at 60, the overwhelming majority of affluent boomers are as busy as ever, even hitting their peaks of experience-based knowledge and capability, while at the same time being bedeviled by sudden and significant diminishment of physical capabilities, energy, stamina, good health, emotional tolerance for wasted time, incompetence, and hassle. When you consider all this, the first two items on Gronbach's list are obvious.

It's also worth noting that affluent boomers already own a lot of stuff. Their needs are fewer and get increasingly fewer with passing years, thus they are less interested in or seduced by *things.* Many of us now have the experience of paging through a favorite catalog or visiting a mall, able to buy just about anything we might want without second thought but finding nothing to buy. Consequently, **boomers are *service consumers* more than *product buyers.* We want nothing as a thing; we want a thing that gives us time, convenience, freedom, or ease.**

The third item on Gronbach's list is too often forgotten or misunderstood when selling to boomers. They have had more than enough life experience of being disappointed or feeling ripped off by a number of purchases and marketers. And they are not eager to repeat the experience. Boomers still think in terms of "classic credibility" while younger consumers do not; for example, brand names matter more, credible and relevant celebrity endorsements matter, years in business, professional affiliations, access to live humans for resolving problems, all matter more to boomers than to younger buyers (and more to seniors than to boomers). You need to increase the reassurance for each year of your customer's age.

Beyond Gronbach's list, I would make number four that they want what is *for them*—but not if pandered to or made to feel old by the specialization or customization. Affluent boomers are, frankly, elitists. To quote somebody I can't name, "If you can't have things everybody else can't, what the hell's the point of being rich?" Further, affluent boomers, especially affluent leading-edge and aging boomers, know (but prefer not to enunciate) that they have special needs and want them accommodated without a lot of fanfare.

One of the Toughest Challenges for Marketers
(The Death of Age-Based Advertising)

Age used to be a straight line, a continuum from birth to death, with benchmarks that were extremely predictive of behavior and therefore consumer spending. Many marketers still act as if this were true. People used to progress from college or military to office to family life to empty nest, retirement, and the golf course on a predictable schedule. These days, the schedule's been tossed out the window. Some 50- and 60-year-olds are starting second or third families, so a 55-year-old couple is in the market for a larger home (not a smaller one) close to a good school (not a golf course) and is a prospect for a Disney® Vacation Club time-share (not a condo in a retirement community). Instead of ending careers at 60 or 65, boomers are extending careers, starting new ones, and buying or starting businesses. **We boomers have made a helluva mess out of age-benchmark-based advertising, marketing, list segmentation, and product and service offers.**

This mess we're making requires an entirely new way of thinking about demographics, a far greater reliance on psychographics, and a much more serious commitment to such things as lead-generation advertising so boomers self-select; precise list segmentation and message-to-segment matching; sophisticated database management with the best possible tools; and smart use of response lists rather than compiled lists. It also requires literal reinvention of businesses to meet the desires of the segment(s) they choose—with recognition that hardly any business can be all things to all boomers. Frankly most businesses—large or small, national or local—WILL FAIL MISERABLY at capitalizing on these opportunities. The fresh and creative thinking, the agility in adapting, the financial and other commitments required will be beyond their owners' or leaders' ability or willingness to provide. As a result, I believe a number of big-name companies will be bankrupt and gone ten years from today, literally driven extinct by boomers' refusal to patronize then. And most small-business owners will feel it is all beyond them.

The tiny number of business owners willing to dig in and figure all this out and adapt accordingly may find the next 6 to 12 years of boomer boom to be the greatest wealth-creating time of their lives.

None of this means FREELY IGNORING the historic patterns of spending tied to passages from 30 to 40, 40 to 50, 50 to 60, etc. My friend Harry Dent Jr. is uncanny at his ability to predict the booms, stalls, and busts in various product, service, and business categories based on his study of the rising or declining populations within age groupings, and the historical precedents for their present and future spending. Every marketer should pay attention to Dent. You can start free, at www.DentResearch. com. However, you can't be dogmatic about this either. You have to be able to spot the disruptive factors that differ so significantly from the past that they will prevent history from repeating itself perfectly or precisely. You have to recognize substantial, artificial interference with the natural order and pace of things—for example, the Bernanke-to-Yellen years of super-suppression of interest rates, artificial support for the stock market (building a big bubble), and printing of money. This is the sort of thing that causes deviation from otherwise imminently predictable patterns much like a once-in-100-years drought causes deviation from otherwise predictable crop yields, harvests, and commodity prices.

Above all else, though, it is the attitude and mindset of the affluent consumer that matters most. This is uniquely true of the affluent consumer. If, for example, a barely-mass-affluent consumer loses 20% of his $250,000.00 net worth and his household income also drops by 25%, he is not only emotionally traumatized, his actual ability to spend is also compromised, more likely crippled. But if the truly affluent consumer and even more so the ultra-affluent consumer suffers the same percentage cuts, he still has a comfortable or beyond-comfortable cash reserve and asset base, and he still has far more income than he needs for necessities. For the ordinary consumer, his normal, customary, by-age attitudes can't govern spending when such reversals occur. For the affluent and ultra-affluent consumer, the normal, customary, by-age attitudes can still rule.

A Look at the Attitudes Governing Boomers' Spending

Boomers' Attitudes toward Aging

The advertising insider term for the earliest boomers is *abbies:* aging baby boomers. But these boomers would decry the term.

To say that these boomers expect to stay young isn't just a vague idea—it's verifiable through hard data from quality statistical research. Yankelovich Partners, one of America's respected research groups, found early boomers surveyed placed "old age" as *starting* three years *after* average life expectancy (82.3 years). Irrational as it may be, boomers do not feel bound by facts. They fully expect advances in health care, genomics, and other areas to have them living to or beyond 100. And the big wave of boomers behind them is even more expectant of long life. This has great significance for marketers. It means, in general, that a large number of those 60-plus are not thinking in terms of slowing down, aging gracefully, or retiring (as retirement has been known in the past) but instead are thinking about new options and changes.

An extensive survey of women ages 50 to 64 by Dove® beauty products found that they do not see themselves as older women, and they resist such description. Age is, of course, a more sensitive issue with women than men, and the gender differences do need to be considered throughout marketing to boomers, essentially adding a female vs. male division to whatever other segmentation is done.

Boomers' Attitudes toward Health

Boomers now expect to be cured of all sorts of things our parents or grandparents accepted as incurable—including breast cancer and other cancers, heart disease and heart attacks, and other serious ailments. There is an optimistic faith in medical research producing more and better cures for all manner of diseases that is wholly unwarranted by reality; there actually hasn't been a new, complete cure for anything since polio. However, boomers still believe the cure for what ails them is just around the corner and will arrive in time to save them. This makes a segment uninterested in self-help, self-discipline, and so on regarding their diseases. As a diabetic myself, I find many diabetics undaunted, talking about and anticipating easy, readily available organ transplants and expecting other cures, so eating badly and not exercising are irrelevant to them. Fortunately, there is a sizable segment who share similar hope for cures but are also extraordinarily proactive in attempting to influence their own health with alternative means. Thus the boomer boom is fueling the dramatic sales growth in nutritional and dietary supplements, herbal supplements, treatments available only at foreign clinics, organic and bio-engineered healthy foods, and so forth. On top of that, and seemingly in contradiction to it, the pharmaceutical industry is having a field day rolling out new prescription drugs for every conceivable (and newly conceived) ailment and being welcomed by boomers. Viagra® may be the most age-attitude altering of all pharmaceuticals of our time. It radically changed boomers' specific beliefs about their sex lives and aging, but, more broadly, it also changed attitudes about fixing *all* normal aging issues with drugs. It removed stigma; it created new expectations. In short, real medicine, alternative medicine, fake medicine, all are booming with no end in sight.

Dan Kennedy's #3
No B.S. Key to the Vault

Your desired customer's attitudes about things related to your product or service matter much more than any facts about your product or service.

The wellness industry, a new buzzword, has emerged from the fringes to be a major, mainstream business sector. It includes spas, organic foods, nutrition, exercise and fitness, and, given boomer vanities, cosmetic surgeries and procedures, beauty products and services, as well as, to a limited degree (due to the professions' own dysfunction at positioning themselves), chiropractic, massage therapy, dentistry, and integrative medicine. Given the wide range of businesses, practices, products, and services that can be classified as part of the wellness industry, determining industry size and growth is inexact. Various industry sources place the industry revenues from $500 billion to $700 billion. *Business Week* projects growth to reach $1 trillion by 2020.

A wide range of big companies are trying experimental ways to enter or expand their piece of this pie. Hotel chains are putting more emphasis on their spas and spa vacations at resorts. Hospitals are also (awkwardly) trying to position themselves as wellness centers rather than just sick rooms— some getting into the fitness center business, some adding vitamin and herb stores to their pharmacies. The most recent trend in health/wellness is occurring inside your mobile devices, on your smartphone, and in various wearable devices and smart watches: apps and websites and services that measure and monitor your calories consumed, steps walked, heart rate, blood sugar levels, etc., etc., provide coaching and accountability, transmit data to your health- care providers, and otherwise marry tech with your body.

One of the things the big corporations do not grasp about this growing consumer population is that it skews affluent, thus requiring targeted marketing and discriminating products, services, environments, and pricing. They err badly in marrying the wellness-demand growth trend with the boomer population wave as a whole. More than 50,000 corporations are currently identifying themselves as in the wellness industry, and Wall Street analysts specializing in the sector forecast that number quadrupling before 2020. This means the roughly tripled growth in consumer spending will be in play with a quadrupled number of competing marketers—and that does not factor in the much larger number of small businesses and solo practices.

Incidentally, eyeglasses and hearing aids have become fashion accessories, not just functional items. The percentage of people over 55 needing vision help is 88%. There are 60% needing hearing help—and given boomers' youthful affinity for rock concerts and rock music, that number's headed up. Innovative products that address these needs are finding success . . . . from cosmetic cases with magnifying mirrors to computer keyboards with big keys and easy-to-read letters to simplified cell phones that offer no features other than the phone. A mail-order company called FirstStreet® is specializing in such products and identifies itself as "for Boomers and Beyond.™" Care has to be taken never to rub a person's face in a need brought on by aging he is loathe to admit, so, for example, advertising for a lower, easier-to-climb-into SUV with bigger captain's chairs that swivel for easy in and out access cannot say the car is for old, fat people who have trouble climbing in and out. We marketers have to give great thought to finding ways of presenting needed, welcomed products and services without triggering denial, resentment, or other negative responses from boomers.

> "Boomers have redefined every age they've moved through, so there's no reason to believe they will not define the stereotypes of what it means to be retired."
>
> —PATRICK CONROY, CONSUMER BUSINESS ANALYST, DELOITTE & TOUCHE

Boomers' Attitudes toward Retirement

Classic retirement is no longer the goal of boomers. Affluent boomers who do not need to work or create earned income still expect to keep working—Merrill Lynch's New Retirement Survey put the total number at 81% of boomers who plan to work well past age 65. (This connects to their expectations of life span, health, etc.) A similar survey by the Wealth Institute directed at boomers with net worth from $3 million to $10 million had 62% expecting to keep working past age 65. Ken Dychtwald, president of Age Wave, says: "They want the action. They don't want to be on the sidelines." My take on this is that they fear being irrelevant, being bored, and being looked on as old or out to pasture to such an extent that even secret yearnings to relax, do nothing, travel, and golf are trumped. This is demonstrated by countless celebrity boomers and seniors. My friend the late Joan Rivers, in her 80s, absent any economic need, worked furiously to—in her own words—stay relevant. Regis Philbin stayed retired for about a week. The man holding the record for the most on-air hours as a talk show host quickly found his way to a sports talk show on one cable network, frequent appearances as a "celebrity investor" on CNBC, and increased frequency of appearances on Letterman. I believe Cher is, as I'm writing this, embarking on *another* farewell tour. Senior entertainers find ways to step into the spotlight of younger stars. Bob Newhart was robbed of a deserved Emmy, but still captured the attention of the audience of CBS's number-one show, *The Big Bang Theory*, with his guest star role as Professor Proton—made reoccurring by popular response. Senior crooner Tony Bennett, in 2014, released a duets CD with Lady Gaga. What do they all want? *Relevance.*

From a marketing perspective, this suggests two points: First, if your products or services have anything to do with retirement, you're going to need to redefine them. (Even boomer retirees do not like the term *retiree.*) Second, there's opportunity in leveraging their fears.

Sales Strategies, Tactics, and Tools

Basically, we can never know enough. Selling, in person or in media, is about connection. On a primitive level, it can be completely mechanized and some, sometimes satisfactory, money can be made. But on a sophisticated level, the more we understand, the more we are understood, accepted, and trusted.

Language

One way we translate our understanding of a group of people is by the language we use when speaking to them. Far too little effort is made by salespeople or copywriters to get the language right.

Early-edge boomers are quite sensitive about language used to describe them, their options, and aging.

In the 1950s, *they* used the term *old folks' home* without negative thoughts about it; today if you suggested they move into one, they'd pop you one in the nose! Then came *nursing homes.* Then *retirement homes.* Now, *assisted-living communities.* But that industry is scrambling to again redefine itself and reposition itself to be acceptable to aging-resistant boomers, especially affluent ones, who may very well need such housing and service options but are loathe to admit it. This industry's challenge can be seen as the positioning and linguistic challenge for all businesses seeking what dare not be called any longer a senior citizen market. (If anything, that kind of language has moved up on life's calendar, to be used for and acceptable to people in their 80s and up.)

Boomers and Nostalgia

Everyone even barely conversant with NLP (neurolinguistic programming) understands the use of emotional ANCHORS in persuasion. An anchor may be a song or music, a visual image, a person, place, or thing already embedded in the prospect's mind that when recalled and linked to you, your product, or your service produces positive thoughts and warm feelings and/or a sense of common bond, thus less resistance and greater, faster trust. Mainstream, mass advertisers most commonly attempt utilizing anchors by buying rights to and using very popular, well-remembered songs of boomers' youth. The best anchors, though, aren't as simple, brief, or one-dimensional. For example, Roy Rogers is an anchor for (mostly male) boomers of a certain age, but sitting on the floor in front of the TV, still in pajamas, with a bowel of cereal, to watch Roy Rogers, his superhorse Trigger, and Dale Evans . . . that's a better anchor.

Such NOSTALGIA ANCHORS are extremely useful in marketing to aging boomers, leading-edge boomers, and, to a slightly lesser degree, boomers.

The reasons nostalgia itself is so powerful are many, and they warrant an in-depth discussion of psychology. But to abbreviate, we naturally rewrite history and memory to romance the past (in linking to our desire for lost youth and immortality). We are dissatisfied with the present (because no reality can match imagined memory and because we are critical by nature). We fear the future (as it links to mortality).

Even false nostalgia is more appealing than present realities. As example, almost everybody likes—and buys things from—the little fake general store in Cracker Barrel® restaurants, even if the closest they ever actually got to a small-town general store with stuff in wood barrels was watching the *Andy Griffith Show* on TV. The Restoration Hardware® stores have similarly capitalized on nostalgia real and invented. Celebration, a planned community in Orlando originally developed by Disney® (a MUST-tour) is built out of nostalgia anchors. It is the picture-perfect, quintessential American small town appealing to those with a romanticized memory of such a place, but almost as appealing to people with an imagined nostalgia for such a place.

When marketing to boomers, you will benefit greatly from carefully choosing and using age-appropriate, gender-appropriate, geography-appropriate nostalgia anchors. But you can't overplay your hand either. Boomers are hypersensitive to being conned. They have seen a lot, have a lot of life experience, and quickly detect false, inauthentic, pandering attempts at connecting with them—and they resent them.

As an interesting example, I've encouraged my investment partner Darin Garman to increase the small-town anchors in his marketing of American heartland investment properties to investors throughout the country, including many from the coasts. Why? Because one investor enunciated for us what others have not but must be influenced by: He, a New York resident attending his mother's funeral in Iowa, saw Garman's ad, called, and bought several hundred thousands of dollars of small-town Iowa real estate on impulse, based on nostalgia for his youth. We have since seen the power of telling the story of a place where small-town values still rule, where Fourth of July parades and Friday-night games are attended by the whole town, where churches host summer picnics and neighbors meet at the ice-cream stand—even though it has nothing whatsoever to do with a numbers decision for an investor. But this has to be done gently, naturally, authentically—not waved like a big red pennant. Fortunately for Garman, it is authentic. It's where he lives and how he lives.

What Sets Boomers' Teeth on Edge: How to Lose a Boomer in 60 Seconds

If you want to know what will drive boomers away from your business, here's your answer. First and foremost, it is (perceived or real) disrespect. Boomers deeply resent and often react with rage to employees who 1) call them Pops, Ma'am, Old Man, and so on, either as deliberate or accidental offense; 2) dress in ways the boomers view as inappropriate for the workplace and a sign of disrespect for the job and the customers; 3) talk down to them or are condescending, such as "I realize at your age you don't know much about the internet, so…"; 4) use street slang or young slang or references instead of speaking the King's English; 5) fail to clearly explain things; 6) hurry them (beyond their capability); 7) engage in impolite, disrespectful behavior, such as talking on a cell phone while ringing up their sale at a cash register.

Beyond that, boomers aren't fond of having to deal with young employees in a number of settings. SalesDesign® expert Sydney Biddle Barrows did a massive research project about consumer expectations, satisfaction, and unvoiced dissatisfaction in cosmetic surgery, and found the number-one complaint of boomer women was having to discuss their treatment, progress, recovery, or questions with *"20-or-30-year-old GIRLS who can't possibly know what I'm going through."* While it is illegal to discriminate in hiring

Recommended Resource

SALES LANGUAGE is critical. Mark Twain said the difference between any word and just the right word is the difference between lightning bugs and lightning. You can fine-tune your own sales language, develop ultra-effective scripts, and convert ordinary selling into performance art—all dealt with in depth in Sydney Barrows' short-term tele-coaching program. Information at: www.SydneyBarrows.com.

based on age, it suggests going out of your way to recruit and hire age-appropriate staff members when you can, and to be careful how you deploy different staff members.

To do well with boomers, every person in your employ or representing you who comes in contact with your customers must learn to modify his attitude, language, appearance, and behavior to do well with boomers. Otherwise your people will sabotage your marketing.

Big Opportunities and How Businesses Will Adapt to Boomers in Coming Years

Conglomeration of Services

As example of the conglomeration-of-services approach, here's my thought about the retirement community for affluent boomers: I think there'll be a boom in retirement lifestyle clubs that bundle together a primary-residence condo or apartment in something akin to today's assisted-living center for time-share exchanges for other such sites all over the country x number of weeks a year, plus cruise ship weeks, car and driver transportation at all home sites, concierge travel services and concierge medical care, all for one monthly fee or lifetime prepayment.

This may require insurance companies, doctors, hospitals, HMOs, real estate developers, and community operators to all come together in new joint ventures, or a big company from one of the involved industries—say, Marriott (already very active in assisted living and, obviously, in travel)—to be the organizer, or an entirely new type of corporation to be created. For the customer, this will offer the own-nothing, rent-everything option or the time-share-your-whole-life-for-one-fee option. It is a quasi-marriage of today's high-end destination travel clubs utilizing mansions as well as resort properties—with buy-ins in the $200,000.00 to $350,000.00 range plus yearly dues—with retirement communities and assisted-living facilities, with full services, from a driver waiting to take you to the mall to a doctor on call to a refrigerator stocked for you. The consumers may even pay by assigning assets via their wills or transferring assets through irrevocable trusts rather than with present-day dollars, as more and more boomers feel entitled to spending it all rather than stacking it up for heirs. (Buffett has inspired and emboldened them.) This requires new and very innovative thinking about product, business models, financing models. (Charities have gotten very good at securing these post-death payments as well as getting large sums turned over in exchange for income or benefits for life. Why shouldn't other businesses?)

The truly innovative leaders—what I'm calling *lifestyle service inventors*—will make the huge new fortunes in America. Making fortunes from manufacturing is just about over and certainly freakish. Making fortunes from technology alone is on the ebb. Making fortunes in any single category of business being replaced by multichannel, multimedia, multicategory businesses based on high customer value is the coming trend.

Using this as metaphor, you have to start thinking about just how radically your industry and connected or potentially connected industries may change or could be changed, and how you can be in the lead rather than chasing—or worse, watching.

Experiences

"Boomers aren't likely to spend their retirement years sitting in a rocking chair. Instead, surveys suggest they'll continue to SEEK OUT REMARKABLE EXPERIENCES—whether on cruise ships, in RVs, or at hotels and gambling tables."

—*Fortune*, June 2006, a prescient forecast

Boomers are RESTLESS. They are easily bored and in need of a lot of external stimulation. The old idea of the 60s being a time to slow down and take it easy is moving forward, to people in their 70s and 80s, and is more common to NON-affluent boomers and their elders solely because of financial limitations on their options. Today's affluent boomers want to be entertained wherever they go, whether to Las Vegas or to a neighborhood restaurant.

Boomers are unsatisfied with the ordinary. An ordinary store, an ordinary mall, an ordinary hotel or resort, all unappealing. A resort needs to provide the chance to swim with dolphins, not just a nice pool area. Vegas and Disney® set the bar for themed experiences and environments, and retailers and other businesses must follow suit. Even mail-order catalogs and websites need to provide multidimensional experiences, not just descriptions of goods. You may immediately be tempted to engage in the Uncreative "But my business is different" thinking as an excuse for not creating exciting and memorable experiences for prospects and customers, clients, or patients—but boomers will not reward you.

Service Spread Thin: A Crisis and Opportunity in Capitalizing on the Affluent Boomer Boom

Boomers are far more demanding regarding service than, progressively, members of each younger generation. A 30-year-old is not annoyed by—and may even prefer—self-serve grocery checkouts or self-serve online banking. A 60-year-old hates it. Affluent boomers will go out of their way to go where they get exceptional service.

However, the United States is experiencing a significant and growing shortage of service-sector employees. By 2030, America will have twice as many retirees as in 2005, but only 15% more service workers to support them—and that's *with* unchecked illegal immigration. The demand for service is outpacing the workforce required to provide it, now and into the future. Most businesses are reacting to minimum-wage increases, overall increases in costs per employee, and ever-increasing managerial frustrations with quality of employees by reducing the number of service employees per x amount of gross sales or by some other ratio; substituting automation; and substituting self-serve systems, transferring the burden to the customer. This may be mathematically sensible, but letting bean counters create policy is a consistently destructive act. (Bean counters should count beans. Period. Kennedy's First Law of Investing: Never invest in a company run by the accountants.)

For success with the boomer boom, and especially with affluent boomers, a business needs to alter its fundamental economics in order to do the polar opposite: Increase the number of service persons . . . pay above-average wages and offer incentives to attract and keep superior people . . . invest in continual training (including training on satisfying boomer customers) . . . and integrate exceptional service promises into its advertising and marketing.

My favorite business success tactic is to engineer a business to be able to substantially outspend all its competitors on advertising and marketing, customer acquisition, and customer retention. I would extend this to hiring, training, and motivating people.

Social Networks and Organizations that Attract Boomers

AARP (www.aarp.org) is one of the largest membership organizations in the United States. It began as—and, to a great extent, is still a mask for—a business selling insurance, financial services, and other services to seniors, and selling ad media and other access to its members to companies marketing to seniors. In short, it is a marketing and media business presenting itself to a group of customers as an association working for them, serving them, even representing them politically. It is a terrific example of a tollbooth business. And of an illusion.

With its current size and success, its masquerade has become more real, but it is still not a true or classic social organization, like, for example, the Elks. In fact, AARP has no local chapters or meetings it organizes, although it does have its own speakers bureau and other support for member-organized gatherings. AARP's only official meeting for its members, its annual convention, draws more than 25,000 attendees and features speakers like Terry Bradshaw, Raquel Welch, and Bill Cosby.

AARP's media is expensive but pretty much essential if you are going to be a serious national marketer to the 55-plus, boomer, and senior markets. Many companies err by not integrating to the greatest extent possible with AARP, via advertising in its media, exhibiting at its conventions, providing editorial content for its publications, renting its lists, and offering discounts and benefits to its members. AARP is *the* big kahuna in this market, with nothing but growth in size and influence ahead.

AARP is also evidence of a "joiner bias" among boomers. Boomers are membership oriented, having grown up with many more affinity groups of influence than have younger generations. This is an exploitable bias. There is ample room for niched organizations serving boomers or only affluent boomers, largely copying AARP—for example, an association for affluent boomer travelers or affluent boomer real estate investors or affluent boomer golfers.

The Elks (www.elks.org) organization has, by comparison, only one million members and is struggling with declining membership. The group's average member is 65. It has lost moe than 600,000 members to old age or death since 1980 and has only recently begun serious efforts—with mixed success in different cities—to attract younger boomers. The organization does have 2,100 lodges throughout the United States. It has potential for reinvention. Unfortunately for the Elks, they do not skew affluent and tend not to attract affluent boomers… essentially they are trying to pump life with weak blood. They should not, however, be overlooked in developing a complete marketing plan for boomers (or seniors). They have effective and reasonably priced media **and** exploitable affinity.

The Red Hat Society (www.redhatsociety.com) has enjoyed terrific growth since its 1998 launch, largely thanks to generous media attention. Geared to women over 50, the organization has over 41,000 chapters (many very small), national publications, an online community and so on, but it revolves around local tea parties, luncheons, shopping trips, and the like. Over one million members proudly wear the trademark purple outfit with a red hat. While the organization makes no effort to attract affluent women, estimates are that better than half of its members are wealthy. The organization also has a very active licensing department, for fashions, accessories, gifts, merchandise of all kinds, books, and consumer service.

My take is that integrating a societal or community element into just about any boomer-oriented business is, at very least, in the no-harm, no-foul category—and can be very useful. It's a way to create added value mostly from thin air, and to involve your customers with you and with each other. Ideally, you'll find a way to use it to create "pain of disconnect," discouraging departure or fickleness and encouraging continued or frequent patronage.

Boomers Buying Businesses (and Selling Businesses)

Well over 50% of all sellers of businesses turn around and start or more often buy another business within 12 to 24 months.

There's no indication this is less true of people in their 50s, 60s, and beyond. The franchise industry reports that boomer buyers, especially early retirees encouraged to exit their corporate careers, are a prime source of buyers. A growing number of franchisors specifically target this market. There is no reliable research I've yet located on the relationship between boomers, homebased businesses, and in-home offices, but ample anecdotal evidence suggests a major trend there.

There are three key themes.

1. **One reason boomers start or buy businesses, franchises, or business opportunities is to prepare for and begin their next life.** They have no intention of actually retiring in the classic sense, and they look to self-employment or business ownership for their sense of purpose for the years from 50 to 60 or 60 to 70. In many cases, they are pursuing dream businesses—that's how bed-and-breakfasts, small restaurants, antique stores, and the like come about.

2. **The other reason is to make up for lost time.** Several of my clients have had considerable success aiming prepackaged part-time or second-business opportunities at affluent professionals ages 45 to 55, who, while affluent, still have not amassed enough wealth to comfortably retire. They see the second-income business as a means of pouring additional income into retirement savings and/or quickly creating equity in a saleable asset.

3. **A third area of opportunity is in selling lifestyle businesses to boomers,** such as info-marketing or internet-marketing businesses, mobile and portable businesses, and absentee-owner businesses. The "have your cake and eat it, too" theme is working well for countless promoters of businesses that lend themselves to spare and flexible time operation, outsourcing, and automation. And, claims about

large income potential are not as important as lifestyle claims . . . a common mistake is focusing on the money.

Boomers Investing and Investing in Boomers

In the financial services industry, there is a current—and likely to continue—explosion of investment products, advertising and marketing programs, prepackaged seminars, sales tools, sales training, info-marketers, and coaches all aimed at reaching the boomer market. There is even a separate trade journal, *Boomer Market Advisor* (www.thinkadvisor.com). Predictably and sadly, virtually all the ads and the editorial content in this publication is product and platform oriented, not focused on understanding and communicating with the boomer client. As is all too common, all these fools think is about their products. But the growing number of such products is illustrative of the size, scope, and potential of this market . . . and the need to customize for it, even if most financial companies and advisors are relatively clueless about how they ought to actually go about that.

Fact is, boomers have a lot of money invested but *also a ton of money underinvested.* Boomers, especially leading-edge boomers, have hundreds of millions of dollars parked in bank CDs, money market accounts, regular checking, bonds, and, still, in their mattresses. Those selling businesses or selling large homes and buying smaller ones; those getting paid bulk sums to retire early; executives with golden parachutes; and those inheriting money from their parents combined have a boatload of investable assets and are uncertain and anxious about where to put it. (Note: Anyone going after it needs to remember the three key wants mentioned on page 66.)

Boomers Buying Homes

According to the National Association of Realtors, boomers account for 50% to 60% of second-home purchases—a record high for the age group and a reminder that the old rules of age-based marketing are broken. Boomers used to buy second homes for only one reason (preparing for retirement), and only the ultra-affluent bought vacation homes. Today's affluent boomers may have a second and a third home .... and they have multiple buying motivations: leisure or vacation; preretirement; retirement; gathering places for geographically scattered families; and investment.

Affluent boomers who intend to buy new homes when they retire—59%; 45% in a different state than their current residence; 36% intend to downsize. One of the most sought-after in-home amenities: "spalike bathrooms." To me, this means the way the real estate industry works with boomer clients has to change, or the boomers will replace Realtors® with other means of meeting their needs. Boomers ready to relocate do not want hassles or uncertainties. This presents growing opportunity for real estate investors rather than agents to immediately relieve the boomer-owner of his current property, but somehow whoever is at that end of the process must also be able to support the boomer in finding and purchasing the new home, and vice versa. The opportunity here is in a seamless outcome for the boomer. Regardless, though, it tells you that this is a viable market for homes and condos—and a market less affected by price and market highs and lows than the general housing market, because when they're ready, they're ready, and they can afford the luxury of NOT waiting for better timing.

How Old Do You Think Grandpa Is?

Grandpa was born BEFORE:

- ❏ Television
- ❏ Penicillin
- ❏ Polio shots
- ❏ Frozen foods
- ❏ Xerox®
- ❏ The pill
- ❏ Credit cards
- ❏ Ballpoint pens
- ❏ Pantyhose
- ❏ Electric typewriters
- ❏ McDonalds®
- ❏ Pizza Hut®

Grandpa says:

Your grandmother and I got married first, then lived together. Every family had a father and a mother. Until I was 25, I called every man older than me Sir. You could buy a new Chevy for $600.00— but who could afford one? Pity, cuz gas was 11 cents a gallon. Grass was mowed; Coke was a cold drink; hardware was found only in a hardware store. If you saw anything made in Japan, it was junk no self-respecting American would buy. We were before dual careers, day-care centers, draft dodging, group therapy, fast food. We had 5-and-10-cent stores where things sold for 5 cents and 10 cents.

OK, now, how old do you think Grandpa is?

Most I've tried this on guess from 80 to 90 to dead. In fact, he is 59, my age.

The younger you are, the more distant in the past you are likely to place Grandpa and his frame of reference, his life experiences. Thus, the more difficult you'll find it to connect with boomers. What you can't conceive of anybody still walking the earth having experienced we recall as if yesterday and, as we age, recall with increasing fondness and nostalgia. The emotional gap between

How Old Do You Think Grandpa Is?, continued

boomers and those in their 30s is the size of the Grand Canyon. Boomers resent the lack of knowledge, understanding, and respect for their history. To connect with boomers, you must be familiar with, respectful of, and reference where they came from.

CHAPTER 8

Those Who've Gone from Poor to Rich

"I don't think of myself as a poor deprived ghetto girl who made good.
I think of myself as somebody who from an early age knew
I was responsible for myself, and I had to make good."

—OPRAH WINFREY

I've gone from rags to riches, so I think I get these rich customers better than any others.

A very significant percentage of the affluent population did, in fact, pull themselves up by their bootstraps, and they strongly identify with that cliché. Many came from stark or relative poverty or other difficult circumstances and are still very much governed by having been poor or put down. They never disconnect emotionally from this past, no matter how successful and wealthy they become. Some romanticize their past struggles. All keep them as touchstones. I doubt it coincidence that Jay Leno's star on the Hollywood Walk of Fame is located precisely at the street corner where he was twice arrested for vagrancy. Can't help but think he had something to do with that placement. Or that his massive collection of classic cars may have roots in his having to sleep in his car while homeless, when starting out. I settled for a little model of my first car, a 1960 Chevy with leaky floor and roof, bought for $25.00 on $5.00 monthly payments in 1971.

Walt Disney was once driving home from Disneyland® when he saw and stopped briefly to admire a particular new car in a showroom window. Then driving home, he said aloud to himself, "Gee, I wish I could afford one of those." It was a half hour later that it occurred to him—"Hey, I can afford that"—and he turned around, drove back to the dealership, and bought himself the car. This reveals a little something about self-made affluents: They may have nearly unrestricted spending power in reality, but not necessarily mentally and emotionally. Most are conflicted about money. They know they need to think, feel, and act rich to remain attractive to money, as I explain in my book *No B.S. Wealth Attraction in the New Economy*. But they also battle guilt, fear, anxiety, and abhorrence of waste. Those who have worked for their wealth, rather than inherited it or gotten it in some amazing windfall, as a movie star or athlete signed to a $50 million contract, can be self-indulgent and profligate, but are not casually so. A yacht salesman told me: "I always show them an outrageously pricey one first, a very expensive but slightly smaller and less luxuriously equipped one second, and a stripped-down bargain model third. They buy the middle one and are able to feel good about not spending as much as they could have. They feel like they acted responsibly."

Selling to the Self-Employed Affluent

A very valuable subsegment of these self-made affluents is business owners and entrepreneurs. Here you may very well find your best customers, clients, or patients.

Self-employment is one of the most reliable paths to first-generation wealth, supplemented by real estate investment. All the research into the rich done by Dr. Thomas Stanley, summarized in his books like *The Millionaire Next Door,* showed that self-employeds make up a slightly growing 20% of the U.S. population, yet account for about 70% of the affluence. The net worth of a U.S. household in which its head is self-employed is nearly 500% greater than one in which the number-one breadwinner works for somebody else. Frankly, we business owners tend to pay ourselves a lot better than we do anybody else! And among the ultra-affluent, just shy of 50% own a business that is their primary source of wealth. The other 50% is fragmented, with wealth amassed from inheritance, marriage and divorce, pedantic investment over time, and a number of other sources.

The personality of these affluent business owners and entrepreneurs is sharply drawn, with little ambiguity, so they can be the easiest of all affluents to market a wide variety of goods and services to.

One of my multimillionaire clients owns a large home services company. He grew up in a house with no indoor plumbing. He started in business with a box of tools and hard work. Another multimillionaire client was divorced by his first wife and shunned by his own family for being a wild-eyed dreamer who refused to get a decent job. Only when his brother, a doctor, saw an article about my client in *Forbes* did the family make overtures to patch things up. Another multimillionaire client now traveling around in his two private jets and living in what can only be described as a palatial estate in Florida was once working as a car mechanic, and recalls having to explain to his wife that they could not afford to have the clothes dryer repaired and having to borrow the money to go to his first seminar on real estate. These examples are more typical than atypical of the affluent entrepreneur profile. They have never been handed anything. They've worked and sacrificed for everything they've gotten. They got it by "taking no shit" from anybody and have no intention of doing so now.

Won't Take No for an Answer

First and foremost they view themselves as fiercely independent. They chafe at rules and tend to exit, stage left, immediately upon hearing rules language from anyone marketing to them. The fastest way to repel this customer or client is tell him "No, you/ we can't do that," and when asked why not, say, "Policy."

I have stayed at every imaginable kind and brand of hotel, from the much-lauded bastion of service, Ritz-Carlton, to the orange-roofed Howard Johnsons; top-rated resorts, city business hotels, rural motels. I and my companies have spent millions of dollars putting on meetings, conferences, and conventions for groups of 20 to 20,000 in these same facilities. Since this is self-described as the service and hospitality industry, you might expect service and hospitality. But you'd be wrong. In 30 years of this patronage, I have been in only two of these places where no matter what I asked, I never heard the word no or can't. The properties where this occurs consistently are Disney's® in Florida, notably Animal Kingdom Lodge® and the Grand Floridian®. Everywhere else, you get no's. I've stayed in a lot of resorts once. I take a vacation at a Disney property nearly every year. If not already, I'll certainly generate a million dollars in lifetime customer value for Disney®. Only $10,000.00, give or take, for just about every other resort I've ever stayed at but will never stay at again. That's the value of being able to say yes to the affluent.

If They Admire You, They'll Reward You with Their Business

Second, the self-made affluent are great admirers of the qualities that got them where they now are. Every one of them is doing business with somebody who reminds them of themselves when they were starting out. I got my first bank loan from a 70-year-old entrepreneur who owned the small-town bank outright, and the mill, and the main street restaurant and hardware store, and most of the real estate as far as the eye could see in any direction. I met him for lunch at his diner on a Wednesday, not knowing his bank was closed on Wednesdays. Afterwards, he unlocked the bank, found its checkbook in a drawer, wrote out a check to me for $50,000.00, and told me he'd have somebody draw up the paperwork and mail it to me to sign. He said I reminded him of himself when he was a young buck too dumb to know what couldn't be done and tough enough to do it. I regretted not having asked for $100,000.00.

These people reward ingenuity, drive, persistence, and salesmanship. They have a *spiritual reverence* for these virtues.

An axiomatic example was given me by a fellow who was charged with selling a new kind of pizza-making conveyor oven to New York restaurants. In the city of pizza, only fixed ovens with real pizza stones were acceptable. To crack the market, he determined he would need the number-one restaurateur as a reference, the owner of a couple famous, high-end restaurants as well as five different franchise chains. It just so happened this entrepreneur had just secured the area rights to a new pizza franchise and would soon be opening dozens of locations. The salesman sent him a letter requesting an appointment. Then he sent him one of his business cards with a handwritten request, along with some brochure or article about the ovens or the restaurant business in general, every day. Every day for two months. Finally, his phone rang and the famous restaurateur asked—in good humor—"What do I have to do to get you to stop sending me your business cards?" The salesman told him he'd bought the cards by the thousand, so there was a long way to go, but a brief appointment would put an end to it. The ending is happy. More than 100 of those pizza locations have the "odd" ovens.

On the other side of this coin, the self-employed affluent genuinely detest sloth, weakness, wimpiness. They are hustlers who not only respect hustle but find those lacking it pathetic and untrustworthy. That does not mean they respond well to desperate hustle; they don't. But aggressive hustle, they do.

They Are—More Often than Not—Searching for Value, as They Define It

Third, they know the value of a dollar, and tend to pride themselves on being smart about money, getting good deals and bargains, negotiating successfully, even being seen as frugal. Donald Trump likes telling the stunts of buying the bankrupt billionaire's oceanfront manor as a foreclosure bargain, of recouping his investment in his famous Mar-a-Lago resort by replacing all of the antiques, antique furniture, and art that came with it with reproductions and selling the originals, and of buying his huge 727 airplane rather than a smaller private jet because there was less of a market for 727s so it could be had at a bargain price. The late Sam Walton and Warren Buffett, famously, symbolically frugal: old pickup trucks, off-the-rack suits, even brown paper bag lunches.

When you step down from these ultra-affluent business leaders to the merely affluent, you find even more serious frugality. While they all have one or two things they will spend wildly on, most abhor waste and have an emotional need to buy smart with most things they buy. I believe this is rooted in two things: 1) a patch of thin skin about others' perceptions of the rich as drunken-sailor spenders who are fools about money, reinforced by the news stories featuring those who are, and 2) a vivid memoir of and residual paranoia about from whence they came, when spare change from the couch cushions was needed to buy dinner. Most affluent entrepreneurs harbor a nagging fear of losing it all or having it all taken away from them and winding up broke. This anxiety is always there, like a low-grade infection. If they feel they are wasting money, that anxiety flares up.

It's important to know that the price these people will pay for something has to do with how right and justified or queasy and irrational they feel about it. Not about intrinsic value or their own ability to pay.

In marketing to the affluent, you will mostly be marketing to these people who have made themselves affluent through ingenuity and initiative—not rich heiresses roaming Rodeo Drive between two-martini lunches and hours at the spa, not rappers and rock stars or superstar athletes draped in bling. The way you present yourself to them must be in sync with their values.

Reprinted from: *No B.S. Marketing to the Affluent* Letter. Diamond Membership. www.GKIC.com

---

I want to tell you about four people.

One drives a $400,000.00 Maybach (a luxury auto I also own) and a $360,000.00 Bentley, wears a diamond-encrusted one-of-a-kind wristwatch, lives in a two-floor penthouse in New York in which he removed walls in order to create a big home theater. He is as new-rich flashy as can be.

The second guy splurges on $500-a-box cigars, his custom shoes cost $500.00 a pair, his oddball vehicle stable includes an actual M47 tank, and he has ownership interests in over 100 businesses and is a significant stockholder in companies like Weight Watchers and Walmart.

The third guy wears only perfectly tailored Armani suits, has a large motorcycle collection, and has several homes each worth upwards from $10 million.

The fourth calls himself a beer-and-pretzels guy, wears jeans and rugby shirts every day, drives a five-year-old car, and owns a huge

---

home with only a few rooms in it furnished, but owns and uses a Gulfstream V, and famously makes large purchases and investments.

The first guy was expelled from high school and never finished, and after being rejected by every company in his industry that he submitted his demo product to, produced it himself and started selling it out of the trunk of his car. He is worth an estimated $300 million.

The second guy is an immigrant, was rejected by many potential employers, and made some of his first money with a kitchen table info-marketing/mail-order business. He began buying cheap real estate before he owned a home of his own or even had an apartment of his own, while bunking with friends. His estimated net worth exceeds $400 million.

The third guy grew up in a trailer, with his mother and a series of "stepfathers." He worked in a rock quarry, as an adding machine salesman B2B door to door, and at an ice cream stand, before being hired as an announcer by his biological father—from whom he later bought the small business in 1982, grew it, took it public, and made it a multimillion-dollar enterprise. His estimated net worth exceeds $500 million.

The fourth guy has benefited from a little luck and fortuitous timing—he sold the second company he built to Yahoo! for $5.7 billion, before the dotcom crash. But *he's from a blue-collar family background, and he started his first business after working, selling, scamming, and paying his own way through college.* He became a millionaire from it by age 31. His estimated net worth exceeds $1 billion.

The first rich guy is Jay-Z. The second, Arnold Schwarzenegger.

Third, Vince McMahon. Fourth, Mark Cuban. You see him now on *Shark Tank.*

How They Spend Their Money

Cuban is most transparent in not caring about some things and thus being relatively cheap in spending on those things, while caring a lot about other things and spending on them, ludicrously. Nobody needs a Gulfstream V; not for speed, security, or convenience. But if you could closely examine the other three, you'd uncover the same fact. To Arnold, fine cigars and enjoying them is of earth-shaking, prime importance. You can be certain he reads *Cigar Aficionado* magazine. As Governor of California, he even challenged the anti-smoking rules at the state capitol. He also cares passionately about ownership of iconic American companies and quality real estate, like shopping malls. I am certain we could find other things he has no interest in at all, and may very well be buying ordinary goods at ordinary prices in those categories. Jay-Z is about "bling" impressive to fellow rappers and entertainers, but he is not an accumulator of large residences around the country.

Appearances, status, peers' opinions seem to matter to them all, although maybe less to Arnold than the others. Cuban bought an NBA basketball team, McMahon took a stab at a new pro football league and his wife poured money into a U.S. Senate campaign. Jay-Z wants to be known as something much bigger than a rap music mogul; he has a vodka brand, an apparel company, and minority ownership in a pro basketball team. The rich and super-rich buy things that reinforce or raise their prestige. The self-made rich tend to (try to) buy respect and respectability. They are also intensely, perhaps obsessively, competitive. Visibly, notably winning, leading, having the biggest, the best, is important to them.

They all indulge themselves, expensively, *and openly*. There is none of the (artificial) humility of a Warren Buffett here. Schwarzenegger recently retold his story of buying the tank on the Kimmel show—and clearly relished the telling of it. Cuban is happy to have you know his $41 million Gulfstream is the largest online purchase in history. Jay-Z didn't just buy a fantastically expensive watch—he had a custom Audemars Piguet made.

And what do you think *they* think about their indulgent and lavish and mostly showy spending? They are obviously uninhibited. I would imagine, if challenged about it, they would say—contrary to Obama's ideas—that *they* created it, *they* built it, *they* earned and earn it, and they're fully entitled to keep it and spend it any damn way they please. They share hard-scrabble starts, and they appreciate and respond well to "hustle" and hustlers. They have all been underestimated underdogs.

This gives you valuable insight, as a marketer or sales professional, engaging such people—whether worth a mere million or ten million or hundreds of millions of dollars.

CHAPTER 9

The ¾-Full Glass

"In all likelihood, world inflation is over."

—The Managing Director of the
International Monetary Fund, in 1959

A very important thing to understand about the psychology of affluence is optimism.

In the first edition of this book I reported on this: In the very same month late in 2007 that Gallup released and publicized a poll showing some 92% of the population purportedly in a state of angst and depression over the state of the economy, Rush Limbaugh sent factoids out to his newsletter subscribers saying, "Here are the facts about the actual robust economy, a continual surprise to mainstream reporters":

- The GDP grew by 3.9% in the third quarter—faster than expected, according to the *New York Times*.
- Productivity surged 4.9% in the third quarter, the fastest pace in four years.

- Since January, 1.25 million non-farm jobs have been created, 84 million since the Bush tax cuts.
- The GDP is up 18.5%, about $1.8 trillion since the start of the Bush presidency.
- The deficit has fallen to just 1.2% of GDP.
- Discretionary income for U.S. consumers grew to a record high going into the fourth quarter.

Limbaugh presented these facts in the context of a two-page "lesson in Economics 101," debunking the gloom and doom being spread at the time by Democratic presidential contenders and complicit media. You may or may not think he cherry-picked his facts of the moment, to fit his own consistent premise that the economy is strong, the gap between poor and rich is good news of expansive opportunity, and good times are ahead. But it really matters less what you think than what his gigantic audience featuring mass-affluent and affluent business owners, entrepreneurs, and professionals think. And they think Limbaugh is right. And they reward him by tuning in for hours every day to hear this optimistic message. No one spreading a pessimistic message can boast of an audience even a fraction of his. They also reward his advertisers, and his program has been a market maker for companies ranging from builders of pre-engineered commercial and industrial buildings to hardwood floors to computer software.

In September 2007, the American Affluence Research Center conducted its yearly fall survey of affluent and ultra-affluent consumers and investors. This was immediately after a very volatile August in the stock market, amid much negative noise about the subprime mortgage crisis, and a slowing, weak housing market. The media was a gloom-and-doom machine turned on High. Still, the survey respondents were "cautiously optimistic" in their outlook for the economy, and expressed a "positive outlook" about the stock market and their own personal incomes. The percentage expressing no plans for major expenditures in the next 12 months was neither up nor down from the previous five surveys. And about two-thirds of the wealthiest of the households reported plans for major expenditures in the coming 12 months, including automobiles, home remodels, and cruises.

This is but one illustration of the optimistic attitude of the affluent. If you are alert, you can find plenty of the very same expressions of contrarian optimism aimed at affluent listeners, viewers, readers, and buyers on any day, any week, any year, regardless of the prevailing news of the day. As I'm writing this, a very pro-market investing "personality," Charles Payne, has emerged from the ranks of Fox and Fox Financial network pundits to host his own nightly show, pretty much a cheerleading for optimistic investing infomercial. I happen to like him, and I have profited from some of his advice, carefully chosen. There is no doubt, though, that he is popular by preaching to the converted, just as Limbaugh is. The cynic might think it's easy for the affluent to be optimistic because they have so much money, but that ignores the fact that the majority of the affluent got to this point through their own initiative as entrepreneurs,

Dan Kennedy's #4
No B.S. Key to the Vault

Be a good-news merchant. Sell optimism along with whatever else you sell.

business owners, and investors and, themselves, cite optimism as a cause rather than effect. At their core, they are optimists. And they tend to be most responsive to optimistic messages.

In my own survey of millionaire entrepreneurs, I found that the overwhelming majority ranked Ronald Reagan as the best President of our lifetimes and ranked John F. Kennedy as second best. The title of worst went to Jimmy Carter. If you carefully examine the speeches, addresses to the nation, interviews, and overriding themes of these three men and their presidencies, you can easily see Reagan and Kennedy as representatives of optimism, Carter as a representative of pessimism.

I have several clients in the investment real estate field, who have been largely unaffected by the troubles that began dominating the news from mid–2007: the mortgage meltdown, tightening of available credit, slow housing market, drops in values. Many of their competitors have seen their investor clients freeze new investing. Not my clients. Why? Because they quickly became passionate preachers of a positive message. Citing John D. Rockefeller's famous "buy when there is blood in the streets" advice, they have beat the drum of now as the best time ever to find bargains and buy, buy, buy.

Most affluent entrepreneurs are very familiar with Napoleon Hill, author of *Think and Grow Rich*, and his admonition that "in every adversity lies the seeds of equal or greater opportunity." This is a belief already in place that any marketer can link himself to when his industry, product, or service category or clientele are actually facing difficult times or are being told they are by the media.

Optimists are naturally attracted to other optimists. If you seek to go where the money is, you will find yourself unwelcome if you lack and fail to express an attitude of optimism. I have long told my clients, "Whatever else you are a merchant of, be sure that you are also a merchant of good news."

What the Wealthy and Successful Believe That the Poor and Unsuccessful Do Not

If you roam the libraries and bookshelves in any ten affluent or ultra-affluent individuals' homes and offices, you will find at least seven well stocked with what I call the literature of the rich. Books like *Think and Grow Rich*, *The Power of Positive Thinking*, *The Magic of Thinking Big*, and other classic, perennial bestsellers of similar theme. If you visit the homes of any ten poor people, you will likely find none of these books in none of the homes. It is not coincidence. It is causative. The possession of such books reveals a very particular and specific mindset on the part of the affluent—that there is a profound and direct link between their thoughts, attitudes, and beliefs and their prosperity. Consequently, the affluent of this belief are conscious, even forced, optimists. They deliberately resist their own pessimism or pessimism delivered to them by others. The poor, on the other hand, are extremely pessimistic and welcome delivered pessimism as proof that their lack of success is rooted in circumstances beyond their control. The rich explain the poor as "poor of mind, poor in purse." The next logical extension of this is that the rich tend away from skepticism, the poor tend to it. Pessimism and skepticism are close cousins. Because the rich strive not to permit themselves to be pessimistic, they automatically tend not to be skeptical.

So, whom would you rather be selling to—a skeptical and pessimistic person, or an accepting and optimistic person?

CHAPTER 10

Peer Deep into
Their Souls

*"I do not wish to be in any club that would have
me as a member."*

—GROUCHO MARX

T he affluent are segregationists. Even those loudly
proclaiming their liberal or socialist politics and social
consciousness. Segregationists all.

In the old South, white people didn't want to drink water
from water fountains used by blacks. In the new *Richistan*, rich
people do not want to drink the same water or use the same
entrances or, God forbid, sleep on the same sheets as ordinary
folk. *Richistan* is the "place" described by Robert Frank in the
fascinating book *Richistan: A Journey Through the American Wealth
Boom and the Lives of the New Rich*, a must-read for every marketer
to the affluent. Among other things, it gives insight to the tiered
and aspirational elitism of the mass-affluent, affluent, and ultra-
affluent, each group emotionally validated by its purchased
privileges that those one level lower are denied.

First of all, segregation has been the NATURAL order of things since cavemen. We form tribes. In elementary school, junior high school, high school, and college. At work, at the office, within our professional and trade associations. In our cities and neighborhoods. We form tribes. We form tribes more to exclude than include. We seek separation, differentiation, and disassociation from unlike as well as association with like.

In an episode of *Mad Men*, the outstanding AMC dramedy about the advertising agency business—and life—in the 1950s, a new woman moves into the suburban community, and she is, horror of horrors, a mother of a young child, divorced, without a husband. All the other women are married, of that tribe, and quickly close ranks to protect their husbands and themselves from the dangerous influence of this foreign, exotic creature. It reminded me of an episode of the old *Andy Griffith Show*, when a stranger comes to Mayberry, and everyone becomes convinced he's an international spy, just because he is a stranger. This speaks to the fear, paranoia, loathing, dislike, and disdain we have for the different even as we seek to feel different. The tribes we form try to reinforce our differences as superiority by excluding a majority of those we can label as inferior.

Assimilation has remained a theoretical goal but never realized. Each tribe voluntarily segregates. If this were not the case, there would be no BET or NAACP, there would be no gay pride parades or gay and lesbian magazines and websites, no Italian or German neighborhoods, no Chinatowns, no women's health clubs like Curves®, and, in economic examples, no private schools or colleges. No one would want such things. Everyone would want only to be fully and completely assimilated with everyone else. But this is not what you want or what I want. Nor is it what liberals want; if it were, their kids wouldn't be in private schools and there would be affordable public housing in ZIP code 90210. It is certainly not what affluent people want—

they have worked very hard to arrive at the financial ability to segregate themselves.

As a political exercise in America, we keep trying to desegregate society in terms of race, ethnicity, gender, economic status; we have geographic redistribution schemes engineered into the code. Just about as fast as we democratize something, the people affected resegregate themselves. Hotels were once used only by the rich and by business travelers; they democratized prices, but then, added concierge floors, then higher- and higher-priced hotels, even to the point of putting a Four Seasons inside the Mandalay Bay. When I started flying on business in the mid–1970s, I was the young oddball in first class. With very rare exception, it was all 50-year-old white guys in suits and ties,

"Sure, you're in, but it's not really heavenly until you upgrade to premium Heaven."

frequent business travelers—the riffraff could not afford sitting there, and the divider was firmly policed by the stewardesses who brought us drinks, food, and even *Playboy* magazines and on long flights sat and played cards with us. Today many flights have no first class, and those that do have seats dispensed at cheaper prices than 30 years ago (inflation adjusted) and often to people getting up there with frequent flier points. Air travel has been price democratized and desegregated, and even the crowd that used to go Greyhound® now flies the unfriendly skies. What happened? A giant boom for private aviation, featuring fractional jet ownership. You can't stop segregation. And you damn sure can't stop those with money from segregating themselves from everybody else.

What the Gates Really Are

A gated community is not really about protection from thundering hoards of criminals, as was a drawbridge and alligator-infested moat for the affluent tribe's early predecessors. You are, of course, at far more risk of home invasion, burglary, and other crimes living in an inner-city ghetto than in a suburban gated community. Today's gates are symbolic far more than functional. They are the grown-up version of the boys' tree house with rope ladder pulled up after only the chosen few in the club have climbed up. A symbol of exclusion. We are in, you are not, *nah, nah, nah.* The gates are symbolic of exceptional achievement, accomplishment, and status. Symbolic of the very existence of an elite tribe. Mostly, this is simple economic segregation. But as another example, consider the Florida city envisioned by Domino's Pizza® founder Tom Monaghan, into which he poured hundreds of millions of dollars, his intent to create a *Catholic* gated community devoted to Catholic life. As a legal practicality, he can't ban heathens or Baptists or Jehovah's Witnesses; he can

Dan Kennedy's #5
No B.S. Key to the Vault

Create the tribe your desired customers are
eager to be a member of.

only design every brick, every cultural icon, every tribal activity to make them feel unwelcome. Gate at community's entrance or cross in its town square, symbols of tribalism.

As a marketer to the affluent, it is vital you fully understand tribalism in general, and the affluent's devotion to membership in smaller and smaller, seemingly more and more elite and therefore profoundly exclusionary tribes.

The affluent tribalism is simply an extreme variation of all tribalism. The most important thing to understand about it is its emotional driving forces, so that you fully incorporate those same forces into your marketing. Those forces include those common to all tribalism: acceptance, recognition, peer approval, like-mindedness, elitism. But **the overriding driving force of affluent tribalism is validation of superiority.** The affluent believe—whether through heritage or achievement—that they are inherently and profoundly superior to all others. The majority have arrived through accomplishment born of ingenuity and innovation, discipline and persistence, work ethic and related behavioral characteristics, as well as philosophy they see lacking in the masses, so they do not view their affluence as luck or gift but as product of and then as proof of their superior character.

In short, their affluence is a special form of moral authority and superiority. This is the belief system that gives affluent liberals and socialists their moral authority to dictate to others how they should live: Barbra Streisand telling people to dry their clothes on clotheslines rather than wasting energy on electric dryers, although it's doubtful she has James Brolin out on the Malibu beach with laundry basket and clothespins. Al Gore preaching energy conservation to save the earth from global warming while flitting about in gas-guzzling private jets between giant, energy inefficient homes. Warren Buffett insisting "the rich" should pay more income tax while virtually all of his income is not subject to it, but instead taxed as capital gains. Nothing new here. Limousine liberals have been with us since first wealth. And, for the most part, they do not perceive themselves as disingenuous hypocrites. In their minds, they possess their special moral authority as superior beings.

This is the same belief system that gives affluent conservatives their moral authority to dictate to others how they should live: Limbaugh, of whom I'm a fan, but still, Limbaugh railing against drug offenders from his radio pulpit while indulging his own addiction to painkillers not just by doctor shopping, but allegedly by sending his housekeeper out to buy stolen drugs from back-alley dealers. This is the belief system that keeps the rich's reaction to the homeless fellow in the doorway "Get a job" rather than "There, but for the grace of God, go I." Affluent conservatives believe their affluence is result of superior initiative and discipline, certainly not luck of the draw.

If you are an affluent by accomplishment yourself, this may seem an unflattering glimpse in the mirror. Be that as it may, accurate, honest, realistic, and pragmatic assessment of the deep-seated beliefs of those you seek to sell to is valuable beyond price. Even the price of turning one's self-portrait to face the wall. We are what we are.

So, what do Superior Beings want? It's really quite simple. Recognition as Superior Beings. The sort of segregation that kings and queens have always had, that is *appropriate* for kings and queens. Special privileges. Fawning service. Products, services, and places inaccessible to anyone but kings and queens.

Recommended Resource

A Comprehensive Course on Tribalism-Marketing (to the Affluent)

My book *No B.S. Guide to Brand-Building by Direct Response* features insight into the development of a brand-tribe connection, and use of the tribe to further build the brand (rather than pouring money into traditional brand advertising). Today's online social media can be a powerful ally in such an exercise. My co-authors, Forrest Walden and Jim Cavale, are developing the fastest growing, most successful brick-and-mortar fitness franchise system featuring group workouts, appropriately named: Iron Tribe Fitness. Their fully illustrated case history in the book along with accessible videos for readers of the book are a great demonstration of **tribalism-marketing to the affluent.**

CHAPTER 11

The Affluent E-Factors

"There is perhaps no feeling more acute than being left out."

—MARK PENN, IN HIS BOOK *MICROTRENDS*

A short preface . . . since publication of the first edition of this book in 2009, I've gotten more unsolicited, favorable comment about this chapter than I would have guessed. Marketers and merchants of every stripe have told me of very practical applications—reworking their marketing, rewriting or replacing their advertising, altering the sales presentations and scripts they and their staffs use. A dentist conducting public seminars to get implant patients sent me his "before" script, his "after" script, and reported a 170% improvement in booking of appointments at the end of his seminars—accounting for over $600,000.00 more dentistry performed, year to year. I tell you this so that you don't miss its importance. An investment firm retooled its lead generation advertising, making sure to embed all seven of the extra affluent E-Factors on pages 116 to 117, and more than doubled response. I could go on. I tell you *this so that you don't somehow miss the importance and usefulness of this chapter. We have laminated cards with all the E-Factors, and will be glad to send you one or several—simply request them by faxing your full contact information to: 602-269-3113.*

E-Factors are the emotional drivers of buying behavior. For years I have taught sales professionals and marketers a generic list of E-Factors and done my level best to get them to rely on that list, whether selling to the CEO in the boardroom or Mom 'n' Dad in the kitchen at home. The most common mistake made by marketers is an egotistical belief that *their* customers are smarter, more rational, and more sophisticated than others, thus not controlled by E-Factors. It's a costly egotism. *Everybody's* buying behavior is driven by emotions, justified as necessary, after the fact, with logic.

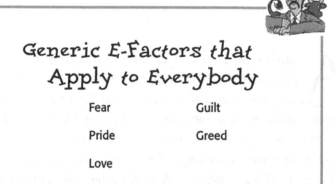

Generic E-Factors that Apply to Everybody

Fear	Guilt
Pride	Greed
Love	

In addition to the E-Factors affecting everybody, the affluent have a particular set of E-Factors to consider, some of which may surprise you:

- insecurity,
- fear of being found fakers,

- desperate desire not to commit a faux pas,
- today, not passé,
- feeding emotional emptiness,
- giving selves gold stars, and
- after all, what's the point of being rich.

The affluent are insecure in many ways. They certainly worry about going backward, about losing their money, status, or privileges. If you've never been rich, you have no frame of reference, but if you've been rich then poor, you know what you're missing! They are acutely aware of the aggravations, inconveniences, and financial difficulties endured daily by the ordinary mortals that they have left behind—and lose a few winks every night worrying about waking up *back there* again.

More importantly, they are concerned with being *found out*. Affluents who have gotten there largely or totally on their own become keenly aware that everybody else thinks of them as profoundly smarter or more talented or privy to special information or otherwise superhuman. Many actually use this in the attainment of career or business success, making themselves into and being accepted as wizards. I've been in the wizard business myself for three decades and have wound up hanging out with an entire community of them. (We even have our own trade association! The Information Marketing Association, at www.info-marketing.org.) Yet we know wizardry is more illusion than reality. I often say if ordinary people realized how ordinary in capability most millionaires are, there'd be a lot more millionaires—what holds most back isn't lack of opportunity or lack of capability, but the illusory belief that millionaires possess some special abilities they do not. The affluent are also very sensitive to judgment by their own chosen tribe or other affluents and are worried about "using the wrong fork" one way or another, showing up in an out-of-fashion dress, not knowing what the others know and converse about during cocktails at the club. Think of the whole thing as a high school clique, and everyone in it as desperate for acceptance by the others and secretly feeling the others may be superior.

These anxieties actually spur a lot of productive behaviors and ironically contribute to the successful becoming more successful, the rich becoming richer. They may eat healthier and exercise more to look better as a path to status with peers. They may read more, read more eclectically, and stay more abreast of political and financial news, leading to more successful investing. They may contribute to charitable and civic organizations and activities as a means of self-validation and validation within the tribe. These anxieties can obviously be used in selling to them, and both for-profit and nonprofit marketers should pay heed.

Then there is the matter of emotional emptiness—the long-standing debate, and joking about, whether or not money can buy happiness. People without money like making themselves feel better about their situation by insisting that the rich are no happier and may be less happy than the nonrich. Having been poor and now relatively rich, I can assure you that money buys a lot of access to opportunities, experiences, comforts,

Dan Kennedy's #6
No B.S. Key to the Vault

**Make owning your product or being your client
signify something.**

and conveniences that can lead to happiness, but I don't think it directly and in itself buys happiness. Other than Disney's® character Scrooge McDuck®, I don't know of anybody who gets joy from going into his vault and playing with his money like a child playing with toys. But I know quite a few affluent adults who buy some very expensive toys and enjoy playing with them very much.

There is, however, an underlying level of disappointment in most affluents with the fact that their affluence isn't a true Easy Button™ that works without fail or a crown everyone recognizes and bows to. When I switched from driving old, bad, cheap, beater cars to my first shiny new Lincoln Continental, it was a supreme disappointment to discover that birds crapped on its hood with impunity, just as they had my bad cars. You'd think the birds would show some respect! And it is true that a lot of affluent consumers' purchasing is done as a means of showing themselves respect and giving themselves recognition for their hard work and accomplishment they don't feel they are getting from others. Being told, subtly, that "you deserve this (and most others don't)" and "owning this signifies accomplishment and status and commands respect" is extremely persuasive to the affluent.

Recognition Does Matter

Should you, for a moment, think the affluent are not motivated by this seeking of recognition, you should familiarize yourself with the fundraising modus operandi of the Republican and Democratic parties and candidates. Much of it revolves around motivating affluent individuals to be bundlers and bring together groups of maximum donors, thus raising $50,000.00 to $100,000.00 or more in clumps, for which the bundler is rewarded with invitations to special events like cocktail receptions at the

Vice President's home or dinners with a Congressman seated at every table of eight, photos with the politicians, little trinkets like presidential seal cufflinks and suitable-for-framing parchment certificates. I have seen it as a donor myself and used it to help political candidates as an advisor. It is every bit as pin-and-medal driven as a direct-selling organization like Mary Kay® or Amway®, except money is being raised rather than made, and it is millionaires and multimillionaires vying for the emerald or ruby or diamond pin, rather than cosmetic, vitamin, and soap sales agents.

The mass-affluent also have their own special E-Factors:

- the aspirational acquisition,
- I own therefore I am, and
- Knowing the secret handshake and having those who know it know you know it.

This is all about being part of the clique. It once was all about having stepped up. Having visibly arrived. In the post-World War II era, when the suburbs were becoming both a place and a way of life, it was called "keeping up with the Joneses." Auto, TV, home improvement, and similar industries—as well as credit companies—benefited by this force of nature; if one driveway on the street suddenly provided home to a new station wagon, a fleet of station wagons was sure to follow. But today, there is a more complex collection of emotional drivers behind the purchases of the mass-affluent. There is some of the "Look, we've arrived" going on, but a lot of purchases are made as a forward statement of "where we're going." I call these *aspirational acquisitions*. The woman with a full-time career and two kids who is too exhausted to cook anything you can't microwave in its own dish still buys a $75,000.00 custom kitchen with a cooking island and state-of-the-art equipment, as she aspires to be more Martha than Rachael, and intends to devote more time to the art of cooking very soon. If you carefully tour the typical mass-affluent's home, you'll find ownership of all sorts of things bought because his peers have them, other things bought with strong intention of investing time and energy in them sometime soon—from nearly empty home wine cellars to rarely used home gyms and saunas.

The affluent seem to mature in their attitudes about owning things, and the longer they are affluent and the more affluent they are, the more they choose and buy luxury goods and services for practical and functional reasons, regardless of symbolic statement made. But for the mass-affluent, the things they buy and own and their self-images are tightly linked. "I own, therefore I am" is a powerful driving force. *If the most popular and perceived-as-sophisticated mom in the neighborhood wears x, drives x, enrolls her child in x, and I do the same, I am as sophisticated as she.* Ownership equals being.

You can profit significantly by giving serious thought to how you may present your products, services, and business in sync with these E-Factors.

Bonus Guest Expert Chapters

Chapters 12 through 18 provide more and deeper understanding of how to be motivational, inspirational, interesting, and influential with affluent consumers. This information comes from my friends and colleagues Nick Nanton and J.W. Dicks of the Dicks+Nanton CELEBRITY BRANDING AGENCY, and authors of the book *STORYSELLING*™. The agency has over 1,800 clients spanning 33 countries, including entrepreneurs, private practice professionals, sales professionals, executives, authors, and speakers.

Nick is an Emmy-Award-winning director and producer who frequently produces documentary films that are used to position individual businesspeople and companies as apart from and above all their competitors. These documentaries always air initially on networks like Bio! (The Biography Channel), CNBC, or Discovery, then are used as online media and in DVD form as promotional tools. He also produces unique TV shows integrating clients with people like Steve Forbes, Brian Tracy, Jack Canfield *(Chicken Soup for the Soul)*, and Michael Gerber *(The E-Myth)*. Nick has also led the marketing and PR campaigns that have driven more than 1,000 authors to bestseller status.

Nick has appeared on CNN, Fox, CNBC, and MSNBC, and been seen in *The Wall Street Journal, Inc.* magazine, the *New York Times, Forbes, Fast Company.com,* and *Entrepreneur* magazine.

J.W. Dicks is a business, franchise, entertainment, and intellectual property attorney, personal branding authority, and serial entrepreneur. He has been extensively quoted in *USA Today, The Wall Street Journal,* and is *Fast Company's* resident branding expert for their internationally syndicated blog. He is the publisher of *Celebrity Expert Insider.*

You can learn all about Nick and J.W. and the agency at: www.CelebrityBrandingAgency.com.

I am in collaboration with Nick and J.W. on a special, geo-area exclusive celebrity/expert branding program for financial advisors. Information about it can be requested from my office by fax: 602-269-3113.

CHAPTER 12

StorySelling™ to the Affluent

By Nick Nanton and J.W. Dicks

I f you're wondering who these Dicks and Nanton guys are—and how they happened to barge into the middle of this brand-new edition of Dan Kennedy's masterwork, *No B.S. Marketing to the Affluent*—well, let us introduce ourselves.

For the last decade or so, we've been offering innovative personal branding services to entrepreneurs, professionals, and business leaders of all types—services that enable them to elevate their *profiles* above the competition's and become known as the pre-eminent authority in their fields.

If that sounds like a lot of jargon to you, let's make it a lot simpler: We help our clients tell an incredibly amazing story that sets them apart from literally everyone else in the world—*their own story*.

We'll explain that a little more in a moment—but, first, here's how we came to contribute to this book. Luckily, our work in the personal branding arena brought us to Dan's attention—and that, in turn, led to us partnering on a few projects with him. Those projects went very well, so, when he decided to create a new updated version of this important book, we brainstormed with Dan how we could contribute in an impactful way. We figured out that it was a great fit, and we agreed to co-author the book together. And, as you know, Dan wouldn't invite us to a party unless he thought we added something important to the mix.

That special something is a process we call StorySelling™, which we described in great detail in our *Wall Street Journal* bestseller, *StorySelling™: Hollywood Secrets Revealed—How to Sell without Selling by Telling Your Brand Story*.

The concept of StorySelling™ boils down to this—people love a great story. And when you tell the right story about yourself and your business, you create the foundation for a marketing powerhouse, or in story terms, a blockbuster.

Trump, Branson and . . . Kennedy: Understanding StorySelling™

The biggest business legends know the importance of StorySelling™. Think of Donald Trump and his "narrative"—the brash billionaire who always says what he thinks and brushes off anybody who dares take him on. Or Richard Branson—the bold adventurer who dares to do business as no other mogul does. And, of course, we can't forget Dan Kennedy himself—the irascible/gruff No B.S. master marketer who suffers no fools and stands on old-school sales principles that have been proven time and time again.

Now, all of these *gentlemen's* super-successful business stories certainly are based on a huge foundation of reality—each of them has a very distinct personality that meshes with the public image. Each of them, however, also has a very strong *awareness* that they are StorySelling™ an image—and that they need to continually find ways to keep that story fresh and exciting. Trump barking "You're fired!" at the end of each episode of his reality show, *The Apprentice,* played perfectly into his narrative. Branson arranging to make a cameo appearance in the James Bond movie *Die Another Day* was an equally brilliant move. And Dan Kennedy's insistence on avoiding email and using faxes well into the 21st century continues to effectively sell his persona.

But perhaps the most important aspect of all three of these men's stories is the fact that all three *signify prosperity and success.* When Trump, Branson, or Kennedy walks into a room to make a deal with a wealthy prospect, they don't walk in there alone— their *stories* walk in with them. That gives each of them a huge and overpowering advantage in terms of jump-starting their *credibility, trust, and moneymaking expertise.*

Who wouldn't want that kind of clout in a business situation?

Well, the point is, you *can* have that kind of clout, if you follow StorySelling™ principles as these three legends do. And, frankly, it's the best kind of clout to have when you market to the affluent.

Scaling the Affluent's "Sales Wall"

StorySelling™ is an incredibly high-powered tool when it comes to marketing to the affluent. And you'll find the reason in five magic little words that are part of our very long StorySelling™ book title—*"How to Sell without Selling."* How to sell without selling is a concept that's vitally important when it comes to marketing to the affluent . . . and here's why.

Everyone who's affluent has one big thing in common, besides disposable income—that's the fact that most everybody else *knows* they're affluent. They live in the kind of ZIP codes that marketers lust after because those ZIP codes contain lots of high-income residents. The affluent also end up on every marketing list of companies that sell high-ticket items, simply because of their buying patterns. And it's not just businesses that market to the affluent—you can be sure their less-than-affluent friends and family members regularly hit them up for money, too!

Which brings us to this BIG point. Whichever of Dan's categories of affluent consumers you want to consider, whether it be the ultra-affluent, the mass-affluent, or the many other specialty market groups he names elsewhere in this book, the common thread among all of them is *someone is always trying to get money out of them.* Yes, everyone from the biggest corporations in the world down to ne'er-do-well nieces and nephews want the well-off to fatten their wallets. After all, if they have disposable income, why not dispose of it with *them?*

The outcome of all this constant asking for money? The affluent's resistance ratchets up—and any request for money, even in exchange for services or products, is met with skepticism, if not outright hostility. They build up a strong psychic "Sales Wall" that easily repels most hard sell pitches; the only ones that get over that wall are from companies or people they're already familiar with and are *already* sold on.

That familiarity is what StorySelling™ brings to the table. With it, you can actually burrow under that Sales Wall and create the bond you desire with a potential affluent customer or client—without them even realizing you're doing it.

To understand why that bond becomes so strong, you must understand the power of stories themselves.

Our Love Affair with Stories

The fact is the human brain enjoys nothing more than a good story. That's why stories have dominated our culture throughout the existence of our species—and why we've used whatever medium we had at hand to tell them, from cave drawings in prehistoric times to YouTube videos in the 21st century. Think of how many kinds of entertainment focus on telling stories—movies, TV shows, stage plays, songs, books, etc. Even documentaries and so-called "reality" TV are at their best when they have a clear, strong narrative.

That's because we don't just *like* stories—we *love* them.

Literally.

Researchers at the Center for Neuroeconomics Studies at Claremont Graduate University, in Claremont, California[1], discovered that stories activate the oxytocin hormone in our brains—this is actually *called* "the love hormone" by the scientific community. That's because it's associated with romantic attachment, human bonding . . . and yes, sex.

In other words, stories are way sexy. Even when they themselves are very far from it.

Dr. Paul Zak, one of the Claremont researchers, showed volunteers a video that told a story about a four-year-old boy with terminal brain cancer—and also showed the same group a meandering video of the same length about a four-year-old boy going to the zoo without any real beginning or end in place. Those that watched the first video had a 47% higher level of the love hormone. "Of all the stimuli we've developed that release oxytocin, this one was the best," said Zak of the story experiment.

Why do stories trigger that kind of reaction? Other research suggests that it happens because we identify with whoever the story is about—and put ourselves in their shoes. After all, we're

---

[1] Jorge A. Barraza and Paul J. Zak, "Empathy toward Strangers Triggers Oxytocin Release and Subsequent Generosity," *Annals of the New York Academy of Sciences*, June 2009.

all people—and we all experience the same fears, desires, joys, and ambitions.

More fun with brain-scanning confirms that this is true. Jeffrey Zacks of Washington University in St Louis, Missouri, ran functional magnetic resonance imaging (fMRI) scans on people reading a story or watching a movie[2]—and discovered that, when the main character encountered a situation, it activated the same parts of the brain in the subjects that would have responded if *they themselves* had been in the same predicament in real life. And it didn't matter if the story was read or experienced through a movie or a video—it was the content of the story itself that provoked the reaction.

We are addicted to stories in a very real sense—and here's more research that proves it. Read Montague of Virginia Tech University in Blacksburg and William Casebeer of the U.S. Defense Advanced Research Projects Agency (DARPA) in Arlington, Virginia[3], analyzed how listening to a story affects the brain's reward centers—the parts that respond to such wonderful things as sex, good food, and drugs. Casebeer's conclusion? "If I were a betting man or woman, I would say that certain types of stories might be addictive and, neurobiologically speaking, not that different from taking a tiny hit of cocaine," says Casebeer.

Simply put, strong stories key into our emotions in a deep and profound way; we identify with them in a way we don't identify with raw data.

Or, for that matter, a hard sell.

Here's a good example of how StorySelling™ trumps traditional selling. Remember the *Seinfeld* episode where George Costanza buys an old clunker—but he's VERY excited about it

---

[2] Gerry Everding, "Readers Build Vivid Mental Simulations of Narrative Situations, Brain Scans Suggest," phys.org, January 26, 2009.

[3] Jessica Marshall, "Gripping Yarns," *New Scientist*, February 12, 2011.

because it once belonged to the actor Jon Voight? Well, Georgie obviously didn't care about the mileage on the used car or the features or what shape the tires were in—all the things he *should* have been concerned about. Nope, he didn't think twice about any of that. He simply bought the car because the most important thing for him was that he would be *driving the same car that an Academy Award-winning actor once owned.*

He wanted to be a part of Jon Voight's story—even if it only involved Voight's old broken-down car.

Now, in case you think that's a fictional example that doesn't count . . . well, would you believe Dan Kennedy himself made a similar purchase—*for the very same reason????*

As Dan himself tells the tale in his book, *No B.S. Price Strategy*, a few years ago he bought a mint condition 1986 Rolls Royce convertible. And he paid a lot more than he had to. Why? Because it had previously belonged to famed Rat Pack member and show business legend Dean Martin—and, as Dan wrote, "I always had a strong affinity to Dean[4]." Yes, Dan wanted to be a part of *Dean's* story, and for Dean to be a part of his.

Now, lest you think Dan Kennedy would pay more for a celebrity car and not get anything out of it—well, then, you don't know Dan Kennedy. A few years ago, Dan sent out to his "herd" a large color postcard of him at the wheel of Dino's Rolls... basically letting everyone know if they wanted to be able to afford something amazing like Dean Martin's luxury convertible, they should continue to listen to Dan, and we agree!

The Four Key Factors of StorySelling™

Now, a star's car is an *extremely* basic StorySelling™ narrative. StorySelling™ is actually a rich and rewarding discipline with

---

[4] Dan Kennedy, *No B.S. Price Strategy* (Entrepreneur Press, 2011), 102.

many possible avenues that can lead to prosperity, which we explore thoroughly in our book.

The best StorySelling™ narratives, however, share four Key Factors that lead to their success with the affluent—and we'd like to share them here, using Dan Kennedy himself as an example of how he implements each of these Factors to his advantage.

Key Factor #1: Simplicity

How many stories do we hear in a day? How much information do we end up taking in? The answer to both of those questions is the same: a scary crazy amount. That means if *your* story isn't simple and easy to grasp, most of us, unless we're already intensely interested in the story, aren't going to hang on to it. Our lives are too busy and our minds too cluttered to take in something that's not directly relevant to what we're dealing with at the moment. The affluent are no different. If anything, if they're not retired, they're most likely busier than most of us. The simplicity of a StorySelling™ narrative, then, becomes of paramount importance when marketing to them.

Dan Kennedy's personal StorySelling™, of course, completely embraces simplicity without ever being simple. His plain-spoken conversational style immediately cuts directly through to the reader (or the audience, if he's speaking) with strong, easily understandable, and memorable points that stick and make perfect sense.

Key Factor #2: Authenticity

As noted, the affluent are bombarded with marketing efforts night and day—and most of them can smell a sales pitch a mile off. If your story only seems like an effort to get them to buy—or, even worse, if it doesn't have the ring of truth—they're not going to take it seriously (the only exception is if they have already heavily bought into your StorySelling™ and will accept a sales pitch from you based on established trust).

Again, Dan Kennedy displays this virtue of authenticity in spades. First, because he is so NOT the slick salesman, he earns more trust from an affluent audience than he otherwise would with an overly polished presentation. Second, he has decades of genuine experience in marketing to draw from to add credibility. Finally, Dan is not afraid to be who he is—and display his colorful individuality at every turn. This, too, adds to his authenticity—and attracts high-income clients like honey attracts bees.

Key Factor #3: Visibility

The affluent will also more willingly trust someone they have heard of, someone they like, and someone who has displayed an impressive expertise that ties in with whatever they're selling. For instance, a tax lawyer who has written a book on winning business tax strategies will be more trusted than a tax lawyer who may have just as much knowledge and skill, or perhaps even more, but hasn't taken the time to display it in a public arena. Because that lawyer made himself *visible* in the right venue, his StorySelling™ is effective.

The affluent, more than most, covet the services of professionals and entrepreneurs who have made a name for themselves. That's why we focus much of our branding at the Dicks+Nanton Celebrity Branding® Agency on helping our clients do just that, through exposure in major media outlets such as CNN or *The Wall Street Journal*, in books that we guarantee will be bestsellers, and in branded films (we'll discuss all of these tactics in later chapters).

Dan Kennedy, of course, has written countless books and reached out to countless entrepreneurs and marketers through seminars and informational products. In the process, he created a legendary name for himself and set the standard for direct response selling.

You may not reach Dan's heights, but there are many media channels you can utilize to deliver your narrative to an affluent audience. The main point to understand is that you can't expect them to come to *you* to find out your story—you need to find a viable and visible way to deliver your story to *them* in a way they will find credible and impressive.

Key Factor #4: Relevancy

Finally, your story has to be one that the affluent will want to hear—because it is somehow important to their lives. To go back to our tax lawyer example, if this particular attorney does write a book specifically targeted to the well-to-do to help them legally lower their tax liability, those people will want to read it— because it's going to save them money. And, as a result, they're more likely to hire that particular tax lawyer.

Affluent people, as Dan repeatedly makes the point throughout this book, also covet status and prestige—so if your StorySelling™ makes it clear that you can deliver those qualities to their lives, they'll also be excited to hear it.

Dan's StorySelling™, of course, hits a real sweet spot when it comes to relevance. What he's primarily selling is the ability to make money—and what could be more relevant to the affluent? It's a universal desire—and Dan is there to fulfill it.

This is a very brief look at the art of StorySelling™, an art which, when properly accomplished, can pay dividends for a lifetime. In the next few chapters, we'll delve further into some of the most effective ways you can StorySell yourself professionally—and create a happy ending for yourself and your bottom line!

CHAPTER 13

StorySelling™ Your Authority: Adding The X Factor to Your Marketing Mix

By J.W. Dicks and Nick Nanton

Y ou wouldn't expect an astrophysicist to approach rock star status—especially one whose record as a scientist is described by academic colleagues as "sound, but not extraordinary."

You wouldn't expect an astrophysicist to author huge best-selling books, host a multimillion-dollar TV series, or be named one of the 100 most influential people in the world by *Time* magazine.

And you definitely wouldn't expect *People* magazine to create a special category, "Sexiest Astrophysicist Alive," for this individual.

But then again, you wouldn't expect an astrophysicist, in preparation for his first appearance on *The Daily Show with Jon Stewart*, to study interview segments methodically to see how many sentences a guest usually was able to say before Stewart interrupted one with a joke—so he could plan the length of his answers in advance.

Dr. Neil DeGrasse Tyson has become a household name as well as the most famous person in his field since Carl Sagan not because he necessarily knows more about his specialty than anyone else and not because he's accomplished any sort of incredible breakthroughs in his field.

No, he became a huge pop culture celebrity simply because he engaged in the type of StorySelling™ we talked about in the previous chapter—and used it to *communicate his expertise in the most accessible way possible.* That allowed him to gain what we call "The X Factor," something any professional or entrepreneur should acquire in order to presell themselves to the affluent.

The X Factor: Gateway to the Affluent

There are roughly 23,000 physicists and astronomers in the U.S. alone—but very few of those can claim the access to the rich and powerful that Dr. Tyson has. That access is the reason he was able to host the highly rated *Cosmos* TV series; *Family Guy* creator Seth McFarlane met Tyson at a Hollywood event and backed the project, which is why it was able to get a time slot on the Fox Network.

Tyson illustrates a very important principle when it comes to marketing to the affluent. It's not enough to simply *be* an expert—you also have to demonstrate your expertise in a reputable public forum that directly connects you to your target audience. When that's done right, even an astrophysicist can become a media superstar. So why not a doctor, lawyer, fitness expert, real estate agent, or CPA?

StorySelling™ your authority isn't just about going on an ego trip. To quote a *Forbes* article, "There are many powerful aspects to positioning yourself as an authority for your brand. Remember, by raising your own profile, you will, in turn, raise the profile of your company. You'll also significantly widen your reach.... The bottom line is, people buy products from brands that they know and trust. And they'll trust you—once they know where to find you."

Creating that trust is, of course, essential to reaching the affluent market. Which is why working to develop the X Factor is one of the best business moves you can make.

The Oz Effect

Another prime example of the X Factor in action is what's been labeled "The Oz Effect." Dr. Mehmet Oz first became known to TV viewers through his frequent appearances as a health expert on the *Oprah Winfrey Show* beginning in 2004. Winfrey herself, because of her deep connection with her viewers, became, in the words of ABC News, "one of the most influential figures in media" and created several household names, such as Dr. Phil, Rachael Ray, and Suze Orman, simply by conferring expert status on them on her program. In Oz's case, she dubbed him, "America's Doctor"—and Oz took that ball and ran with it.

Dr. Oz went on to star in his own popular syndicated series that began in 2009, but it became only the base of his efforts to add the X Factor to his expert status. Oz's best-selling books, magazine articles, radio shows, as well as his TV show, all cemented his image in the public's eye as THE health expert to listen to.

The result? The Oz Effect. Whenever Dr. Oz mentions a product on his show, sales shoot up dramatically. For example, after the Neti Pot, a relatively obscure device used to ease nasal dryness, was showcased on Oz's show, internet searches for it rose by 42,000%—and sales rose by an unbelievable 12,000%, according to *Forbes*.

Now, we're certainly not saying everyone can take the X Factor to the heights of a Dr. Oz—but even approaching his level of success is obviously a good thing! We've found that with our clients, the X Factor can work just as effectively for a dentist in his or her community as it can for a national figure seeking to bond with an audience of millions.

Connection and Communication

The real key to achieving the X Factor is *effective communication that connects you to your intended audience*. When you find meaningful ways to bond with the affluent, you don't need the power of an Oprah Winfrey to become a success or to come to the attention of the successful. As a matter of fact, all you need is the internet.

John Green is a writer who, back in 2007, was critically acclaimed and had written an award-winning young adult novel, *Looking for Alaska*. However, his book sales weren't so great, because he didn't have the X Factor working for him. He decided to change all that.

That same year, he and his brother Hank decided to communicate solely through YouTube videos. Hank lived in Montana. John lived in New York City. So they barely saw each other and thought this would be a great social media gimmick as well as a fun thing to do. Billing themselves as the Vlogbrothers, they posted several videos a week—and quickly built up a huge following from young fans who loved their in-jokes, their philosophic musings, and their goofy humor. Viewers of the Vlogbrothers described themselves as "Nerdfighters," in honor of one of John's videos where he talked about the concept of being a warrior for internet subcultures and things that were considered "geeky."

With this massive prebuilt audience in place, what happened with John's next book was nothing short of phenomenal. From a *New Yorker* article about Green: *"Publishing executives talk about successful books as if they were lightning strikes, but the popularity of 'The Fault in Our Stars' was no accident. Nerdfighters, who by then numbered in the millions, were evangelical about it, tucking notes into copies of the book and encouraging readers to join their movement. In fact, 'The Fault in Our Stars' reached the No. 1 position on Amazon six months before it was published, when Green announced its title online."*

That success continued with the movie adaptation of the book. The movie opened in the number-one position at the box office after the online trailer for the film had 20 million views.

Now, what's really interesting about John Green is that the expertise he demonstrated in his online videos had little or nothing to do with his actual novelist skills—and everything to do with bonding with his audience. By keying into their feelings and entering into authentic discussions with them, he built a base of trust and credibility that translated into massive sales of his book. He showed himself to be an expert at understanding his readership—which may have, in turn, been more important than his actual writing ability.

In other words, although his literary prize for his actual writing talent did not translate into success, his reaching out to his base did—to such an extent that, through the first half of 2014, *The Fault in Our Stars* was the best-selling book in 49 out of 50 of the states in the USA.

Attaining the X Factor

We know that the X Factor can be an invaluable asset to real estate agents, attorneys, medical practitioners, small-business owners, and entrepreneurs and professionals of all types and stripes; it allows them to connect with the affluent on a deeper level than normal marketing can achieve because, again, it creates the all-important element of *trust*. When affluent consumers see someone visibly treated in the media as a known expert, they lower their guard and become more open to what that person has to say. That takes care of a lot of potential roadblocks to making a sale.

In the next few chapters, we'll talk in more detail about how to use media to its best advantage, as well as how to connect specifically with values of the affluent, but for now, we'd like to offer a few proven strategies for bringing the X Factor into your business persona.

Exhibit

Sometimes all that's necessary to be recognized as THE authority in your field is just being able to *exhibit* expertise when the opportunity arises—even before you've reached a higher level of experience and knowledge.

For example, a doctor, who, when he was still only a medical student, appeared as an expert on a local Sunday night radio call-in show entitled *Ask a Surgeon*. After he graduated, he became a regular co-host on a relationship advice program that aired every weeknight on the same radio station. The program became so popular that it went national after a few years, and then made the jump to TV.

Three years later, Dr. Drew Pinsky was ready to start his own media operation. Based on his celebrity brand alone, investors put $7.5 million into the pot in October of 1999 when he was ready to start DrDrew.com, an online community designed to give health advice to young adults. Talk about reaching an affluent target group!

Heidi Roizen, managing director of the Softbank Venture Capital Fund, said at the time, "Dr. Drew has the ear of a large and important audience. He's earned their trust and respect. We hope to build on this great franchise with ever expanding content, community, and commerce opportunities."

Clearly, Dr. Drew from the start understood the power of the X Factor and made it an essential part of his highly successful career path.

Explain

Because effective communication is all-important to the X Factor, professional jargon and overly technical phrasing should be avoided at all costs when you're out there talking about your field. The idea is to *explain* everything in clear and easy-to-understand language, so you keep the average person's attention and help them "get" what you're talking about.

As previously discussed, X Factor master Dr. Neil DeGrasse Tyson works hard to make difficult scientific concepts comprehensible to the average person—even going so far as to use a reference to such network comedies as *Family Guy* or *The Simpsons* to make a point.

Similarly, former president Bill Clinton has often been called "The Explainer-In-Chief" during Barack Obama's residency in the White House. When Obama had difficulty making a policy clear to the American public in a way that resonated, Clinton would be called upon to do it in his stead—which is exactly what he did when he spoke at the 2012 Democratic Convention. Here's how *Time* magazine defined Clinton's X Factor at that event: *"There have been a lot of analyses of Clinton's political style — empathy, people skills, wonkiness — but one that may be underestimated is the fact that the man can explain the hell out of a thing. Clinton didn't deliver poetry; he gave a talk and told a narrative."*

Expand

Most professionals and entrepreneurs are content to market themselves through normal advertising venues and techniques. We encourage our clients to use a different approach that *expands* beyond those conventional methods—by generating *useful and credible content* in one's field through these platforms, which distinguishes them from those that merely trumpet their greatness through paid advertisements.

For example, a fitness expert who writes a book has a verifiable, tangible item that both promotes expertise as well as delivers added prestige. A real estate agent who contributes a home buying and selling advice column in the local newspaper or a call-in show on a radio station accomplishes the same feat. In both examples, the professionals are a) the featured attraction, b) demonstrating mastery of their field, and c) immediately raising the value of their names by providing content through a respected media outlet. That's a whole lot more effective (and credible) in reaching the affluent than buying a commercial or print ad that any competitor could easily duplicate.

This is why generating content is of primary concern to X Factor adherents such as Dr. Oz. Here, a *New York Times* article describes the incredible amount of information Oz and his staff delivered outside of his TV show at the beginning of its run:

> *Oz is also on the radio every day . . . Oz is in bookstores, where you can find half a dozen titles in the ongoing "You" series— including "You: The Smart Patient," "You: On a Diet," and "You: Having a Baby"—that he has written with Dr. Michael F. Roizen, the unofficial co-chairman of what might be called Oz Industries. There are about nine million of their books in print so far. Oz is in magazines and newspapers. In February, he wrote what will be the first of six "Prescription" columns a year for Time magazine. In the fall he will start writing one column every other month for the AARP magazine. He reaches out to men with a monthly column for Esquire, to women with regular contributions to Winfrey's magazine. All of this comes on top of the newspaper writing that he and Roizen, under the "You Docs" banner, produce for King Features Syndicate.*

It's hard to conceive of one man putting out that much content. But presumably, that's a large part of how he earned his title of America's Doctor.

Exceed

If you want to gain the X Factor, you also have to *exceed* the profile and exposure of your competition. As we just discussed, generating content is one method of doing that; another is simply finding new venues for exposure and new paths to influence that competitors aren't exploiting.

In the early 1990s, David Letterman and Jay Leno were both up for the job of replacing Johnny Carson on NBC's *The Tonight Show*. Both had a strong case for the job; Letterman had hosted his own 12:30 A.M. show for ten years and enjoyed strong ratings, while Leno had filled in for Carson on a regular basis and had also done well.

But, while Letterman relied strictly on his performance on his show to get him the job, Leno went out of his way to build relationships with NBC affiliates all across the country. He would do stand-up at their meetings, fly in to a station to help them sell their commercials, or do an interview with the local press. He went beyond the normal bounds to connect with the NBC decision-makers who would influence the network's final decision in his favor.

Similarly, a dentist who specializes in implants and spends two or three hours a month speaking directly to affluent clubs with older members and informing them about the advantages of implants stands a better chance of growing his or her business than the dentist who doesn't do any outreach.

Excite

In order to fully galvanize an affluent audience and motivate them into buying a product or utilizing a service, your message has to *excite* that audience on a deep psychological level. By keying into who the audience is and what their wants are (something we'll discuss in a later chapter), you're able to build a strong relationship that goes beyond standard marketing interactions.

As already detailed, author John Green did exactly this with the series of YouTube videos he and his brother posted online. He connected with his readership in a vital and exciting way that bonded them to him.

This aspect of the X Factor can also be obtained simply by your charisma and ability to engage a crowd. Contrary to popular belief, these qualities can easily be taken on when you're willing to train and learn. To quote the *Harvard Business Review*,

> . . . *charisma can be learned through deliberate practice. Bear in mind that even Winston Churchill, one of the most charismatic figures of the 20th century, practiced his oratory style in front of a mirror.*

The X Factor—being seen as a visible, engaging expert in one's field—can go a long way towards launching your business to a new level of success within the affluent marketplace. In the words of *Forbes* magazine,

> *You are an expert on your brand—and more than likely on your industry, too—and you can leverage that expertise to help your brand further its reach. When you share what you know, you'll start to gain visibility in your industry and build a community around you—and when a big product announcement comes along, that community will be ready to engage with you on your news.*

By putting to work the building blocks of Exhibit, Explain, Expand, Exceed, and Excite, doctors, lawyers, financial analysts, business owners, or entrepreneurs can make the all-important X Factor a vital part of their professional portfolios. That, in turn, will become a huge factor in generating an ongoing success story that will reap rewards for years to come.

CHAPTER 14

Mastering the Business Trifecta:
The Magic Formula for Marketing to the Affluent

By J.W. Dicks and Nick Nanton

I n the previous chapter, we discussed how you can StorySell your expertise to connect with hard-to-please niche audiences like the affluent.

In this chapter, we're going to get more specific—and tell you how, once you have your narrative in place, you can successfully reach your target group by utilizing what we call The Business Trifecta®.

The more you establish yourself as a noted and reputable expert before you attempt a direct sale of your product or service, the more chance you have at making that sale. You're creating the kind of invaluable and positive buzz that makes your well-to-do prospects:

- Aware of who you are,

- Aware of what you do, and
- Aware that you're very good at what you do.

This is similar to how Hollywood studios get the movie-going public excited about one of their blockbusters before it appears in theatres. They release a teaser trailer in advance of the real trailer that is introduced by the hosts of *Extra* or *E! News Daily*; they leak a particularly effective clip on the *Huffington Post* or CNN; the stars give exclusive interviews to popular entertainment websites like HitFix.com or *The Onion*'s AVClub.com. There is a steady impactful stream of information about the film released through influential and established mass media outlets that's designed to accomplish the same sort of three-point process as we're talking about: Make audiences aware of the film, aware of what it's about, and aware that it's supposed to be *awesome*.

You can create the same kind of excitement about yourself and your business when you put the Business Trifecta® to work for you. More importantly, you can *pre-sell* yourself to the affluent audience. The Business Trifecta® does all of the heavy-lifting for you.

Before we discuss how the Trifecta actually works in practice, let's first reveal just what the three different "legs" of the Business Trifecta® are—and then discuss how we make this threesome work together for our clients in the most powerful way possible.

Business Trifecta® Leg #1: Media

When most people think of media, they think of different communication platforms, such as TV, radio, newspapers, and the internet. In reality, that type is only one category of media—*mass* media. Mass media is about numbers. That means these kinds of platforms want to attract the most users, so they can't really mess around; they *must* produce content that's genuine and interesting to the most people (or at least the most people in their target audience) or they lose money.

All of us put the "mass" into mass media—we seek out these platforms every day when we watch our favorite shows, read our favorite newspapers, listen to our favorite music, and so forth. And because the mass media has no other visible agenda than to entertain and inform the most people, it automatically brings two things to the table—awareness and credibility. If there's a story about you on CNN, people 1) see it and 2) think more of you because of it. (Unless, of course, you just murdered somebody or something . . . but we won't get into that here!)

The other type of media is known as *direct* media. This is generally a targeted informational sales tool that takes the form of a CD, DVD, newsletter, direct-mail piece, sales letter, website copy, etc. The entrepreneur, professional, or business creates this kind of media usually for the sole purpose of selling a product or service. The huge advantage to direct media lies in the fact that because you're paying for the creation of the direct media, *you completely control the message and the content.* This is vitally important to entrepreneurs and professionals, of course, because the business can be portrayed in its best light.

Most people are anxious to have access to both kinds of media in order to raise their business profile. There are three different methods of doing this:

1. *You can appear in media* naturally. Let's say you're a high-profile plastic surgeon in your community and the local TV station is doing a story on more and more residents getting "work done." They call up your office, arrange an interview, and use clips of that interview in their final report. Well, congratulations! You just received great free advertising simply because you were the right person in the right place at the right time! More importantly, because you were chosen as an expert by a third party (in

this case, by the local news), your *credibility* was given a significant boost.

2. *You can buy media access.* Maybe you want enough time to fully demonstrate your product or service—so you buy some half-hour blocks of time on local TV and produce your own infomercial to run during those times. Or you buy an ad in the local paper or city magazine, or put a radio commercial on the community airwaves. Advertising is the conventional approach to buying media access by businesses; unfortunately, it ends up lacking the credibility of *naturally* appearing on mass media through a respected third party's invitation as in the case of our plastic surgeon example. Advertising can obviously be effective, but, too often, the time is not spent to get the messaging and the creative approach right. That makes it a very expensive gamble that won't pay off the way you want, especially when it comes to attracting the affluent customers.

3. *You can create your own media.* Professionals and entrepreneurs, especially since the dawn of internet marketing, often create their own direct media, in lieu of either spending for or waiting for mass media exposure. This is generally the form of direct media we discussed earlier (i.e., CD, DVD, newsletter, a documentary film, etc.).

   The advantage of creating your own media is the control of the finished product. You carefully script what you want to say, target the exact market you want to reach, and present the story in the exact type of media your market is most attracted to. This type of media done right and continuously can create a very lasting relationship with the market you are trying to reach. Created media can also be sold if you provide enough real content to your target market. For instance, a real estate agent could write a book on buying and selling luxury homes. That book could then be sold on Amazon, even though the specialist's main business is, obviously, helping clients with their home transactions. The book serves as an indirect promotion for the agent—and, in this case, also targets the affluent segment of potential clients, as it focuses on luxury homes.

Whichever approach is used to gaining access, media is vitally important in terms of delivering actual *content* that allows you to demonstrate your expertise in a credible way, which is what makes it so valuable.

Business Trifecta® Leg #2: P.R.

P.R., or public relations, is all about creating *awareness and third party endorsement when it is picked up by outside media.* The awareness comes primarily from press releases and media appearances. For example, when you're offering a top-level product or service for the affluent, you want them to know about it. That's why you want to put out a special online and offline press release about what you're offering.

If that press release hits at the right time or falls into the right hands, it could land you a story in the newspaper, in a magazine, on the radio, TV, or online. It can also get you invited on radio and TV interview shows to talk about what you're selling. Or, if it's an online press release, it could drive more traffic to your website— which, if you've got your ducks in a row, could end up being far more profitable than any media appearance you could get.

(By the way, that's why we mostly concentrate on the online press release, rather than the old-school offline variety. Online press releases boost your internet presence and, because they're written in the third person, also act as powerful online testimonials to anyone Googling you or your business—and its ROI is pretty much guaranteed.)

Should you nab those special media appearances, stories, and the traffic to your website, the great thing is you got it all *totally free*. Your main cost might come from hiring a P.R. company to help you make all of that happen, but, if you end up getting mass media access as a result, it's more than worth it for the extra credibility you'll gain from that exposure. Even if you don't get that mass media shot, the P.R. will still be out there on the internet for a very long time, and that, in turn, will boost your Digital DNA and your Google Search results.

BUT . . . if you haven't gotten your StorySelling™ together and don't have a strong narrative in place, you're throwing your money away. The important thing is to use P.R. when you've developed the most effective story to tell—that, in turn, makes your P.R. as compelling as possible and gives you the best shot at gaining attention.

Business Trifecta® Leg #3: Marketing

The third and final leg of our Trifecta is marketing, a topic that volumes and volumes have been written about. The American Marketing Association defines marketing as "the activity, set of institutions, and processes for creating, communicating, delivering, and exchanging offerings that have value for customers, clients, partners, and society at large." To put it more simply, it's everything you do to make everyone aware of what you do, what you sell, and what you can do for them. And we mean everything. All of the media and P.R. we just discussed can be part of a marketing plan—but, then again, so can a pen with your logo imprinted on the side that you use as a giveaway.

The most important word in that last sentence is "plan." Marketing is most effective when you coordinate all the different ways you promote your business so that a) your marketing messaging is consistent and b) you're able to successfully deliver that message to a substantial segment of your target group. Ideally, that plan should make prospects want to buy from you or, at the very least, give you a long, hard look.

Of course, a marketing plan is only as good as its ingredients will allow. For example, if you're really thinking a pen with your logo on it is all you need to bring crowds to your door...well, you should write off that idea right now, and you can use the pen to do it. That's especially the case if you're aiming to reach an affluent audience—that requires a high-powered strategy to deliver results, a strategy that includes elements designed to impress.

Which brings us to . . .

The Secret Formula for Media Success®

How you put all three of the Business Trifecta® elements together—media, P.R., and marketing—is critically important when it comes to marketing to the affluent. Again, they have a greater amount of sales resistance than other segments of the population, simply because so many marketers target them.

That means only *one* element of our Trifecta is generally not enough to make a sale. You need to put all three together in the right mix. If you don't allocate enough money and resources to each one of them—and/or if you don't use each of them in the right way—again, you'll end up spending a lot of money without much to show for your efforts.

Which brings us to the magic ingredient of our secret formula . . . . *Melding Media.*

As we previously discussed, there are two types of media— mass media and direct media. Mass media is preferred by most because it delivers a higher degree of awareness and credibility; that's why people hire P.R. companies to get them on mass media outlets. The problem is, you can't "eat" awareness and credibility—in other words, if there isn't a direct solicitation involved with a mass media appearance, in all but the most unusual of circumstances, it doesn't generate any real revenue. You're a story for a day, and then it disappears (another reason we prefer online P.R.—it pretty much *stays* online forever!). Just think about it, when was the last time you saw someone being interviewed on TV or quoted in a newspaper, and you stopped what you were doing and said, "That person is so smart, I'm going to stop everything I'm doing right now, and hire them!" Right, you don't. Also, with mass media, you are not in control of the message—as a matter of fact, you are at the mercy of the outlet you end up appearing on or in. If they decide to make you look like an idiot, you don't have much say in the matter.

Direct media doesn't have that problem. Again, you completely control the message, so it's up to you how your business is portrayed. However, direct media traditionally doesn't always have the same level of credibility as mass media because you *are* producing it yourself. And if you're distributing the media through traditional marketing means, such as direct mail or email, to the affluent consumer, it will may be perceived as an advertisement, no matter what the content happens to be. Again, the affluent are constantly getting lots of sales pitches from many different kinds of businesses.

That's why we advise our clients to meld *both* kinds of media—mass media and direct media—into one marketing system.

Here's how we do it. We create direct media that *looks* like mass media—and then place that direct media on a mass media outlet.

For example, we create interview shows built under various business umbrellas—such as *The Brian Tracy Show* (hosted by legendary business coach Brian Tracy), *The New Masters of Real Estate*, *Health and Wellness Today*, and *America's Premiere Experts*.

Our clients are interviewed on these shows, which are produced at the same quality level as other shows of their kinds. We then place these programs on a variety of mass media outlets—ABC, CBS, NBC, and Fox affiliates as well as such cable channels as CNN and Fox News—where they appear to be mass media shows. We also produce branded documentary films (which we'll also discuss in a later chapter in this book) for our clients that feature high production values; these too are placed on such prestigious outlets such as the Biography channel, where, again, the level of quality is such that it looks like one of their standard half-hour program profiles.

We do the same thing with print. We create special inserts in such publications as *USA Today* and *The Wall Street Journal* that resemble standard newspaper editorial pieces, but are actually direct media designed to shine a bright spotlight on our clients' expertise, with the emphasis on usable content for the viewers, so they get value out of it on their end.

This approach allows our clients to get the benefits of *both* kinds of media. They can completely control the message, but they also get the huge boost in credibility and awareness that mass media can deliver. Not only that, but they can then use their mass media appearances in their marketing and P.R. to get them even *more* positive attention. When one of our clients does directly approach an affluent prospect, and their materials feature the logos of all the prominent media outlets they've appeared on, the prospect is going to regard them a lot more seriously than they would otherwise. The client is suddenly elevated in their eyes to a national expert—which makes selling a great deal easier. That mass media "stamp of approval" can mean the world to a potential customer.

So ask yourself—don't you think that kind of mass media stamp of approval is of critical importance to get you into the running with affluent customers or clients? We can tell you, based on literally hundreds of clients we have worked with, it absolutely will get them to seriously consider what you have to offer.

So get yourself some mass media credibility with direct media content control, or let us help you make it happen. When you successfully combine the Business Trifecta®, media, marketing, and P.R., you can reach your intended affluent audience—and bring about guaranteed business growth and increased revenues. Correctly using the Business Trifecta® raises your enterprise to the next level—and trust us, you'll enjoy the view from up there!

CHAPTER 15

How Authors Attract the
Affluent: The Write Process
for Marketing Success

By J.W. Dicks and Nick Nanton

Writing books? Is it really a viable marketing strategy?

Well, let's consider the living legend whose book contains this particular chapter—Mr. Dan Kennedy. Head over to Amazon.com and do a search in the "Books" department for his name. You'll get 862 results.

Now, many of those 862 entries are duplicate editions of the same books and some merely feature a contribution from Dan K. Oh, and there's some *other* Dan Kennedy who's written five or six books, as well. But the point is, even taking all that into account, that total is mighty impressive. And it makes the point that this master marketer has made writing books a prominent feature of his overall marketing strategy.

Now, you could respond to that by saying, well, Dan Kennedy is first and foremost a writer, so it's natural that he would write so many books. Well, yes and no. You can assume Dan makes most of his writing income from sales copy, which is what he's known for. Spending time writing books instead of that sales copy probably *costs* him money in the long run.

Or does it?

We don't think so. The real story here is that Dan Kennedy knows if any potential rich client should question his credentials, he can simply point to the same Amazon book results that we did—and that well-heeled individual will see that this guy he's thinking about hiring to help him with marketing has written what appears to be *hundreds of books on the subject.*

That's a real foundation for Dan's ongoing StorySelling™ success.

Books in the 21st Century

Now, your other response to Dan Kennedy's mammoth mountain of books might be . . . well, Dan's kind of a throwback. However, nobody really cares about books anymore. People today text and Facebook and email and IM . . . . to the point where, sometimes, it seems the longest you can get someone's attention is for 140 characters or less.

Talking in Twitter-sized bites, however, doesn't really help you get a lot of meaningful ideas across. For example, here's how Honest Abe Lincoln's Gettysburg Address would have gone if he had tried to tweet it from his smartphone . . .

Four score and seven years ago our fathers brought forth on this continent a new nation, conceived in Liberty and dedicated to the propositi

Never really was able to get even close to the point, did he? And we even took out two commas!

Of course, a speech would naturally be hard to nail in 140 characters. So let's try putting out the 23rd Psalm on Twitter—that's a little more direct:

The Lord is my shepherd—I shall not want. He maketh me to lie down in green pastures—he leadeth me beside the still waters—he restore

Restore what? Well, you'd either have to wait for another tweet to finish the thing or you'd never know. Turns out it's your soul, which is kind of an important detail.

Our point is, even though social media and today's instant communication interfaces occupy an important place in the marketing scheme of things, one thing they *can't* do is really put your ideas fully out there in a meaningful and substantive way. We're not saying social media can't be meaningful or substantive, but they simply can't hold a candle to the credibility of books.

Think of it this way. What's the first thing someone seriously considering running for President does? *They write a book.* Barack Obama did it. Mitt Romney did it. John McCain did it. Hillary Clinton did it. Even Rick Perry and Herman Cain did it. Why? Because their books become the basis of their StorySelling™. To them, a book is the perfect method of establishing who they are, where they came from, and what they believe—and, more importantly, they can tell their story in a way that *they totally control.*

The only other way they could pull that off is through a branded film (which we'll discuss in a later chapter)

So, how else do you have the kind of lengthy conversation you need in order to build your circle of influence and establish your name? How do you communicate who you are and what you have to say in a way that has lasting impact and in a way that has a long marketing afterlife? And how do you articulate your specific business/professional philosophy in a complete and satisfying manner?

The best answer still happens to be in a book.

The Oldest Form of Social Media

We quoted the Bible before—and that wasn't a random choice. Books like the Bible were the original form of social media. Would Christianity have grown to the size it is today without having the Bible as a cornerstone of the religion—a book with all the religion's philosophy contained in it that could easily be passed around? It would have been a lot more difficult, at the very least. And consider the fact that, in its time, the Bible was even interactive, as prophets and apostles of the time added on to it as events kept occurring.

Books have usually been the basis of any major movement— and that fact still holds true today. Major motivational speakers like Anthony Robbins and Jack Canfield depend on regular book releases to continue to grow their base. And superstars in sports, politics, and entertainment make it a point to get a book out, even though it's usually ghostwritten, to expand their brand and put out their side of the story, without a reporter or interviewer beside them ready to instantly poke holes in it.

That's why we say books are the oldest form of social media. Social media is anything that starts a conversation—and for hundreds of years, books have prompted millions of hours of discussion, and still do. That's why thousands of people participate in social book groups all around the world—there's even this woman named Oprah who happened to have a very famous book club of her own, don't know if you've heard of her . . .

At the same time, authors are also seen as unique and *smart*. It's a hard, time-consuming task to finish a tome of your own— especially when most of us really don't like to write. It just feels like leftover homework from English class in high school. That's why most people would never think of attempting to write a book—and anyone who actually does finish one, let alone have it published, is instantly held in a higher regard.

And that's always a good thing.

How a Book Attracts the Affluent

Let's return to what we talked about at the beginning of this chapter—how hard it is to impart your ideas to an audience when everyone is chattering away in short, slang-ridden texts and updates on their electronic gadgets.

A book is the ideal base for you to have the conversation you want to have with people. It gives you the opportunity to craft your message and have it delivered without any interruptions. When somebody reads your book, you get to go inside their head for hours and hours, so you can make your case in the most impactful way possible—and again, no one's there to argue against you, except the reader. You're no longer just a sound bite or a one-liner—you're someone who has a fully realized vision of how something should work. And again, that brings you instant respect.

Especially with the affluent. As we've already made clear in previous chapters, the affluent gravitate to those with prestige and established authority in their fields. If you've written a book, you immediately establish BOTH of those all-important attributes. And we haven't even gotten to the best part yet . . .

It doesn't matter if affluent people read your book or not.

Now, some will . . . but most probably won't. A lot of people just don't like to read, and, if they do read, they'd rather read entertaining fiction (fictional ebooks sell twice as many copies as nonfiction ones). In any event, again, it doesn't matter if they do or they don't! Just the fact that you have published a book—with content that displays your expertise and, better yet, demonstrates an understanding of affluent consumers—is impressive enough to your intended audience.

Not only that, but publishing a book plays perfectly into the Business Trifecta® (which we discussed in an earlier chapter), which really can make for a marketing slam dunk. Let's walk you through how we use our books together with the Trifecta at our CelebrityPress® publishing house, simply because our all-in-one process is a great example of how you can use a book as the foundation of a powerful marketing effort.

Books and the Business Trifecta®

As you recall, the Business Trifecta® begins with creating effective **media**. Obviously, in this case, the media is the book we publish with our clients as the authors. But we don't just simply put out a book by one of those clients and call it a day. We feel it's our job to make each book an "event" that will give our authors the maximum marketing leverage.

That's why many of our books are actually done in conjunction with a personality who already has a great deal of influence in the marketplace—people like business legend Brian Tracy, authors Jack Canfield and Mark Victor Hansen (the men behind the mega-selling Chicken Soup series of books), financial leader Steve Forbes, and . . . Dan Kennedy himself!

When we do put out a book under one of these thought-leader's names, we then have a hand-picked selection of our clients simply contribute a chapter. This allows the client to say to his potential clients, "Hey, I just wrote a book with Brian Tracy." That means not only does that client have the book to boost his or her business profile, that book also *connects them directly to an internationally prominent figure.* This system also makes it easier for our clients who may not want to write an entire book—it's obviously much easier to generate only one chapter of content rather than try to come up with an entire book (although many of our clients prefer to do their own complete books, and if you are interested in having a book, you can contact us at CelebrityPress®, 800-981-1403).

And by the way, if you're intimidated by the thought of trying to find time to write, be aware there are plenty of ghostwriters out there who can help you get your content structured and written in a professional and compelling way. Many of our clients work with our ghostwriters on a regular basis, usually through telephone interviews, and the process makes it easy for them to put out a polished product without much effort.

We also employ still another method to up the marketing power of the finished book. We employ our own system to make sure, the day it's released, it becomes an automatic Amazon bestseller. That takes the prestige factor up another notch. While it is impressive simply to write a book, it's a whole lot more impressive if that book attains bestseller status—it grants even more prestige to the author.

With our media in place, we move on to the next member of the Business Trifecta®—**P.R.** High-profile media, such as a best-selling book co-authored by somebody like Dan Kennedy, makes a great story for P.R., both during prepublication and publication. For example, one press release will focus on a client signing with our publishing arm for a book deal—and a subsequent one will announce that the book has reached bestseller status. In addition, those P.R. proclamations are also trumpeted through social media mentions—tweets, Facebook statuses, etc.

The real value of this online P.R. is that it makes media live forever. The press releases stay online and continue to show up in Google results—even though the book in question may have been released months or even years ago. If someone is searching on the internet to find out more about you, it's awesome to have those kinds of mentions show up in your search results!

Which brings us to the third member of the Business Trifecta®—**marketing**. Because you have the media (i.e., book) already published and available through Amazon and because you've done the P.R. about the book, you now have a real ace up your sleeve when you begin to market specific products and/ or services to the affluent or other market segments. Your P.R. and media efforts have already established your credibility and visibility to an enormous extent.

And that gives you a much better shot at convincing the affluent to buy from you. A bestselling book, especially if it features a Jack Canfield or a Brian Tracy on the cover, automatically separates you from the herd and automatically makes you a preeminent expert in your field. When you're trying to market to the affluent, you need this kind of impact to differentiate yourself from the rest of the pack.

A book properly leveraged by the Business Trifecta® does just that.

Just make you sure your book has a lengthy afterlife *after* publication—it should become an important part of your professional profile. Make sure it's added to your official bio, your website homepage, and even put the name of the book in your email signature. You can also break down a chapter and make it into an ongoing free special report, available on your website through an opt-in box. Definitely rework the material into speeches or seminar material for your personal or recorded appearances.

Your office should also reflect your author status. Put a framed copy of the cover of your book on the wall in your reception area or office. Also, leave copies of your book on the coffee table in your office with "Take Me" stickers on the front. You should also donate copies to the local libraries in your area. Make sure your contact information is contained in these copies—either put a business card in the book, or have your info stamped on the back page. You never know who will run across it—or just how eager they'll be to become a client.

You may never end up authoring hundreds of books on Amazon like Dan Kennedy, but even just one book is a whole lot better than none. A book establishes you as an authority in your field. It gives you credibility and influence—and it also gives you the launching pad for an incredible marketing effort that has an excellent chance at landing scores of affluent clients. So—write on!

CHAPTER 16

StorySelling™ Hollywood-Style: Making a Movie that Will Gross Millions . . . for Your Business

By J.W. Dicks and Nick Nanton

When Stanley Lieber hit 40, he found himself running a comic book company that was rapidly going broke. He had been working there since he was 17, thanks to his uncle who owned the place, but he still only saw it as a temporary stop until he had the chance to write the Great American Novel. But somehow, that masterpiece never got written. Now, in 1962, the comics business was in a severe downswing—Stanley was down to having only three or four staffers working full time for him, grinding out stories about monsters from outer space for the boys and harmless teen romances for the girls.

But DC Comics, the perennial industry leader, had just had some success with a new superhero group title, The Justice

League of America, which brought together Batman, Superman, and a bunch of other costumed crusaders—so Stanley's uncle suggested that his nephew create one as well. Stanley wasn't happy with the whole idea. Superheroes were kind of silly, and they had been out of fashion for years. He didn't want to write another copycat comic—instead, he was convinced he needed a career change if he was ever really going to make his creative mark.

So he went home and talked through his frustrations with his wife. She finally told him, "Look, don't just quit. Do this one the way you want to do it. Put everything into this new comic, and see what happens. You can always quit later."

Stanley thought about it and finally decided, why not? He didn't have anything to lose—he might as well go for it. So, using his pen name of Stan Lee, he created The Fantastic Four with artist Jack Kirby—and was as shocked as anybody when the sales figures came in a few months later; kids were buying up the new comic like crazy. His uncle wanted more—so, in short order came an incredible creative burst that produced Spider-Man, The Incredible Hulk, The X-Men, Iron Man, The Mighty Thor, and The Avengers. It was like something inside Stanley had been finally unleashed.

Even more important than the breakthrough characters he created with his team of artists was the StorySelling™ Stan Lee used to sell his new approach. He called the line "Marvel Comics" and gave every cover the same distinctive design. He pushed the boundaries of traditional comics publishing and storytelling in every way; in-jokes abounded, and adventures were continued from issue to issue for the first time, just like soap operas. Stories were also more adult; they were an entirely new combination of the boy-girl dramas Stan had concocted for his romance comics, traditional superhero sagas, and, for the first time, an irreverent humor that permeated almost every page.

The world at large took notice of the big Marvel movement. Soon respectable magazines like *Esquire* and *Rolling Stone* were publishing serious profiles of Stan and Marvel. Their readership now didn't stop when kids turned 12; college kids were reading his stuff and loving it.

BUT . . .

Even though Stan Lee had story-sold his way to super-powered success, it didn't really extend far beyond the world of comic book fans. The mainstream media still looked down on that whole world—and the few movie and TV adaptations of Marvel heroes were low-budget ludicrous embarrassments. It was this way until 2000, when technology advanced to the point where producers could make affordable and believable films of superhero characters. *The X-Men* was a big success—and then *Spider-Man* was an even bigger blockbuster. More and more hits—along with a few misses—made their way to theaters, and Marvel's money-making ability grew and grew.

In short, it took the *movies* to really make Marvel's fortune—expanding its sights from niche comic book readers to audiences around the world. Yes, Stan Lee's StorySelling™ had provided the crucial foundation for this success—but only *films* took that StorySelling™ to incredible heights, culminating with the Disney® Corporation purchasing the company in 2009 for *$4 billion.*

The Power of the Branded Film

Now, the Marvel example is obviously an extreme case, but it does illustrate a very important point: A film opens up your StorySelling™ to a whole new audience that most definitely includes the affluent consumers you most want to reach. Not only that, but it's much more effective at *engaging and converting* that affluent audience.

Here are some stats that will demonstrate the power of movies and videos over print:

- Some 90% of information transmitted to the brain is *visual; those* visuals are processed 60,000 times faster by your brain than text. (*Sources*: 3M Corporation and Zabisco)
- About 40% of people respond better to visual information than plain text. (*Source*: Zabisco)
- Visual content drives engagement. When a brand uses visual content on Facebook, it creates a 65% increase in engagement. (*Source*: Simply Measured)
- Viewers are 85% more likely to purchase a product after watching a product video or movie. (*Source*: Internet)[1]

Statistics like this are what led Forrester Research's Dr. James McQuivey to state, "A minute of video is worth 1.8 million words."[2]

But beyond its potent scientific power, a film also elevates your stature in a way that completely differentiates you from your competition. That highly prized prestige factor is vitally important to earning the affluent's trust—as well as giving them the confidence to buy from you.

Branded Films and StorySelling™: Powerful Partners

The fact is, there is no better way to StorySell than with a properly produced branded film—because there's no better way to tell a *story* than with a film. You can actually bring whatever

---

[1] Amanda Sibley, "19 Reasons You Should Include Visual Content in Your Marketing," *Where Marketers Go to Grow*, August 6, 2012, http://blog.hubspot.com/blog/tabid/6307/bid/33423/19-Reasons-You-Should-Include-Visual-Content-in-Your-Marketing-Data.aspx

[2] Yahoo Finance, accessed June 18, 2014, http://finance.yahoo.com/news/minute-video-worth-1-8-130000033.html

narrative you choose to life—and craft it to appeal to high-paying customers and clients in a persuasive and dramatic fashion.

For example, Morgan Spurlock is a documentary filmmaker who made sure to insert himself into all his films, such as *Supersize Me* and *The Greatest Movie Ever Sold* (which was, ironically, a movie about product placement). His increased visibility, as a result of this choice, made him into a bona fide celebrity and media success— because of it, Spurlock is able to host his own TV shows and finds financing for other projects to be a much easier process.

And you don't have to be a documentary filmmaker to make this work for you. Anybody remember the inspirational sports movie, *Rudy*, about a 5' 6" kid with bad grades who worked his butt off to get into Notre Dame and into one of their games? Well, the guy who made his dream come true, Rudy Ruettiger, ended up working in a boring insurance company job after that moment of glory—but became obsessed with finding a way to make Hollywood turn his college triumph into a feature film. Ten years later, he somehow made it happen—and, after the movie was released in 1993, he got a call from a motivational speaking bureau and began a whole new career, earning tens of thousands of dollars telling his story to adoring crowds, including at our 2013 event in Hollywood, The National Academy of Best-Selling Authors® Best-Sellers' Summit.

It took a branded film to make that happen.

And, by the way, Hollywood even produces branded films for its *own* projects. When you see one of those "First Look" featurettes on HBO about an upcoming release, you're looking at a branded film *about* a film. These shorts are done documentary-style—but they're anything *but* real documentaries: They're actually advertisements produced to *look* like the real story behind the movie—but, of course, you'll never see any material that might be interpreted as being negative, unless it helps their cause. They don't have to put any in—and neither do you.

There are many reasons branded films are essential to realizing the potential of your StorySelling™ efforts—here are a few of them.

Films Make "Stars"

In the early days of Hollywood, there was no "star system." Actors were not credited and no one thought twice about what actor to put in a film. It was the *audience* that created movie stars—by demanding more movies featuring performers they saw and liked in different films. Producers finally figured out it was worth it to pay these performers a premium in exchange for the increased audiences they brought in to see them.

In a branded film, you are the "star"—the central figure in your own story, who is presented as a likable and magnetic individual. The audience responds to you on a gut level that just can't happen with the printed word. As we've already noted, the affluent have a hugely powerful sales resistance that can only be overcome with familiarity and trust. A properly produced branded film accomplishes both those aims.

Films Tell Stories

When the narrative behind your StorySelling™ is actually brought to life in a branded film, people take it in on a very deep level—and they *remember* it. Why? Because you're able to do your StorySelling™ in the most compelling and dramatic way.

In any action movie, Western, romantic comedy, or other popular film genre, various time-tested film techniques, such as how you use editing, music, lighting, and camera angles to create moods and effects, are put to work in order to make the story as exciting and suspenseful as possible. An effective branded film uses those same sophisticated techniques—and combines them with real people and real locations to give your narrative an authentic power that a Hollywood film can't match. Just ask the controversial, but very successful, filmmaker Michael Moore—the only movie he made with actors and a concocted story (*Canadian Bacon*) bombed badly at the box office.

Films Control the Message

The long-running CBS news series *60 Minutes* built its reputation initially by "ambush" interviews. The reporter would show up, without warning, at the office of the person being investigated and ask very confrontational questions. That person had no control of the message. If he answered honestly, he might incriminate himself. If he didn't answer at all, he risked looking incredibly guilty.

A branded film should be as opposite as you can get from this nightmarish scenario. Interviews and location shooting must be highly planned and scheduled, and the interview questions designed to shape the proper StorySelling™ narrative. It's one of the secrets of Michael Moore's success, by the way—he's been called out repeatedly for deceptive editing and shading reality to make the StorySelling™ in his films more pointed and dramatic. We aren't Michael Moore fans in any way, but we think the illustration helpful.

Films Allow People to Know Who You Are

In a book, you can write that someone is well put together. In a film, you can *see* that a person is well put together. The difference is crucial. In the first instance, someone is telling you something that you have to accept as being true; in the second instance, *you see it for yourself.*

Books are great at conveying ideas and demonstrating your expertise on a subject; they are essential to personal branding. Films do something else entirely. They allow your audience to experience *who you are*—how you walk, talk, and look—and respond to you in a *personal* way. All of that can obviously be shown to your best advantage with a knowledgeable director and production crew.

There's Never Been a Better Time to Make One

A branded film is a relatively new arrow in the marketing quiver of entrepreneurs and business owners, for two key reasons, both having to do with technological advances.

Reason number one is that creating and editing *high-quality* films has become much more *affordable* in recent years. You no longer need millions of dollars to create a professional Hollywood-level production. Equipment is much cheaper, more people have access to train on that equipment, and post production can be accomplished on computers not that much more powerful (or expensive) than your average home or office PC. But, be forewarned not to interpret that last statement to mean "anyone can do it." That couldn't be further from the truth. There are a lot of people out there with a camera who point and shoot, but that is just part of the process. You have to know how to write a winning script that tells the story, and you have to edit what you shoot in a way that the final cut is able to sell what you offer, including you. Making it look like a movie is a *very* different skill than most people have.

Reason number two is that online video has exploded on the internet, becoming incredibly prevalent and powerful. That means a branded film can be shared not only through YouTube, but also through popular social media sites such as Facebook and LinkedIn.

Of course, for your StorySelling™ to really engage an affluent audience, you need to stand out from the herd. Most branded films fall far short of the mark in this regard. Even though there is an incredible number of videos and films being posted to the internet, most of the ones that attempt branding do it in the most basic way possible. The person merely speaks to the camera and explains who he is or what he does. This is effective as a quick introduction to a website or for explaining a specific product or service, but as far as StorySelling™ a brand goes, it only can do so much—especially if it ends up looking more like a clip from *America's Funniest Home Videos* than a real *movie.*

And that's an approach the affluent are bound to reject. They like to see a high gloss on the people, products, and services that are marketed to them. (Unless, like Dan Kennedy, the lack of gloss is actually a virtue of what's being marketed, and again, *part* of the story.)

For a branded film to genuinely appeal to the affluent, it needs to look as if it has high production values—and it has to tell an impactful, emotional story. An entrepreneur or professional must present the most polished and professional brand possible, while, at the same time, make the strongest possible emotional connection to the potential audience.

It all comes down to this: When you watch a well-produced movie, you become involved in the characters' lives and what's going to happen to them. You root for them to do well and succeed. And you want to see more of them—that's why Hollywood is so big on sequels.

There are a lot of reasons for this; but mainly, it's this: By telling your story through a film, you (and your company or practice) become a *shared experience* with the affluent consumers you want to reach on a deeper level. They are magnetically drawn into your professional and personal life, they feel like they're a part of your success story—and they want to see you continue to do well.

And that, in turn, makes them *want to do business with you.*

This all happens on a deep psychological level because a properly produced branded film triggers an amazing amount of empathy that draws viewers closer to you and your business. And, again, it doesn't matter what kind of business it is!

For example, on paper, one of the branded films we produced, *Car Men*, would seem to be a ridiculous concept: Make an emotional, even touching film about an incredibly outrageous car dealer (we mean that in the best way, and he would take it as a compliment!). But for one of our clients, Tracy Myers, it turned into a huge success that resonated with his entire community. Because it was so well produced, the local TV stations ran the film—and reran it!—at absolutely no cost to Tracy! Can you imagine how much free advertising that was for his business—especially when one station ran it right before its coverage of the Super Bowl?

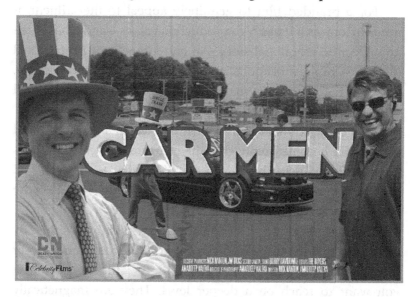

And again, the fact is, if you work with the right kind of production team, getting that level of quality is entirely affordable—and it pays off again and again down the line. Tracy even gave *Car Men* its own premiere at a local movie theatre— and it sold out! In Tracy's words:

> *When you're there, watching it, it looks like a film when it's on the big screen. It doesn't look like a television show or a cheap*

production that's been half put-together. It looks like something you would actually see in the movie theater.[3]

So create your own quality blockbuster—for the strongest possible StorySelling™ success when it comes to the affluent. It will certainly win you some valuable business.

[3] Nick Nanton & J.W. Dicks, *StorySelling: Hollywood Secrets Revealed—How to Sell Without Selling By Telling Your Brand Story,* hardcover edition (Celebrity Press, 2013) 139.

CHAPTER 17

The Extraordinary Power of Exclusivity: Courting the Affluent "Tribe"

By J.W. Dicks and Nick Nanton

"The world is a big place. The brands that understand how to speak to the shared values of the Global Affluent Tribe can transform that big world into one that is smaller, more united, and more within reach."

—MARK MILLER, CHIEF STRATEGY OFFICER, TEAM ONE

I f you're active on any social media platform, you routinely see virtual fistfights break out between people who have different beliefs or support different things. And you also see those fistfights quickly transform into organized warfare as those who think the same as one side unite against those who think the same as the other. Savage name-calling and personal attacks often result, ending in a defriending frenzy—the middle ground doesn't seem to exist.

The simple cause of this, a kind of us vs. them mindset? That fact that we all see ourselves as members of various "tribes." We identify with other people who are similar to us, and we want to surround ourselves with them. In turn, our belief systems harden along with the other people in our group. Organizations of individuals we think don't "fit in" with our tribes we often view with suspicion and alarm. Go ahead, put somebody who only watches MSNBC and somebody who only watches Fox News on the same couch. Or put a New York Yankees fan and a Red Sox fan in adjoining seats at a ballpark. You'll understand what we're talking about pretty quickly!

The funny thing, though, is it's not as much about politics or sports in the above examples as it is about science; humans are wired to be tribal. As biologist E.O. Wilson wrote,

> . . . *everyone, no exception, must have a tribe, an alliance with which to jockey for power and territory, to demonize the enemy, to organize rallies and raise flags. And so it has ever been. In ancient history and prehistory, tribes gave visceral comfort and pride from familiar fellowship, and a way to defend the group enthusiastically against rival groups. It gave people a name in addition to their own and social meaning in a chaotic world . . . Human nature has not changed. Modern groups are psychologically equivalent to the tribes of ancient history."*[1]

Are the affluent clients and customers you're pursuing above this sort of tribal behavior? Of course not—because they are, in fact, their own tribe!

The Global Affluent Tribe

As Dan Kennedy explains elsewhere in this book, the point of affluent gated communities isn't about protection from

---

[1] E.O. Wilson, "Why Humans, Like Ants, Need a Tribe," *Newsweek*, April 2, 2012.

dangerous and darker social forces; it's about the gate itself. It's about physically creating a "home" where an affluent tribe can gather together and exclude others.

But times have changed, and affluent tribes are no longer defined by a shared location.

Mark Miller, who works for an ad agency with global expertise and proprietary research in premium categories, is an expert on the affluent consumer. Through his company's research, he's determined that the affluent, in his words, *"are more united by what they love than by where they live."*[2] In other words, just like everybody else these days, their tribe goes beyond geographic borders and, instead, builds virtual villages on online platforms.

That's actually good news for those who want to sell to the affluent. By keying into the values of what Miller calls "The Global Affluent Tribe" and, more importantly, creating a tribe within that tribe composed solely of your customers, you radically increase your chances of successfully marketing to them.

Miller has pinpointed five core values that the Global Affluent Tribe has in common,[3] and they're worth quickly reviewing in this chapter because they hold the keys to successful communication with them.

Shared Value #1: Mobility

The affluent like to feel that they're beyond being identified by a single home location. They like to journey and journey far; Louis Vuitton, the upscale luggage brand, successfully tapped into this theme with its "Life is a Journey" campaign.

---

[2] Mark Miller, "The Five Values of the New Affluent Consumer," *Forbes.com*, accessed July 2, 2013.

[3] Ibid.

Shared Value #2: Success

The definition of success has changed in recent years for the affluent; it's not just about what they acquire but also what their money gives them the power to create and do. This ties in a little with the Mission-Driven Marketing we'll discuss in the next chapter. The point is that the affluent now define success as being about more than just having the most lavish possessions; it's also about having an impact on society or their community.

Shared Value #3: Status

Status, like success, has undergone a transformation in its definition. It's no longer about collecting expensive art objects; it's about having the best *experiences*. That's why a company like Virgin Galactic can continue to sell high-priced tickets for flights into space, despite the fact that they have yet to operate a regular commercial service to the stars. Members of the affluent tribe want to be the first in line for this kind of incredible experience.

Shared Value #4: Belonging

Global Affluent Tribe members are pursuing networked relationships across social, mobile, and digital channels, which, again, puts them in many more active groups with members from all over the world. This is a great opportunity for a marketer to both tap into as well as create these kinds of groups that specifically attract the affluent.

Shared Value #5: Consumption

According to Miller, consumption is more sophisticated, educated, and purposeful than in years past. Again, the emphasis is more on experience than simply the amount they're spending. They are looking for something that will deliver a great memory, not just bragging about spending a fortune on a lavish trip.

Keeping the above affluent values in mind, we're going to take things a step further—and reveal some of our favorite Tribal Tactics that you can use to "infiltrate" the tribes of high-income prospects.

Tribal Tactic #1: Create a New Tribe

"Membership has its privileges." That was one of American Express's longest-running ad slogans, and the credit card company still uses it to this day. Why? Because it's traditionally gone after affluent consumers and has always understood that the elite like to belong to what they perceive to be elite groups.

Tapping into that tendency is easier than ever before in your marketing efforts. As noted, the Global Affluent Tribe is much more flexible and open to forming groups that go beyond geography than ever before. With that in mind, you can create your own tribe, where you control the conversation and create valuable connections with the level of clients you're after.

For example, we formed such organizations as America's PremierExperts® and the National Academy of Best Selling Authors® to help our clients establish themselves as international authorities on their particular specialty. This allows them to StorySell® their expertise with these added credentials for credibility; but it also creates a new tribe for them that includes other affluent movers and shakers that they, in turn, can connect with.

You can do a similar thing on a smaller scale. By creating informal Mastermind groups designed to draw in affluent members, you'll be able to attract and market to them as you go along. For example, if you were an investment advisor, you could create a Mastermind group for local dentists that would meet one night a month to discuss what investments are a good option for them. Of course, along the way, when they begin to trust your advice, some will invariably turn to you to handle their money.

Tribal Tactic #2: Build an Elite and Exclusive Experience

In 2005, Amazon.com, the biggest online retailer, introduced Amazon Prime—now, for a flat yearly fee, Amazon shoppers would get unlimited and no-cost two-day shipping when buying Amazon products. Regular Amazon customers loved the idea.

Wall Street, however, hated it.

The program was instantly deemed an unprofitable disaster by most financial analysts; it would be costly and drag down profits. And, as a matter of fact, both the stock and profits were negatively affected at first. But Jeff Bezos, the Amazon CEO, held firm and said the program would end up paying off. Within a couple of years, it had. Amazon Prime upped customer loyalty to Amazon, so that sales consistently rose— after all, if you were guaranteed two-day free shipping by one shopping site, that would be the first place you'd go to buy something, right? Profits followed along, jumping a whopping 257% from 2006 to 2007.[4]

Even now, however, Amazon continues to be questioned by financial analysts for focusing too much on infrastructure that will generate big-time future benefits. Bezos doesn't care because he wants Amazon to be a very far-sighted company, continuing to risk short-term loss for long-term gain. That vision accounts for a lot of its singular success today. It's also garnered it tremendous repeat business and locked its customers in for the long run. It's perceived as *an exclusive business like no other*.

As we know, exclusivity is important to the affluent, as is having a great *experience*. With Amazon Prime, Amazon put those two together, and that may account for why it's the number-one online retailer for the affluent consumer.

---

[4] Ben Steverman, "Amazon's Spending Pays Off," *Bloomberg Businessweek*, July 25, 2007.

The question is, what can you do to combine exclusivity with a great experience? Whether it's turning a dental office into a dental spa or offering special reserved seating in a movie theater, with cushy easy chairs and access to a premium coffee and snack bar, there are always ways to upgrade the delivery of a product or service that's tailored to an affluent buyer.

Whatever the approach, it's important to have your staff (as well as yourself) take on the proper mindset to provide this kind of exclusive experience. The Ritz-Carlton luxury hotel chain has built its success on this level of service[5] because it has articulated its philosophy extensively and persuasively for the benefit of guests and staff alike—and displays it publicly on its company website. On one webpage entitled "Gold Standards," you'll find its service philosophy spelled out in various sections, including *The Three Steps of Service, Service Values, The 6th Diamond,* and *The Employee Promise.* But perhaps The Credo states its service objectives most powerfully:

> *The Ritz-Carlton Hotel is a place where the genuine care and comfort of our guests is our highest mission. We pledge to provide the finest personal service and facilities for our guests who will always enjoy a warm, relaxed, yet refined ambience. The Ritz-Carlton experience enlivens the senses, instills well-being, and fulfills even the unexpressed wishes and needs of our guests.*

With this kind of mission statement, everyone knows the mindset that needs to be in place for this level of service to be carried out. This is an excellent step for any organization to take, especially one serving the affluent.

Now, when you are creating an innovative way of boosting a customer's experience, always make sure a) you legally own

---

[5] Kelly Kearsley, "Taking Cue from Ritz-Carlton's Customer Service," *The Wall Street Journal,* March 1, 2013.

that process and b) you remind your clients that they can only receive the benefits of that process through you. We do this by trademarking our ideas (we are lawyers after all!) and making sure that when we talk about those ideas, we use all the correct identifiers (such as ®, ™, and ©) so that our prospects know these processes are exclusively *ours*—and, by hiring our agency, they are in the exclusive tribe that benefits from those processes.

Tribal Tactic #3: Sell It with a Star

How many of you out there have heard of Michael Boehm?

No clue? Well, that's the point of this tactic, because Boehm created one of the most famous and successful products of the past two decades—but his name isn't the one you think of when it comes to this particular item. And even though the product was an obvious winner, when Boehm had it ready to go to market, he couldn't find a corporate backer to help him put up the money and marketing to make it happen.

That's when he decided he needed some star power. His invention was a portable contact grill that cooks food items faster and more healthfully—and he knew boxer George Foreman ate two burgers before every fight and that he and his two sons loved to cook meat. He approached Foreman's management and all agreed that the product and the star were an amazing fit.

Once Foreman was on board, Boehm had the credibility to get the corporate backing he needed—and to ultimately sell over 100 million George Foreman Grills.[6]

Similarly, when we began publishing books, we looked for some star power of our own that would attract clients who were thrilled beyond belief to be between the covers of a book co-authored by motivational legends like Jack Canfield and Brian Tracy.

---

[6] Hope Hamashige, "An Inventor's Success Story," *CNN Money*, November 7, 2000.

The affluent are as star-struck as any of us, and when you give them access to a name they know and respect, they'll quickly flock to your side. Celebrities again signify exclusivity and provide a great experience to clients. They are suddenly part of a new and special tribe that has access to the rich and famous, and that's great when it comes to fulfilling their status values.

Of course, the other way to work this is to make *yourself* the star and the unique brand. It, of course, helps if you have a certain level of star power, savvy, and charisma. People like Richard Branson and Donald Trump know how to capture the spotlight and keep it firmly trained on them. They're experts on how to build their names to the point where they can slap it on anything and easily make a few million. That's why we help our clients establish themselves as the *experts* in their fields (as we discussed in an earlier chapter) through authoring books, doing TV interviews on CNN and other networks, and getting press in *USA Today*, the *New York Times*, and other national and local publications. We provide the coaching and training as well as the opportunities for professionals and entrepreneurs to effectively pull off all of the above.

These are just a few of the most powerful and effective ways you can push your business or enterprise to the front by making it one of a kind. When you create a unique and exclusive marketing platform, you make yourself the *only* choice in your business category—and that means you become the only game in town. And when you're the only game in town . . . you generally win at it!

CHAPTER 18

Mission-Driven StorySelling™: Do Better by Doing Good

By Nick Nanton and J.W. Dicks

"The rich don't care."

How many times do you hear a pundit say that in the media?

The conventional wisdom is that the affluent only care about themselves. Once they get theirs, everybody else is on their own, right?

Wrong. Dead wrong.

The affluent are *people*, and most people like to believe they're *good* people (and wonder of wonders, most actually are!). It boosts their self-esteem if they can lend a helping hand to some worthy objective or charity, especially if it's easy to do. For example, when they make a purchase they like to know that the business they're buying from is contributing in some way to a meaningful cause.

That's why aligning your marketing or business with that kind of meaningful cause is incredibly appealing to the affluent. By buying a product or service from a company or professional that is actively and publicly doing something praiseworthy, an affluent consumer feels they are helping out as well—*without having to do anything besides make a purchase they were probably going to make anyway.*

Think about it. All things being equal, would you buy a luxury car from a dealer who donated part of the sale to a cancer fund—or to one that didn't? In most cases, we're pretty sure you would choose the former—because . . . well, why not? You get the car you want at the price you want, *and* you do good without any additional effort on your part.

When a business engages in what we like to call "Mission-Driven Marketing," it gives itself *a clear and distinct advantage* that its competition lacks. Again, it's all about StorySelling™, and Mission-Driven Marketing gives you a narrative that's almost irresistible.

Is this cynical? No. Because the fact of the matter is, it's wonderful if you can combine business with a worthy cause. Why *not* elevate your company above the dollars-and-cents mentality and actively contribute to society?

Especially when it will draw the affluent customers you're after right to your door?

Ongoing research continually confirms that the affluent not only *like* a business that's mission-driven, they believe it *should* be. As Kayla Hutlzer writes in *Luxury Daily*, ". . . affluent consumers have now come to expect that luxury brands act responsibly and align themselves with social causes." The numbers back her up: Research shows that 66% of affluent consumers are loyal to brands that are socially conscious and *will* choose those brands over competitors.

The rich do care. So make them care about what you're doing with Mission-Driven Marketing.

Rocketing to the Top

The ultimate example of just how powerful Mission-Driven Marketing can be is the story of Peter Diamandis, an incredible individual we're proud to be partnering up with on a documentary project.

Peter graduated from MIT and then entered Harvard Medical School to become a doctor. But, a couple of years in, he couldn't let go of his dreams of pursuing space exploration, so he put his medical degree on hold and went back to MIT for a master's degree in aeronautics and astronautics. (Then, believe it or not, he went back to Harvard and got that medical degree, because this guy is a machine!)

A couple years after all that high-level education, Peter decided he wanted to put everything into his own special brand of Mission-Based Marketing. As NASA was winding down its exploration programs, Peter was frustrated at the fact that nobody else was willing to pick up the slack and continue to pursue flights into space. So he decided to do something about it. He founded the X Prize Foundation, an organization that promised to deliver a $10 million prize to whoever created a new generation of private passenger-carrying spaceships.

Only problem? Peter didn't have the $10 million—or really know where to get it! But because so many people were inspired by his mission, he attracted enough sponsors to pitch in the prize money—and in 2004, a winner took the prize. And the first nongovernment-backed flight into space was suddenly a reality.

But that was only the start of Peter's success story. Because his mission had drawn so much attention, he soon had his own publishing deal and his own *New York Times* bestseller, *Abundance*. Not only that, but he suddenly had the ears of the rich and powerful who were intrigued not only by his vision but by how he had actually gotten *results*. Prominent moguls like Richard Branson and Microsoft co-founder Paul Allen became part of his circle, and Peter now began to put together exclusive events where these kinds of notables would brainstorm new scientific initiatives designed to improve our world.

By tapping into a mission that captivated so many influential (and affluent) followers, Peter not only inspired new and amazing breakthroughs but also created the conditions for many more to come. You might say his entire success stems from his unique approach to Mission-Driven Marketing.

The Advantages of Mission-Driven Marketing

While Peter's story is, in many respects, one of a kind, the advantages of Mission-Driven Marketing to the average professional, entrepreneur, or business owner are large and ongoing. We'd like to cover just a few of those substantial benefits, especially when it comes to connecting with the affluent.

1. Increased Profits

Yes, we can be mercenary about this; when properly done, Mission-Driven Marketing drives well-to-do customers to your door. Here's a good example: *Conde Nast Traveler* magazine polled its roughly 810,000 affluent subscribers on travel companies and their social responsibility. The outcome?

Some 58% said their choice of hotel was influenced by the support it gives to the local community; 86% said they'd like hotels to explain how they're contributing to their communities and the environment while 80% said the same thing of airlines. And 93% said travel companies should be responsible for "protecting the environment."

The above numbers indicate that the affluent have a very strong preference for choosing companies that are about more than "business as usual." Again, it makes them feel good to contribute to the success of a company that also demonstrates a commitment to the common good.

2. Increased Loyalty

"If marketers don't have a real handle on the emotional side of the purchase and engagement process, they end up with a 'placeholder,' one whose name people know but don't know for anything in particular, and have absolutely no [brand] advantage. You might as well spend your entire marketing budget on coupons, deals, and promotions," says Robert Passikoff, president of Brand Keys.

We agree. And research shows that Mission-Driven Marketing supplies this elevated and emotional level of engagement. It gives affluent customers a reason to come back to the same business again and again.

3. More New Clients

In addition to being very good at keeping old customers, Mission-Driven Marketing also excels at bringing in new ones. Fully 91% of global consumers said they would switch to a brand associated with a good cause, according to a recent Cone Communications/Echo Global CSR Study. Again, all things being equal, Mission-Driven Marketing is magnetic to affluent consumers who want to do good things with their purchases— and sometimes, even when all things *aren't* equal! Some 50% would be willing to reward such companies by paying more for their goods and services, according to Nielsen's "2013 Consumers Who Care" study.

4. Stronger Awareness/Positive Image

Obviously, a business that is visibly doing good is going to be held in much higher regard by its customers, as well as by its noncustomers. It's also going to gain awareness through its good works, either through joint ventures with nonprofits or through the people it helps. When you align your business interests with a higher mission, you are seen to be operating for a greater good, rather than your own good. In an era where businesses are routinely seen as selfish and uncaring, Mission-Driven Marketing differentiates you in an incredibly significant way. According to the 2013 Cone Communications Social Impact Survey, 93% of consumers have a more positive image of a company that supports a cause.

Ben & Jerry's ice cream company is a prime example of just how successful Mission-Driven Marketing can be. It began as a lone ice cream stand in Burlington, Vermont, located in an abandoned gas station. From the beginning, the owners gave back to the community, by sponsoring a free movie night once a week in the summer, where the film was projected on a wall by the ice cream stand. As the company grew, so did its commitment to the area; the owners sponsored concerts, festivals, and fairs and also made a point of supporting local farmers. The milk and produce that went into its ice cream was always purchased locally. And, when Ben and Jerry first sold stock, they did it through small community meetings where every one of their customers was invited to share in the success. The company continues to be extremely cause-oriented to this day. Of course, making awesome ice cream didn't hurt the bottom line either!

5. Attraction and Retention of Quality Employees

This particular advantage may not apply directly to your marketing and sales, but it definitely impacts the overall health of your business. The fact is that when you engage in Mission-Driven Marketing, you have a much better shot at building a great team underneath you to help you run your business at a higher level. Here are the facts: 77% of Americans look at the corporate citizenship of a company before deciding whether they want to work there, 72% of those who already hold jobs want their employers to show commitment to social causes, and a whopping 85% of employees say they'd quit if it came to light that their employer had *negative* social responsibility practices (Cone Cause Evolution and Environmental Study).

6. Heightened Investor Interest

If you're interested in attracting affluent investors, Mission-Driven Marketing also gives you a big advantage. The Cone Cause Study also determined that as many as 66% of investors consider a company's dedication to social causes before investing their money. Maybe that's why socially responsible investments in the United States actually grew 4% faster than any other sector of U.S. stocks in the last few years.

7. You Do Good Things for Others—and Yourself

Most of us do enjoy doing things that will improve the lives of others in one way or another. If we can link that kind of altruistic effort to our businesses, so much the better. Backing worthy causes isn't just good for your business, it's good for *you*. International studies show that engaging in pro-social pursuits actually results in a longer life, as well as greater personal happiness and even lower blood pressure, according to a 2013 survey in *Psychology and Aging* journal!

Making the Most of Your Mission

Our company endeavors to use Mission-Driven Marketing because we enjoy giving back as a business; the side benefits are just the frosting on the cake. Our first foray into the world of documentaries was called "Jacob's Turn" and was about a young boy with Down Syndrome who played youth baseball. The wonderful story led to Nick winning his first Emmy nomination as director of the film. From that first step we have gone on to build a film studio that creates documentaries for profit and nonprofit causes internationally. Doing good led to rewards we hadn't expected, more Emmys, and a new successful business. If you're interested in pursuing your own cause, here are a few tips on how to do it right, based on our and others' experience.

Make Your Mission One You Believe In

If you don't have some passion for the cause you've chosen, you'll find you won't be engaging with it on the level you need to be. It's like anything else—if you don't feel an emotional connection to what you're doing, you won't be inspired to achieve what you should. Remember, your cause can be almost *anything* as long as it's intended to produce a positive outcome for all concerned.

Share Your Story

Whenever you do something for your cause, don't be shy about talking about it or posting about it on social media. This isn't just about publicizing your business; it's also about publicizing your cause and getting more and more people involved in it. Sharing your story is the first step toward connecting with others who may want to get involved in what you are doing and make your mission part of their own.

Team Up with a Major Player

This is a rich area for the Mission-Driven Marketer. When you team up with a nonprofit organization to tackle your cause, that organization naturally will want to promote your business to its membership and supporters; the better you do, the more you will be able help them with *their* mission. If the cause you're helping to champion is a local one, you'll find yourself quickly being seen as a positive force in the community. As the affluent have the time and money to involve themselves in these kinds of efforts, you will form strong connections to that group and also be seen in an extremely favorable light by them. You also build the all-important element of *trust*—a critically important element when it comes to marketing to the affluent. Finally, you can also team up with noncompeting businesses who are also interested in your cause. You gain access to their client base and they get access to yours: win-win.

Have a Plan

Imagine if you started your business with no endgame in mind. You'd end up flailing around and finally going under. If you have no direction, you usually end up nowhere, which is why goals are important. Well, that goes for the cause you're championing as well. If you don't set up specific projects, fundraising efforts, or events that have realistic objectives, you won't advance your mission or your own interests. And your Mission-Driven Marketing won't be as impressive to your prospects.

Don't Be Divisive

When your business decides to back a political rally for one group or another, you're automatically insulting half of your audience, especially in these polarizing times. That's why it's best to pick a cause almost everybody can get behind. There are certainly exceptions to every rule. At times you may find it advantageous to be divisive, but in general this is not a wise practice. Keep your mission separate from organizations that people may not necessarily agree with everything they stand for. Make your business efforts all about the specific mission. As an individual you have greater freedom with organizations you may want to be part of, but as a business, there's no point in alienating potential customers you don't have to alienate. The affluent are as opinionated (if not more so) than the average consumer, so why drive them away when you're actually trying to get them in the door?

Do Your Homework

Remember that if you are pursuing the affluent marketplace, the best endgame possible is to find a cause that you're excited about—and they are as well. American Express shows a lot of genius in promoting events that they *know* their well-heeled cardholders will love—and giving them early access to those kinds of events. When you tap into a cause that the upscale side of your community supports enthusiastically, they will also end up supporting *you* enthusiastically. Again, you establish an invaluable trust—as well as a deeper kind of relationship that can't be built *within* a business framework, where money always ends up raising a suspicious eyebrow.

When you make Mission-Driven Marketing *your* mission, you open the door to reaching your affluent prospects on a whole different level than a strictly business approach can manage. Do good *and* do good for your business. It's an undeniably awesome combination that has great upside to it.

BOOK TWO

What Are They Spending
Their Money On?

By Dan S. Kennedy

BOOK TWO

CHAPTER 19

What Are You a Merchant Of?

"To be an Imagineer, it's important to keep reality at arm's length."

—CHRISTIAN HOPE, CONCEPT DESIGN DIRECTOR, QUOTED IN
THE IMAGINEERING WAY ABOUT DISNEY'S IMAGINEERS

There was a time when coffee was coffee. Ice cream was ice cream. A phone was a phone. Even a pair of shoes was, well, just a pair of shoes.

At one level, at the lowest price and profit level, there are still merchants stuck in this time warp, continuing to conduct business as if people still bought products.

Today, that cup of coffee comes with more options than a Lexus®. Would you care to add . . . vanilla or caramel syrup? A double shot? Foam? Cinnamon sprinkles? Thus, the $5.00 price for the $.50 cup of coffee. But even that is only half the story. Ordinary products morphing into complex arrays of choices, options, add-ons, brands, and luxury brands is one way prices have been inflated and margins inflated even more. The profit margin of the double shot of extra something or other far exceeds the profit margin of the cup of coffee itself. The designer-name bag selling for $11,000.00 does not cost 100 times more to make than the similar-appearing bag sold at Target® for $110.00. This is a path to profit—and to greater acceptance by affluent consumers. But, as I said, it is only half the story.

Starbucks® does not define itself as a coffee shop or even more elegantly as a coffeehouse. The company describes itself as being in the "third-place business"—home, office, Starbucks® in between. It is not a merchant just of jazzed-up coffee drinks. It is a merchant of place, of feelings, of status, and maybe most of all, of experience. Its inspirations are more Disney® than Denny's®. One of the many students of the Starbucks® phenomenon, Ken Herbst, assistant professor of marketing at Wake Forest University's Babcock Graduate School of Management, makes the obvious point: "If you walked up to someone about to buy a pound of coffee at the grocery store (at about $4.00 a pound) and tried selling them just a cup for $5.00 they would tell you that is too expensive. But if you are at the coffeehouse, you are going to pay for the experience."

Dan Kennedy's #7 No B.S. Key to the Vault

Break the chains that bind in your own mind. More success and prosperity will start materializing instantly.

This means that price is not tied to product. As soon as you disconnect those two things in your own mind about your own products and services, you'll be liberated to make a great deal more money and to have much greater success appealing to affluent customers or clients. To be redundant for emphasis, most business owners are severely handicapped by keeping price and product linked in their own minds. What I call the *Price-Product Link* is as restrictive and antiquated as the *Work-Money Link* that I take apart in my book *No B.S. Wealth Attraction in the New Economy*. These links are imaginary. They exist only in your mind, not in the marketplace, yet they are ties that bind as if real, physical, 1,000-pound chains.

The Price-Product Link becomes ingrained religious belief in most business owners, beginning with textbook formulas for setting price. Retailers are taught the doctrine of keystone pricing, meaning double their own cost. If you buy it for $1.00, it should be priced at $2.00, then, at times, discounted from there. In my line of work, direct marketing—what was once called "mail order"— we're also taught formulaic markup as doctrine, although ours is eight times rather than two times. In businesses where raw materials are converted to finished products, like printing, there is a plethora of price-calculating software to do the thinking for you, using standardized markup formulas. In every case, the price is chained to the product. There is the fundamental idea that a particular product is worth only a certain multiple of its cost and not a penny more, period, end of story. Unfortunately, this widely and deeply held belief is completely and utterly stupid.

The two biggest chain cutters that de-link price from product are who is buying the product and the context in which the product is presented, priced, and delivered.

The *who* is what this book is all about. The simple act of selling whatever you sell to more affluent consumers may allow its price to rise, with no other modifications.

Price for the same product also varies by context. This is easy to see with commodity items like food, even though many restaurant owners still never grasp it. When is a third pound of peanuts not a third pound of peanuts? In a jar, on the shelf, that's all they are, unless dusted with Starbucks® mocha latte powder and packaged in a fancy tin. But when served hot, from a vendor's cart in the park, scooped into the bag and sprinkled with cinnamon by a handlebar-mustached man in red-and-white striped jacket and straw hat, with calliope music playing from the CD player in the cart, they are not peanuts at all. They are an experience that evokes emotional feelings. Even as you read my words, your mind may have flashed to Mary Poppins in the park or a trip to the circus as a child. While it is not so easy for most to transfer this idea to other businesses, it does, in fact, transfer to any business. Context alters or liberates price. Move the exact same product from one context to another and its price can easily be altered.

What It Is Needn't Determine What It Is

A visit to the dentist can be just a visit to the dentist. Cleaning and checkup, a routine experience and a routine price. Or it can mean being picked up at your home by the dental office's gleaming white limousine, brought to the elegantly appointed office with grand piano playing itself in the lobby, neatly uniformed staff rising to greet you at the door and escort you to a comfortable chair, get you a fresh-brewed latte, offer you a choice of magazines (just like what stewardesses used to do for first-class passengers on airlines a decade ago) . . . then, only a few minutes later, escort you to the spa room for your complimentary manicure and hand massage . . . then to the dental hygienist for your regular cleaning, plus a whitening treatment while you relax in a dental chair with a full-body massage pad and gentle heat and listen to your favorite music, not piped-in elevator music or, worse, the radio . . . then back to the spa for some anti-aging skin treatments . . . and back to the limo, carrying a complimentary gift basket of little soaps and skin lotions along with your tote bag containing your next three months' supply of specially formulated toothpaste, whitener, and breath freshener. The charges for the cleaning, whitening treatment, and products are all evened out during the year as a monthly membership fee automatically charged to your credit card, so there is no plebian act of standing at the front desk at the end of your visit, reviewing charges and writing out a check, nor any such bill arriving in the mail.

We can give just about anything a comparable makeover. A meeting with the financial advisor or tax accountant, a visit to the sporting goods store, a stay at a hotel, even a true business-to-business experience, like buying and receiving printing from the printer or industrial parts from a manufacturer. Somewhere in the process there is opportunity to alter the experience and the way the buyer feels about it. It begins with determining the feelings you want to create for the buyer: security and peace of mind. Being pampered like a queen or king. Nostalgia. Whatever. It is this that unties price from the anchor of product and allows it to float upward like a helium-filled balloon on a slightly breezy day.

Different buyers want different experiences and the feelings they invoke in different circumstances.

I choose to fly private rather than commercial, at substantial expense, with practical rationalization tied to the extremely high value of my time and the urgency with which I need to get where I'm going or to get home and get to work. But, as confession, it is at least as much about being and feeling special. For one person using private aviation, that might mean status lorded over others. That's not it for me. For some, it might be about the pampering. Not for me. For me it is—after 20 years of suffering the ever-worsening indignities, inconveniences, and stresses of ordinary air travel—about escape from the way ordinary folk must travel, to a better experience. The feeling to me is similar to the one I get going downstairs to my basement office and being at my chosen work in minutes, in comfortable clothes, knowing that outside, thousands of ordinary people are slogging through snow, waiting for cars to warm, enduring bumper-to-bumper traffic in hour-long commutes. In short, it is about a feeling of superiority.

Yet I get my hair cut at a walk-in, no-appointment hair cutting place. There's nothing about it that makes me feel special. To the contrary. I prize the in-and-out speed and simplicity more than anything else. There are no Kennedy's Barber Clubs open yet in my area. When there are, I'll join the many men of my same age and income who profoundly prefer a trip to a very upscale men's salon with mahogany paneling, plasma TVs playing sporting events, and relative quiet that takes four times as long and costs ten times the price. Not necessarily because the haircut is any different. Because the feeling he gets from the experience is meaningful and therefore valuable to him.

Affluent consumers do not simply choose the priciest option of *everything* in *every* category. Different affluent consumers value different experiences differently. It's up to you, the marketer, to find the group of affluent consumers you can match up with an experience you design and can deliver, that disconnects price from product.

CHAPTER 20

Value in the Eye of the Beholder

In a *60 Minutes* story broadcast in 1973, an astonished Morley Safer
was told that a Saudi prince and his three bodyguards were traveling
to Syria aboard the Orient Express "to shoot swans with a
chromium-plated submachine gun."

I n response to an article of mine in my *No B.S. Marketing
to the Affluent Letter*, a GKIC Member sent me this note:

I have to confess, we **worry** a lot at our company about
pricing. So I was astonished to find out about Williams-
Sonoma's prices: for Halloween Caramel Apples . . . .
mini-apples, no nuts, set of four, "only" (!) $29.50 plus
$7.50 shipping and handling. Or a larger single apple,
with or without nuts, $19.50. For ONE apple! Plus $6.50
s/h. Or your own personalized Halloween cookies,
3 cookies, $24.00. You could combine the apple and
cookies at $43.50. For a discount on shipping, buy $150.00
worth. Though **I am appalled**, it appears that there is a
large enough set of people for and to whom these things

appeal, as Williams-Sonoma does a very good business. Reaffirms the adage that "you are not your customer," or perhaps more accurately, "you are not *necessarily* your customer."

That you are not your customer is an astute observation and brings me impetus for a very important discussion.

First, note that Williams-Sonoma® is a cataloger focusing on the Mass-Affluent, not Ultra- or Super-Affluent. Its products are *routinely* purchased by hundreds of thousands of households with annual income in the $100,000.00 neighborhood. The $19.00 apples are NOT being nibbled only by a few eccentric multimillionaires who also clean their eyeglasses with hundred-dollar bills. It is VITAL that, through this book, from catalogs like Williams-Sonoma's, and as many other sources as possible, you get, accept, embrace, fully internalize that the Mass-Affluent Class of Consumers in America is spending like crazy on premium-priced luxury goods and services, buying all manner of things that will shock you. (I recently reserved a suite at a Disney® hotel—where *families* go on vacation—at $1,800.00 a night, and it was the last of two remaining rooms in the entire hotel in January.)

Second, of all possible reactions to discoveries like these, being appalled is *least* appropriate. Let's consider the reasons somebody might be appalled (my subscriber didn't enunciate his). One would be the "children are starving somewhere" idea, that if people didn't pay $19.00 for caramel apples, somehow starving urchins somewhere would be fed and cared for. Gee, if it really were that simple to solve poverty and world hunger, I'd give up my $19.00 apples and my luxury SUV and my $800.00 cowboy boots tomorrow. But that's just not how money really moves around, how wealth or poverty is caused or affected, and I'd refer anybody wrestling with that idea to my *No B.S. Wealth*

Attraction book. Until you come to grips with the truth about prosperity NEVER being a zero-sum game, where one person's wealth or, by your judgment, waste deprives someone else, you are hamstrung, handcuffed, hog-tied mentally, emotionally, and practically in your own attraction of wealth. The supply of wealth to which all have ready access based exclusively on their own chosen behaviors is not a debit-credit system at all. This is contrary to what 95% believe to be true about money, but it is not coincidental that 95% have comparatively little while 5% have most of it.

Or somebody might be appalled at the wretched excess, the foolish spending. I've been broke; I have a gut-level, visceral reaction to what I judge as waste. But that imposes your value judgments or mine on others. A devout atheist opposed to all religion might very well view your $20.00 put into the church collection plate en route to the Vatican with just as jaundiced an opinion as your critical view of his purchase and enjoyment of a $20.00 apple. One man's wretched excess is another's highest and best value.

There are better (more profitable) reactions than being appalled. One is to use this information as fodder for your own continuing inner thoughts, dialogue, and (probably, hopefully) reorientation of your understanding of price, value, consumer behavior. Another is to be inspired and motivated to re-examine your beliefs about your own customers' or clients' attitudes, spending, interests, passions, and to search for opportunities to 1) design and offer premium-priced goods and services (options or levels) to your present clientele and/or 2) seek out a clientele that places price very low in its list of Buying Decision Factors. (As example of that, imagine how many restaurant owners, grocers, gift shop owners, and so on will read this chapter but will never bother to go to www.SRDS.com, find the Williams-Sonoma mailing lists, contact the list manager, and rent the best Williams-Sonoma buyers they can in their area, to promote their businesses to! Refer to Chapter 29, "We Know Where They Live.")

Back to understanding value: No, a $19.00 apple a day won't keep doctors at bay any better than a $1.00 apple, at least as a result of its nutritional properties. (It might, based on its effect on the consumer's positive attitude. But that's not my principal argument here.) *The value that motivates the Williams-Sonoma buyer to pay $19.00 for the apple is not in the apple at all.* It may be in the impact of it given as gift or served at a party. It may be in the feelings of success or prosperity or of rewarding oneself with indulgence that come with making the purchase (even before ever taking a bite of the apple). It may be a sense of superiority, of buying or serving the best or something unique and unusual. Bragging rights: It's a trophy apple, because, after all, we can't really frame and hang our bank books on the wall for all visitors to see. Instead we opt for other visual representations of our achievement and success: trophy car, trophy house, trophy watch, trophy wife, trophy apple. It may be the time saved and convenience of ordering from the catalog rather than schlepping off to a gourmet store across town. It may be all those things. It is certainly mostly emotional and psychological, not practical. Thus, the $19.00 apple may very well contribute to the person's emotional well-being in ways a grocery-store apple cannot.

When I was young and poor and insecure, just starting in business and routinely asking older, more successful people to give me money, I bought and drove fancy Lincoln Continental Town Cars. And I always flew first class—at the time the only young kid up front, surrounded by 50-year-old executives. I didn't drive the car or fly first class for its impact on others; I did so for its impact on me, for its programming of my own psyche. Neither the value of the car nor that of the first-class tickets for me had anything to do with getting from place to place. The value to me was purchased confidence and feelings of parity and belonging, of having arrived where I was actually trying to get. I never paid $19.00 for an apple, but I did always order Chivas Regal®.

Personally, I don't wear a watch at all. Years back, I owned and wore a Rolex® and a Tag Heuer®, but such things no longer interest me. But I pass no judgment on the fellow who wears one or ten and proudly flexes his cuffs at every chance in order to display them. I also understand that the different motivations different people have at different times of their lives for paying $5,000.00 or $50,000.00 for a wristwatch have nothing whatsoever to do with their need to know precisely what time it is. For that, of course, a $50.00 Timex® will do just fine.

The most successful marketers learn not to question how the public or their customers get value—only to strive to find out about it, recognize it, and capitalize on it. To be of service means offering and delivering what customers value; that's the role of the businessperson. Should you feel a need instead to impose your value criteria on others, you ought to exit business and enter politics or ministry.

CHAPTER 21

Stop Selling Products and Services

"Any fool can make soap. It takes a genius to sell soap."

—Mr. Gamble of Proctor & Gamble

A short preface . . . when I wrote the first version of this chapter for the first edition of this book, published in 2009, even I didn't foresee the rapidly accelerating, expansive wave of fundamental disinterest in things. In stuff. The most functional, basic products are no longer sold successfully based on functionality—phones are a great example. As I was writing this, the iPhone 6 came out, and I happened to be in a room with four of six people who raced to get one, and were lording it over the other two present. But nobody was saying anything about the phone. I have, in very recent years, become acutely aware that it is the poorly compensated, poorly skilled salesman, marketer, or copywriter who defaults to: Product/Service, Features/Benefits, Proposition/Price when selling. People, particularly the affluent, were losing interest in these tried-and-true approaches to *selling when I first wrote this chapter. They have lost all tolerance for it now.*

A cloth bag is not worth $4,000.00 without the Gucci® logo, or some other designer's logo.

You may feel that it is not worth $4,000.00 with the logo either. But that reveals you remain hung up on what a product is, instead of what it symbolizes and represents, what status it confers on its owner, what emotional reactions it evokes, how it feels to purchase and own it, how others important to its owner feel about it.

Few things are intrinsically worth their price. We have all accepted that a diamond engagement ring priced at least equal to two months' salary is a requirement. But the diamond may be far, far, far more artificially inflated from its actual cost of materials than that Gucci® cloth bag. Diamonds are, in essence, polished dirt.

A Great Ad Campaign Can Last Forever

While most businesspeople think of De Beers's dominance in the diamond industry as a result of controlling supply, truth is, it is more the result of creating and manipulating demand, thanks to brilliant advertising delivering a consistent theme for half a century.

Finding rocks is easy. Selling rocks, tough. In the last 50 years, only two markets have opened up for stones. You wear them on your fingers when in love; you put them over the head of a loved one after death. The second was mastered by the Rock of Ages Corporation. The first by De Beers and its holding company, a near monopoly. The product itself—diamonds— was a loser. If you apply ordinary supply and demand, every diamond dug diminishes the value of those already dug because, in fact, diamonds *are* forever. Further, they are plentiful. De Beers recognized the problem with its mundane commodity, so it took the radical move of ignoring inherent value altogether. Instead the company made the product ritualistic and metaphoric, its purchase mandatory without practical purpose. This required the use of advertising to create demand where there was none, and no reason for any. This defies, of course, one of the oldest, most tired business axioms: Find a *need* and fill it.

Before the first ad ever appeared, some of the most extensive market research in advertising history was conducted, including direct questioning of thousands of men and women. The researchers determined that women had to be convinced that the diamond was *the* ritualized representation of love, commitment, and marriage. For women, the "diamond is forever" positioning began in advertising in 1914 and has continued unchanged to this day. And, to solve the forever problem, De Beers created the 10th anniversary ring, 25th anniversary ring, and similar products.

The researchers also determined that men had to be helped past confusion about how to buy this polished rock. For men, the industry's voodoo about carat weight, color, clarity, and so forth was created to provide logic where there was none. Men wanted to know what it was worth. Since it was arguably worth nothing, a logic had to be invented to assign worth to it. But in the cleverest of all gambits, a simpler shortcut for buying decisions was also created, stating the price in the frame of the buyer's own wages: "How can you make two months' salary last forever?" Today, the two-months'-salary rule is widely accepted by the public.

In truth, what De Beers did for diamonds, anyone can do for anything.

You're aware there are wines that sell for hundreds of dollars per bottle. But there is a Samuel Adams *beer* that sells for $140.00 per bottle. How can beer be worth such a price? You may answer: It can't. Or answer: Why not?

To make a giant income marketing to the affluent, you must erase your own deeply ingrained insistence at connecting price to worth and worth to function.

A business associate told me how her neighbors paid a local architect $67,000.00 to draw up plans for a new house to be built on their beachfront lot. She found an architect to do what she judged to be identical work—if not better—for her new house to be built on her beachfront lot, paying just $7,000.00. And she questioned her neighbors' sanity at failing to shop around, at paying such an outrageously inflated fee. She was proud of her bargain. But, contrary to protestations of the psychiatric community, there is abundant evidence that, in our society, insanity is subjective. My kudos go to the architect commanding his $67,000.00 fee. In all probability, he secured it for things other than a tube of blueprints. My associate may very well be correct in judging her $7,000.00 blueprints just as good as the ones delivered for $67,000.00. But her $7,000.00 ones didn't come with the pride, status validation, bragging rights, and other emotional benefits her neighbors derived from searching out and hiring the biggest name, purportedly the most sought-after architect in the tri-state area, an architect, in fact, who had done the plans for a

Dan Kennedy's #8
No B.S. Key to the Vault

Marketing to values is more powerful than the
marketing of products.

famous celebrity's new beach house and who had three homes he'd designed featured in *Town & Country*.

On closer examination, this little story reveals even more. It shows two people's very different values, and why what I call marketing to values is so much more important and powerful than is the marketing of products. My business associate is a woman who, her whole life, has competed with men, has made herself successful in a field difficult for women, has fought being taken for granted as a blonde beauty, and prides herself on her mental toughness, shrewdness, and won't-take-no-for-an-answer-ism. One of her highest and most important personal values is that "nobody pulls the wool over my eyes." Her neighbor is the second, younger wife of a wealthy doctor from a wealthy family—but she came from a poor family, grew up on the wrong side of the tracks, and, in her first marriage, lived a blue-collar life. Her beauty got her the trophy wife position, but she found herself thought of and gossiped about as a classless bimbo rather than accepted into the rich wives' sorority. She has been a relentless social climber ever since, by donating to charities, sponsoring charity balls, patronizing *the* hairstylist, *the* cosmetic surgeon, *the* personal trainer, and being seen in the most current designer fashions, in an orchestrated effort to force her husband's peers' wives to accept her into their circle. One of her most treasured values is their acceptance or their envy. In reality, neither her payment of $67,000.00 to her architect nor my friend's payment of her negotiated $7,000.00 to her architect had much to do with the comparative intrinsic or actual value of the work reflected in the two sets of blueprints.

Another way to look at this, as a marketer, is a choice between selling things with ham-handed, brute force, typically against resistance, or selling aspirations and emotional fulfillments with finesse, typically with little resistance. Which seems like it might be more pleasurable? More profitable?

CHAPTER 22

How the Mass-Affluent
Trade Up

"Kids in Beverly Hills 90210 put on their own unique Christmas pageant,
and the first scene, in particular, was fascinating. In it, Mary and
Joseph are going to Bethlehem to pay their taxes. One little girl
was Mary, one little boy was Joseph, a fit kid was the donkey,
and a kid with thick eyeglasses was their CPA."

—BOB ORBEN, TV COMEDY WRITER AND DIRECTOR OF WHITE HOUSE SPEECHWRITING
DURING THE GERALD FORD ADMINISTRATION

One of the most important facts about the Mass-Affluent is that they do not trade up across the board.
In his research, Michael Silverstein, author of *Trading Up: Why Consumers Want New Luxury Goods—and How Companies Create Them*, found that the typical Mass-Affluent person seeks little steps up in a lot of things, makes major steps up in only one to three things, and remains unmoved by luxury, brand, experience, or other factors in many other purchase categories. To put that in a frame of example, Mrs. Mass-Affluent may indulge in little things like going to Starbucks® rather than Denny's® or to Cold Stone Creamery® instead of Dairy Queen®, may buy luxury-brand drop-downs like the line of Vera Wang® designer duds sold at Kohl's®; may have one category of purchase where

price is literally out the window—perhaps the care and feeding of her poodle—but may also still buy whatever coffee is on sale at the supermarket absent brand loyalty and recoil at the price for a Lexus®, preferring a Toyota®.

She is a complicated creature.

This makes marketing to the Mass-Affluent a complicated thing.

Luxury-goods merchants have caught on, and are very much engaging in what I just referred to as luxury drop-down. The makers of old-line luxury goods like Mercedes® automobiles or Coach® bags have created lower-priced products—usually smaller, with fewer features, but of the same quality and bearing the brand name—enabling the Mass-Affluent consumer to cross the luxury line without qualm. Some luxury merchants have found enormous leverage in leaving a huge chasm between their top-priced items and their new luxury-for-the-masses merchandise. Women who can't afford one, and even those who can, might blanch at a $10,000.00 Vera Wang® dress but be quite happy to pay $99.00 for a Vera Wang® blouse at Kohl's®. But without knowledge of the $10,000.00 dresses, they'd balk at such a high price for that blouse. Some marketers, including several of my clients, even go so far as to create and promote red-herring-priced goods or services they hope no one buys, only to set a standard that makes their actual prices seem imminently reasonable by comparison. I talk more about this in Chapter 34, "Price, Profit, Power."

Their Little Indulgences Equal Big Profit Improvements

Let's go back to the Starbucks® and Cold Stone Creameries® of the world. In these businesses, almost any marketer can find practical inspiration. While many Mass-Affluent consumers easily able to afford high-fee cosmetic dentistry, luxury cars, first-class travel, or designer fashions may find the price tags too big to swallow, they are easily wooed by little luxuries. For what seems like a small uptick in price—yet is a very big increase in profit margin for the merchant—the consumer can feel affluent yet not like somebody just throwing money around, can feel special without guilt. A $70,000.00 sticker on a car, a $35,000.00 fee quoted by the dentist, a $2,000.00 airline ticket—these are all so in-your-face. On the surface, the difference between the $70,000.00 car vs. the $35,000.00 car isn't so great; a car may feel like a car. On the plane, all the seats arrive at the same time. But the fact that you can pick up a half gallon of ice cream at the supermarket for about the same price as a tiny cup of ice cream at Cold Stone Creamery® is more disconnected. The experience is dramatically different. At the creamery, you pick out your flavor, your ground-up pie crust and candy bars, and watch your dessert being made for you on a granite slab. The company, with 1,400 stores, bills itself as "The Ultimate Ice Cream Experience®." The price is still easily found in pocket or purse. It requires no thought, is done on impulse, feels good, and is easily rationalized if need be—*I've had a hard day, I deserve it.*

These little indulgences do add up. It is frequently pointed out by Scrooge-like, annoyingly practical financial experts like David Bach, author of the *Automatic Millionaire* books, Suze Orman, Dave Ramsey, and their ilk that, were someone to forego all the Starbucks® and Cold Stone® and Omaha Steaks® purchases in favor of coffee brewed at home and carried in a thermos, ice cream bars bought at the grocery and kept in the office freezer, and so on, he would quite easily save $25.00 to $50.00 a week, $1,300.00 to $2,600.00 a year, and, if it were all wisely invested even at modest interest rates, could add well over a quarter of a million dollars to his retirement fund or pay off his home mortgage during his working-life years. It is a wildly unpersuasive argument. As Pamela Danziger, author of *Shopping: Why We Love It and How Retailers Can Create the Ultimate Customer Experience,* puts it: "We want our little pleasures and we want them now.

Danziger has termed this inching up of price "luxflation": a form of self-induced inflation, experienced by consumers willing to pay what seems little more for much better experiences—when, in fact, that little more may be a 500% to 5,000% premium. It's ironic that the government, economists, and the media sweat bullets and display great angst over inflation creeping up by a half of a percent or a percent while consumers cheerfully accept 500% inflation in dozens of purchases every day. This is important to grasp, as it affects every business. Mass-Affluent consumers may complain about inflation in general or many items' prices in particular, yet that can have zero impact on their response to your prices.

Dan Kennedy's #9
No B.S. Key to the Vault

Don't forget to offer your customers little indulgence opportunities for self-imposed inflation.

These little indulgences can really add up for you.

This is not really new. The story is now legend of how the dime-store soda fountains survived the Great Depression with the point-of-sale strategy, where the counterman responded to the milkshake order by asking, "Do you want yours with one egg or two?" What hasn't changed is that ATS (average transaction size) is one of the most important numbers to know, manage, and work at improving in many businesses, whether you sell milkshakes to frequent customers or farm tractors to very infrequent repeat customers. To continue the milkshake example, let's say we own an ice cream stand where the cashier responds to each order by presenting the offer of a double flavor shot and an extra scoop of fresh fruit. If half say yes to the extra $.55, and they serve 50 shakes a day, that's $.275 added to every transaction. If the shake itself sells for $1.50, we have increased the average transaction size by 18%. But we may have increased the average margin, invisibly, by much more. Of course, if we can alter the whole experience to support a higher price, still add the extra fruit, and add a big chocolate chip cookie, well, we might take our $1.50 average transaction to $3.50. On a grander scale, we may turn our ice cream stand into a much-talked about, much-preferred destination of the Mass-Affluent rather than just one of a dozen same-as, same-as places in town. Being in the little-indulgence business in a big way can lead to much bigger profits, but even to something more valuable: sustainable unique positioning in your customers' minds and lives.

CHAPTER 23

Spending on Indulgences

"All the things I really like to do are either illegal, immoral, or fattening."

—ALEXANDER WOOLLCOTT, IN HIS PLAY
THE KNOCK AT THE STAGE DOOR (1933)

For your own education, pick up copies of *The Robb Report* and a magazine called *Cowboys & Indians* at your local Barnes & Noble or other newsstand. The latter isn't really about cowboys and Indians, by the way. Examine every ad. You will see a demonstration of how many indulgences are offered to the affluent and get an idea of how much they spend on them. While you're at it, pick up copies of magazines about boating and yachting, private aviation, luxury travel. Go to the next big RV show or boat show that comes to your city. It'll do you good to get out more. Here, I present just a small window into this kind of spending. Some would consider it profligate spending. But, as an early mentor counseled me, denying the existence of cash registers or being a critic of them is guaranteed to be unprofitable. The best thing to do is make sure you are on the right side of them!

Money Spent on Passions

I make this point numerous time in this book: Few affluent consumers and even fewer Mass-Affluents buy premium goods and services or spend freely *across the board*. The greatest dichotomy I personally know of is a person who routinely buys and enjoys expensive, imported caviar but also frequently parks her Mercedes® in the parking lot behind the bread company's store and there, furtively, buys day-old bread. I know a former Fortune 500 CEO who will pay virtually any price without thought for a round of golf, and fire up the private jet to get there, but buys his khaki slacks at Target®, and has been known to pull out Val-Pak® coupons at restaurants. Just getting the more affluent customer is not necessarily the golden key to far greater income. Getting the more affluent customer passionately interested in your category of product, service, expertise, or experience is.

One certain way to connect with affluent consumers is to connect to their passions.

Visit www.bggearco.com, read *Cigar Aficionado* magazine, and you will discover a subculture where people passionate about cigars spend sums shocking to all others on rolled-up weeds you set fire to. As example, consider the elegant yet practical Zino Platinum Cavern Humidor, featuring a cedar tray with palladium plated brass handles on a wooden case finished with 15 coats of lacquer, safeguarding up to 60 stogies. Price: $2,800.00 (www.ZinoPlatinum.com).

In the book *Turning Silver into Gold: How to Profit in the New Boomer Marketplace*, researcher Dr. Mary Furlong writes in-depth about what she calls "the passion and play market," where companies and even entire industries are, pardon the pun, booming thanks to boomers' and especially affluent boomers' willingness to spend without budget and buy without price resistance.

The average homeowner is in his mid-50s. Homeowners ages 55 to 64 already spend more on horticulture than any other age group, but with the rise of the Mass-Affluent boomer homeowner, spending in this category could as much as double in the next five years. Gardening is a $38 billion industry ready to blossom. This same growth of affluent boomers promises positive impact on every passion and play business category, from books to golf to cooking. However, what once was age progressive— meaning you worked to retirement age to then begin indulging, finally playing golf twice a week or finally devoting time to your garden or photography or whatever—is now disconnected from age for the affluent. We have to look at these passion and play businesses as being for the affluent at any age, as their philosophy is to enjoy as you go rather than defer gratification until later. In fact, all age-based marketing thought must change. The idea of seniors on fixed incomes being penny-pinching, reluctant buyers is as inaccurate as is the idea that certain hobbies and pursuits are the province of retirees. Furlong describes the years ahead of boomers as "regenerative" rather than retirement and points out they have plenty of spending power; they earn more than $2 trillion in yearly income and control over 75% of the financial assets in the United States. She writes, "And they are going through more transitions now than at any other time in their lives. Each of those transitions is a tipping point for product and service decisions." Maybe the biggest of those tipping points is the opportunity to indulge their interests and passions as never before. The boomers' kids, though, populate the Mass-Affluent and have a "no waiting attitude" quite different from their parents. So they are *all* spending freely on passions and play.

Consider the wine business. Once a rather narrow, elite, and quite limited customer base predominantly populated by the affluent and Ultra-Affluent supported a closeted industry largely invisible or mysterious and intimidating, thus of little interest to the mass public. Today, the major wine aficionado magazines are sold on newsstands, and the huge public food shows attended by tens of thousands in each city have become wine and food shows. AARP has its own wine club, wine events, newsletters, and programs, but the buying of fine and expensive wines, the installing of home wine cellars, the joining of wine clubs have moved from Affluent to Mass-Affluent, from 50-plus down to 30-plus. This is luxury democratized; a special interest becoming a widespread interest.

Passion and play is the surest way to de-link price from pragmatism. The Mass-Affluent who will grumble about the total change rung up at the grocery-store checkout counter for a week's groceries will separately sign up for Gevalia's® limited edition coffees of the world at $36.95 per month plus shipping and handling, which translates to spending approximately $20.00 a pound (!). And the coffee aficionado will buy pricey coffees everywhere she goes, without second thought.

I once knew a very successful optometrist who complained frequently and bitterly about the costs of supplies for his practice, a year-to-year increase in the cost of his Yellow Pages advertising, his home's property tax, even the local deli's nickel and dime price increases. But, an obsessed Ohio State fan, he had purchased a giant, gas-guzzling motor home painted in Ohio state logos outside, decorated in red and gray furnishings and carpet inside, equipped with satellite dish, big-screen TV, and bar, to travel to and tailgate at every game, home and away, every season. He also purchased season tickets and bought away-game tickets from ticket brokers and scalpers at sky-high pries—all without a peep. Every Friday and Saturday during season, his office was closed, sacrificing whatever income might have been produced, so he could stock the motor home and go to Columbus or wherever the team was playing. Without a thought.

Money Spent Collecting

"Shopping is the museum of the 20th century."

—The Dalai Lama

Should you wish to add a life-sized, real, fully drivable antique fire engine to your portfolio of vehicles, you can find bargains in the $10,000.00 to $12,000.00 range. Buying one of the authentic George Barris Batmobiles at a car auction will set you back considerably more. People collect both. And antique motorcycles, lawn mowers, vacuum cleaners, pocket watches, grandfather clocks, medical devices, board games, toys, dolls, jukeboxes, fountain pens, and anything and everything else you have ever seen. They haunt estate sales, flea markets, and auctions, pay brokers, roam the internet, and respond to countless ads in countless magazines and newspapers in search of an elusive item. When they find it, price is pretty much irrelevant.

I have, in my basement, an antique gambling machine, combining a pinball machine and roulette wheel, with a horse racing motif—horse racing being my passion. It requires old-fashioned picture tubes to function and is frequently on the fritz. I bought it *on a whim*, for, as I recall, $8,000.00. Some whim. The antique dealer who sold it to me has since kindly alerted me every time any item with a race horse on it finds its way to his shop.

Classic car auctions are a great place to see a big population of affluent collectors for yourself. In a magazine promoting one such auction, attended by 200,000 people and selling 5,000 cars in four days, I found an old car I'd want: a 1973 AMC Javelin AMX, a near replica of the 1974 Javelin that was my first ever new car. Inquiring, I was told it had a reserve tag on it of $36,000.00 but would probably sell for more. This is an American Motors, i.e., *Rambler* sporty car. Good grief. The extremely knowledgeable and helpful lady on the phone with me was quick to point out that bidding live from a distance was possible (they would assign an agent to act on my behalf, with whom I'd speak via cell phone), I could watch via the internet, and 100% financing by a major bank could be arranged in 15 minutes. Or, if coming to the auction, I could buy a Segway® and have it waiting for me or pre-arrange a golf cart rental, to roam the acres of cars comfortably. This is but one of dozens of major auctions and hundreds of lesser auctions for classic cars occurring each year all over the United States.

Since that phone conversation at the time I wrote the first edition of this book, I have, in fact, acquired a 1972 Javelin AMX, as well as a 1963 Lincoln Town Car convertible with suicide doors, a 1986 Rolls-Royce convertible owned before me by Dean Martin, and my everyday car, a 1986 Jeep Wagoneer. I've become an avid reader of car collector magazines, watch the Jackson-Barrett auction on TV, occasionally catch Jay Leno's car show. And I am now supporting a car mechanic at roughly the same cost as a famous movie star's alimony.

Collectors are passionate about this one thing and most willing to spend on it, but often, collectors are collectors, so they collect more than one thing. And, of course, are willing to spend liberally on many other things (although not everything).

Consider the lowly pen. I have a habit of losing good ones as soon as I get them, so I stopped buying even ordinary Cross® pens years ago. My office is littered with Bic® pens bought by the gross and Flair® markers. Nowhere to be found, the designer-name or antique pen on its own display stand. But visit www. FountainPenHospital.com for a look at some very pricey pens—and repair services.

It seems that everybody collects something. Affluent people simply have the wherewithal to collect pricier things or to pay more in pursuit of the things they collect. They can and do also spend money on information about what they collect, associate with others who collect the same things, travel to places where they can find or show off the things they collect, storage facilities, insurance, and care and maintenance for their collected things.

Beyond these specific interests, affluent customers are particularly in tune with the very idea of collectible value. So collector's editions and limited editions of just about anything you can think of—book, artwork, wine, home furnishing, golf club, fishing rod—have added cachet and value.

Prices of Sought-After First English-Language Editions of Rare Books

The Fat Man is no longer in pursuit of the actual Maltese falcon—today he wants a copy of the first edition of the book! Here are a few first editions' market values (based on being in their original dust jackets and in mint condition).

Author	Book	Market Value
Dashiell Hammett	THE MALTESE FALCON (1930)	$85,000–$100,000
James Joyce	ULYSSES (1922)	$75,000–$90,000
Ernest Hemingway	THE SUN ALSO RISES (1926)	$65,000–$70,000
J.D. Salinger	THE CATCHER IN THE RYE (1951)	$25,000–$30,000
Tennessee Williams	A STREETCAR NAMED DESIRE (1947)	$15,000–$20,000
Harper Lee	TO KILL A MOCKINGBIRD (1960)	$15,000–$20,000

Source: The Executive's Almanac, by Milton Moskowitz.

Interesting Collectors Clubs

Aladdin Knights of the Mystic Light, founded in 1973, for collectors of Aladdin lamps and memorabilia. Approximately 1,000 members.

American Lock Collectors Association, founded in 1970, for collectors of old locks, padlocks, and handcuffs. Members receive a newsletter and information on upcoming events and lock shows. Number of members not known.

American Pencil Collectors Society, founded in 1958.

Circus Historical Society, founded in 1939, for collectors of historical materials related to circuses. About 1,400 members.

Count Dracula Fan Club, founded in 1965. Research library with 25,000 books, trips to Transylvania, and support for collectors of Count Dracula films and memorabilia. About 5,000 members.

National Fishing Lure Collectors Club, founded in 1976. Newsletter, trading meetings, annual convention. It has 3,000 members.

Source: Organized Obsessions, by Burek, Connors, and Brelin.

CHAPTER 24

Spending on People

"There are three great friends: an old wife, an old dog, and ready money."

—BENJAMIN FRANKLIN

O rphans who live as hermits can reduce spending to a bare minimum if they choose. Affluent individuals tend to be *the* person in their families, in their circles of friends, in their various relationships, most often picking up the tab. Certainly picking up the biggest tabs. It seems that the accomplished, affluent person is often standing in the center of a big circle of others, turning slowly in its center, handing money or support or gifts to each one each time he rotates past them. Because most affluent people are generous, many don't mind. Even those who, from time to time, privately question this arrangement continue with it. This is particularly good news for those marketing to the affluent. Each affluent customer is a conduit to many other consumers. Each affluent consumer spends for a whole bunch of others, not just himself.

Here are a few such scenarios . . .

Money Spent on Kids and Grandkids

"You can get very hungry while waiting, if your livelihood depends on someone's disease. Death does not always listen to the promises and prayers of those who would inherit."

—MOLIÈRE

I recommend a visit to www.LilliputPlayHomes.com as instructive. The company advertises in publications read by the affluent, such as *Billionaire* magazine, an offshoot of the *Robb Report*. In the issue on my bookshelf, its quarter-page ad appears next to one from a law firm specializing in asset protection featuring a John D. Rockefeller quotation, and above a half-page ad for a mergers and acquisitions and commercial financing broker. On the facing page, ads for waterfront homes priced from $2.6 million to $11.9 million. Here, an ad for incredibly pricey backyard *playhouses?*

The perfect place.

Don't leap to the conclusion there's such a tiny market for such things that there can be only one odd company in the business. Visit www.PoshTots.com, where you can have a completely custom-designed backyard playhouse built for your kids or grandkids, replete with lofts, decks, and skylights, or designed to a theme, such as a *Pirates of the Caribbean*-esque ship. Prices from as little as $2,449.00 all the way up to $52,000.00. This company's offerings were featured on the same page in *Upscale* magazine as a fractional jet ownership package priced at $415,000.00 and a unisex, diamond-encrusted wristwatch at $25,000.00.

It is but one demonstration of thousands of demonstrations in my files and among my clients of this valuable fact: Many mass-affluent and affluent parents and grandparents set price entirely aside when buying things for their children and grandchildren.

This is true for all sorts of reasons. Status and showing off. The opportunity to delight somebody, when all the adults in their family including their spouse are thoroughly jaded and very undelighted by the luxury lifestyle they enjoy. Guilt, over shorting the little ones on time or attention. Having been deprived as children themselves. The psychology is complex, but the reality is simple. In this case, you can sell a child's playhouse for more money than a storage shed, garage, or room addition.

It is also demonstration of another very important fact: Marketers of products for the lil' ones are not limited to—and are, in fact, advised not to limit their advertising to—media specifically for parents, about parenting.

A friend of mine selling a very expensive children's product who asked not to be named in this book said that his best clients are the guilt-ridden affluent parents, and he'd discovered the best place to find them is in magazines read by those flying private jets. He says the frequent business traveler, executive, or entrepreneur with young children at home in his second marriage to a younger woman; the very affluent couple leaving the kids at home with nanny, baby-sitter, or grandparents while on luxury vacations; and the wealthy grandparent competitively vying for attention with other grandparents are, far and away, his best customers—and that the best time to catch their attention is when they are jetting across the country.

Money Spent on Women

"If women didn't exist, all the money in the world would have no meaning."

—ARISTOTLE ONASSIS

The Brown Card, nicknamed "the ecstasy card," is sold by Michel Cluizel Chocolat of Paris, actually located in New York, for $50,000.00. Cardholders enjoy limitless access to a private bar with fine wines paired with chocolates, exclusive tasting events, limited edition chocolates, and even a personal introduction to Cluizel himself. Be still our beating hearts (www.cluizel.us).

Is there any sum some men will not spend to attempt impressing, delighting, or seducing women?

No, and many marketers grossly underestimate this sexually stimulated price elasticity. I am constantly dismayed at the unimaginativeness of gift certificate or gift card packaging and pricing by spas, hair salons, jewelers, resorts, stores, and others. Pay attention to Michel Cluizel. He's selling a $50,000.00 gift card, but with a unique exclusive collection of products and privileges attached.

Shortly before Christmas, a cosmetic surgeon, Dr. Stephen Greenberg, appeared on ABC's *Good Morning America* and explained how happy husbands were to purchase his Million Dollar Makeover gift certificates for their wives, unmarried significant others, mistresses, and girlfriends. Yes, they were paying $1 million for the ultimate gift for their honeys: a tune-up from tip of lip to toes and everything in between. It occurred to me that in some marriages, this gift might not be oohed and aahed over with as much enthusiasm as, say, a new car with diamonds in the glove box. Nevertheless, Greenberg said he was responding to men who were coming to him and asking for the *ultimate* package. His *ordinary* $100,000.00 Silver Package and $200,000.00 Gold Package just weren't good enough. The patient on the show with him, an attractive mother of four, a recipient of the Million Dollar Makeover gift, was set to get an eye lift, facelift, neck lift, tummy tuck, butt lift, laser hair removal, enlarged lips, and, of course, breast augmentation. She still missed something; according to a report in *The Wall Street Journal*, hymenoplasty is the ultimate surgical gift—tightening of the vagina or even restoration of virginity, itself starting at only about $5,000.00. Dr. Edward Jacobsen, a Greenwich, Connecticut,

OB-GYN, offers vaginal makeover packages for international patients that include airfare, limousine travel, and luxury hotel accommodations. Cosmetic surgery of all kinds has long ago emerged from hiding and been popularized by celebrities, so it is now more something to brag about than be quiet about. And there is a clientele for the million-dollar gift of it, raising as one question, what ultimate package or ultimate gift ought you to sell in your business?

I can recall a time not that long ago when TV commercials aimed at men at Christmastime touted buying perfumes and jewelry. It's a relatively recent phenomenon that, with perfectly straight face, many car companies run commercials suggesting surprising the wife with a new car. Dealers even furnish big red bows. "He went to Jared®" pales in comparison to "He went to Lexus®." The ante is upped.

However, an excellent lesson in selling a gift of any kind comes from the mail-order jeweler Karats & Facets, which target-markets the Mass-Affluent. A page of outstanding sales copy from the company's catalog appears on page 234. It is headlined "Guaranteed Gasp or Your Money Refunded." This company clearly understands it isn't in the jewelry business but in the gasp business. Or, as the catalog puts it, assisting you with an "investment in your relationship." In selling anything to men for women, this understanding should be yours as well.

Think you've seen it all at Victoria's Secret®? Go to www. Fabriintimo.com for a look at Antinea Paris lingerie and ID Sarrieri lingerie. Or peruse the better-known La Perla® lingerie, like the Black Label bustier (www.laperla.com). It's salient that the La Perla® lingerie is advertised in *Million-Air* magazine, published and provided only to people flying in private jets. The Fabri Intimo® lines, in *Billionaire* magazine. Victoria's Secret's® advertising is conspicuously absent in these periodicals. I can give you my most confident personal assurance that few men know the difference between one bustier and another, but affluent men will buy what they perceive to be the prestige lingerie as a gift. And how will they know which is which? By where they see it advertised.

Guaranteed Gasp or Your Money Refunded

Here is jewelry to capture her heart.

Unique gemworks that make her feel unique. This is jewelry you won't find in department stores (many are one-of-a-kind estate pieces). Nor will you spend hours shopping for them. Just make your choice(s). Dial 800-260-4987, ext. 500, on your phone, and a gift to make her gasp is on its way.

You expect only the finest quality when you purchase Karats & Facets jewelry, and you surely get it. We choose our gems for their immaculate cut and clarity. We use only solid, high-karat gold for our gem settings. Bracelet links are pin-hinged for super flex-strength. And we add not one but two locking clasps to make them vault-safe.

Karats & Facets jewelry is more than an investment in your relationship. Its intrinsic value is one that sustains with the years.

Yet we offer these beautiful pieces at amazing values, unmatched elsewhere. How can we? We buy our gems directly from abroad, eliminating agent and middlemen costs. We smith our own gold in our own workshops (you're welcome to visit anytime). Then we market our jewelry directly to you to avoid distributor, broker and retail markups.

Finally, there's our airtight Satisfaction Guarantee: If you're not 100% satisfied, you have 30 days to return it for a full refund.

Money Spent on Pets

"The Don CeSar hotel is overly pet friendly. Ridiculously pet friendly. They have a pet concierge that comes to your room and describes the services they offer your pet . . . . They said they had aromatherapy for dogs. I'm like, 'Do you have a candle that smells like another dog's ass?' That's what he likes."

—Comedian Ron White, Charter Member of the
Blue Collar Comedy Tour (www.tatersalad.com)

You might want to come back as a dog in an affluent home in your next life. Their future looks bright.

Designers have discovered pets, so, for example, you can buy a Gucci® dog bowl for $900.00. At different upscale pet retailers and websites, affluent owners can buy an Italian-designed doghouse or a Cabitat cat condo, a leather dog bed ($1,450.00), or a Jonathan Adler designer dog dish. One of the humans behind this website says it is "for people who are serious about incorporating their pets fully into their lifestyle."

There is a fast-growing population of such people. In his book *MicroTrends*, author and political pollster Mark Penn called them "pet parents."

My wife and I are admittedly among them. The little dog who lives with us is considered when we choose hotels and resorts to visit—with rare exception, they must be pet-friendly. Preferably *very* friendly. We prefer her with us rather than left behind, so shopping center, store, and similar choices are also made based on whether or not she is welcome. She has her own little couch, her own fur throw, her own blanket. She commutes between our two homes with one or both of us, uncaged, relaxed in the private plane, which she greatly prefers to traveling with the peon pets on commercial airlines, where she must be stuffed in a small cage that fits under the seat. And, yes, she knows the difference between driving toward the regular airline terminal and turning off to the private terminal. She is spoiled. I call her our Million-Dollar Dog. And our Million-Dollar Dog has a bone to pick with you, if you aren't accommodating her as one of the family.

In one city you'll find a Starbucks®-like, upscale coffeehouse for humans under the same roof as the Whole Pet Café, serving healthy meat, vegetable, and whole-grain meals and designer waters to dogs, at $4.00 to $10.00 per item. Next door are a fancy veterinary clinic and a high-end pet fashions and accessories store. In another city, a pet day spa features not just grooming and nail clipping, but fur-beautifying blueberry facials, massages, saunas. Classical music is played exclusively in the fur stylist's salon. Another city boasts a pet hotel with private suites, complete with comfortable beds, heated floors, and plasma TVs. None of these businesses is in Beverly Hills or Manhattan, although businesses just like them are there, as you'd expect. The ones I just described are in Dallas, Texas; Long Beach, California; and Charlotte, North Carolina. In Alexandria, Virginia, near one of my homes, the entire community of Main Street merchants wisely caters to pets and their owners. A local hotel has a happy hour for dogs. The baker features birthday cakes for pets. There is a dog apparel store.

Pets are the new children and grandchildren. Boomers' kids are grown and gone. Families that once stayed in close geographic proximity are now spread out in different and distant locations. Spoiling grandchildren is made more difficult by this separation. So affluents, especially affluent boomers, dote on their dogs, cats, and other pets. And spend truly astounding sums doing so.

In fact, 27% of people now take care of their pets in their wills. Hotelier Leona Helmsley made national news with the multimillion-dollar estate left to her little dogs, guaranteeing them their own staff and exceptional care for life. Posthumous care of pets is but one of the evolving and emerging new businesses catering to the affluent.

No affluent pet owner does the math. The gourmet dog food he purchases in little containers costs more per pound than the steaks he eats himself. The Burberry® dog coat at $200.00 costs more per square inch of plaid than his own Burberry® overcoat. It does not matter.

Pet products are now one of the top ten U.S. retail segments—a bigger industry than toys or candy or hardware. Currently, more than $38 billion is spent each year on pets, double the amount spent just ten years ago. This staggering number may again double within the next ten years. About 63% of American households have pets, up from 55% roughly 20 years ago, and an all-time high. That's double the percentage of households with children. In the last 20 years, the drop in households with kids mirrors the rise in households with pets. As baby boomers become empty nesters, household spending on children is declining while spending on pets is rising. Over a three-year term, spending on toys, games, tricycles, and children's clothes fell by more than 20%; spending on pets rose by 23%.

The fastest growth segment: luxury pet products bought by affluent pet owners. About 40% of all the dollars spent buying things for pets deliver them to only 1% of the pets, the most pampered of the pampered pooches and kitties. Louis Vuitton®, Chanel®, and Burberry® sell designer dog collars, leashes, and toys. Gucci®, Tiffany®, Coach®, L.L. Bean®, and Harley-Davidson® are all in the luxury dog accessories business.

The love of dogs drove the book *Marley and Me: Life and Love with the World's Worst Dog* to the top of the *New York Times* best-seller list—a lofty place this book will never see—and kept it there. If you haven't read it and you like dogs, you must. It even made Howard Stern weep aloud while reading its end, as he told the author in a note. It made me cry. It has made everybody I know who has read it, including those I bought it for as a gift, cry. That speaks to the poignancy of the book, but also to the extreme connection pet lovers have to pets. Even if this is foreign emotional territory for you, it isn't for the majority of your affluent clients.

You Gotta See It to Believe It!

www.inthecompanyofdogs.com
In FetchDog's collection of luxury and designer beds and throws for dogs, you'll find one made to look like a convertible sports car with an open top, windshield, side mirror, rims, door handles, roll bar, embroidered Furcedes logo, and "L.A. Dog" license plate: $279.00. A Furrari is also available. If you'd like something less flashy and more classy, consider the Sniffany & Company bed, a plush, oversized replica of that famous little blue box with the white ribbon: just $129.00. Add a Chewy Vuitton® toy shaped like a purse for just $15.00.

www.ScootersFriends.com
This site features dog coats. Almost endless choices of dog coats. Pink and brown snakeskin with faux fur . . . reversible wool and camel hair . . . multitextured pink wool with pearl trim . . . quilted velvet coat . . . glen plaid raincoat. Separate collection of evening wear. No excuse for your dog to suffer the embarrassment of a fashion fur pas.

www.Muttropolis.com
This company has physical stores that "delight pet parents with the community feel of a friendly dog park," as well as an online cata-log with categories covering every need:

You Gotta See It to Believe It!, continued

Be My Valentine Shop

All Things Pink

Beds and Furniture

Carriers

Collars

Toys

Treats and Supplements

Eco-Friendly Dog Products

Shop by Size/Age

Bowls

Clothes and Accessories

Grooming and Spa

Training & Behavior

CHAPTER 25

Money Spent on Bling

"You asked 'What time is it'?
It's three diamonds after noon."

—SAMMY DAVIS, JR.

There is a special population within the ultra-
affluent who buy bling. This group of bright, shiny-
object lovers tends to include a lot of people who make
a lot of money suddenly or without much effort or through
talent and celebrity or mere celebrity. Think Kim Kardashian.
Hollywood and music celebrities, sports stars. Quite a few
Hollywood celebrities and pro athletes drive themselves to
bankruptcy with wild spending and shopping sprees. Leaping to
my mind, the late Michael Jackson, M.C. Hammer, Mike Tyson.
You might identify these as the affluents with more money than
brains. Personally, I like getting such stupid money just as much
as I like getting smart money. It seems to spend the same. So
affluents with stupid money deserve your consideration.

Some have, in their jeans pocket, a Swiss Army knife made of gold or silver and bejeweled with 800 diamonds, for which they paid as much as $100,000.00.

Traveling to Las Vegas recently, I thumbed through a magazine found in the private air terminal, a magazine I'd never seen before, totally devoted to buyers of pimped-out rides. High-priced sports cars, luxury cars, and SUVs given customized makeovers. I discovered more than 30 full-page and multipage ads for wheel covers. Wheel covers. Most priced from the bargain of $995.00 to more commonly $1,495.00 to $4,000.00 per hubcap. Per hubcap. The most expensive, a set of four inset with diamonds and rubies, priced at $2 million. Extra costs: $100,000.00 a year for the two guys you hire to guard your wheels—and each other—at all times, $50,000.00 for trips to your therapist after seeing your extremely busty, compliant, and talented girlfriend's dog lift his little leg and pee on one of your wheel covers. Talk about emotional conflict.

The more common bling, ultra-expensive wristwatches for men and women and high-fashion jewelry for women, is all quite different for the affluent and ultra-affluent than that on display in the glass cases at your local shopping malls. There is, for example, a Limited Edition Grand Complication Audemars Piguet men's watch priced at $743,600.00 or the more affordable Master Minute Repeater in Platinum by Jaeger-LeCoultre at just $241,000.00. I recommend an investigative tour of the websites listed on the full-page jewelry and wristwatch advertisements in magazines like *Elite Traveler*, and *Town & Country*. Some jewelers' and watch companies websites to visit for an eye-opening education:

- www.DavidYurman.com
- www.Vacheron-Constantin.com
- www.AaronBasha.com

Bling means different things to different people. The affluent person who can't fathom paying $4,000.00 for a hubcap will pay that much or ten times that much for a particular wristwatch that will be recognized by his tribal peers as a symbol of wealth, status, and significance. But even the most conservative individual has something he's bought as bling. And there may be yet-unseen opportunities to inject some bling into your products.

Reprinted from *No B.S. Marketing to the Affluent Letter*. Diamond Membership. www.GKIC.com

This is about the designer of those flashy, paisley and patterned shirts guys wear with the cuffs rolled back to show a different pattern. The shirts are very popular in the Southwest, with the rodeo crowd, rich oil men—one of whom has "collected 130 different designs" and spent so much money, the 2014 "collection" includes a design named after that customer, and quite a few GKIC Members. **The shirts go for $225.00 to over $500.00***, and are sold direct, in catalogs, at Neiman Marcus, Saks, Nordstrom, high-end country western shops, and in several Las Vegas stores. There are two company stores—the original in Venice, California, a second in Houston. Warm weather climates have been identified by the shirt-maker as better than four season or cold because people can wear the colorful shirts year 'round, so they buy more of them. The brand's owner, a Ralph Lauren alumnus, Robert Stock, calls customers "*connoisseurs*." He says he is in the business of selling "feeling good"—getting favorably noticed, getting compliments, getting bragging rights. There's a fraternity: One Robert Graham shirt owner instantly recognizes another. Guys talk with each other about these shirts like the women on *Sex and the City* talk about shoes. Customers who own more than 100 of the shirts (= from $25,000.00 to $50,000.00+) are *inducted* into a special club. Stock is, incidentally, 65 years old, still having fun as an entrepreneur.

*This is at a time when Jos. A. Bank advertises a $199.00 suit, and buy one, get two free. And you can buy dress shirts, as Mitt Romney claimed he did, in packs of three at Costco for $99.00. None of this matters. Not to the Robert Graham shirt connoisseur. Unless and until you grasp that what others are doing does NOT need to matter, you are as handicapped as a one-legged man lugging a 1,000-pound boulder up a mountain.

To dissect, Stock has a) a unique look and design (that's bright and stands out and is *fun*) for a routine item—shirts, b) premium pricing, c) multiple distribution channels and solid place strategy, d) a good understanding that he is NOT in the apparel business, and—maybe most importantly—e) a company and customer culture featuring recognition, and supportive of contagion.

CHAPTER 26

Money Spent at Home

When the Seiberlings—he, a tire magnate—built their home, Stan Hywet Hall, an 80-room Tudor mansion in Akron, Ohio, in 1915, at a cost of $3 million (in 1915!), Mrs. Seiberling ordered workmen to cut scuff marks into the hardwood floors so the home wouldn't look "ridiculously new and unlived in."

Between 25% and 30% of affluents own multiple homes for personal use, with the majority owning two. Ownership of three or more homes for personal use is concentrated among those with the highest net worth and is more common with ultra-affluents. For those with multiple residences, the average value of the second residence or vacation home is $865,000.00; the average value of the primary residence is $1.3 million to $1.4 million. About half of the second homes are within a day's drive of the primary residence and tend to get frequent weekend use. The more distant second residences tend to get seasonal use. What this means to the marketer of products and services for the home is that one in four to one in three affluent customers have opportunity to buy for more than one residence. This is another reason to think globally rather than locally (see Chapter 29).

As an aside, the dual- or multiple-residence owner is an outstanding target customer or client for marketers of a wide variety of goods and services beyond home furnishings, home decorating, home improvement, and home services. Think maid service and landscape maintenance. For example, for insurance, financial services professionals, CPAs, and attorneys, these clients have more complicated needs and interests and tend to respond to professionals' advertising in the national magazines and journals they read, more so than local media.

But, to return to the home itself, as a quick education, you might visit www.DesignerDoors.com to see "picture-perfect, hand-crafted architectural accents crafted by skilled artisans for the re-visioning™ of your home." Should you dare to call them garage doors, they dispatch a tough nanny to wash out your mouth with soap. This is a nice lesson in the fact that no commodity product bought solely as a necessity for its function need remain such a mundane thing when sold to the affluent.

Brian Maynard at KitchenAid, quoted in Pamela Danziger's book *Let Them Eat Cake*, says he views true luxury today "as being an expert at something. It's being a wine expert, a cooking expert, a golf expert. Luxury is about personal transformation . . . In terms of our brand, KitchenAid is for people who love to cook, who have that expert knowledge and love to use it. If it has anything to do with a cooking passion, we provide a product for that. We talk about the brand by communicating why someone would want convection cooking or a wine cellar with temperature zones."

A key part of the KitchenAid marketing program has been the sponsoring or creating and hosting of "experiential events," such as Book and Cook events, where the company brings in influencers like celebrity chefs, cookbook authors, food writers, and kitchen designers to complement product demonstrations and displays. KitchenAid has very deliberately and strategically worked at moving itself from mass marketing of ordinary and utilitarian products to marketing to the affluent, with unique products. Once known for dishwashers, it now strives to be a purveyor of premium-priced kitchen products for true cooking aficionados. It is significant that Maynard is talking not so much about his products as about his customers—people with cooking passions, expert knowledge, and a love for showing it off.

Kitchens, of course, are big business. A friend of mine recently had hers redone, and commented, "Apparently anything not made out of *granite* no longer has a place in the kitchen." You probably know someone—if not yourself—who has recently put from $75,000.00 to $200,000.00 into a complete kitchen makeover. As with all big-ticket purchases made by the mass-affluent and affluent for their homes, whether kitchens, theater rooms, meticulously landscaped and lit backyards with grill areas rivaling the kitchen, and so on, it's not about utility, but about a variety of emotional issues.

And What Might They Buy for Their Homes?

If your family loves pizza, then you may have considered getting a pizza oven. But is an oven that cooks only one pizza at a time enough? A double-deck pizza oven equipped with real pizza stones (the secret of great crust) can be yours for just $180.00 from Brookstone.®

If you've always wanted a tree in your living room—and, hey, who hasn't?—the next best thing is a natural-looking steel art replica tree. Shipped in color-coded sections for easy assembly, so you need not remove your home's roof to get your tree inside. At www.NatureMaker.com.

What Might They Buy, continued

When winter arrives, what backyard is complete without its own outdoor sauna? Prices start at around $4,500.00. One maker is Callaway Woodworks at www.CallawayWoodworks.com.

And when summer rolls around, do not settle for any ordinary hammock. Heavens, what will the neighbors think? Artistically crafted hammock stands made with finely finished North Carolina cypress wood can be had for $595.00 to $795.00, quilted hammock fabrics for $125.00 to $249.00, matching pillows, $45.00 each. From www.Frontgate.com.

Visit www.LuxuryHousingTrends.com for more examples.

CHAPTER 27

Entertainment Spending and the Experience Economy

"Should you have any questions about America's priorities, compare my salary to the Dean of Harvard's."

—JOHNNY CARSON

*S*pending on entertainment is through the roof, into the stratosphere. It has become a 24-7 obsession. The games closet at home, the TV watched only after dinner, the movie theater visited occasionally, the golf course, virtually every diversion and recreation has migrated to the pad and mobile phone, with everybody everywhere, at all times. Coupled with the incredible narcissistic orgy of social media and constant connectivity, itself entertainment, you find a population consumed.

If you are an investor, you can't possibly afford to ignore the entertainment category—and to pick out of other categories the companies not characterized as entertainment enterprises, yet very much into this game. Apple, for example, is categorized as a tech company, but I consider them a 60%+ entertainment company. Disney®, Lionsgate®, Hasbro®, 100% entertainment. (Note: I'm not dispensing investing *guidance*, only commentary.)

As a marketer, you have to look for ways to get your own business above the "50% entertainment" watermark. You want to be where money is flowing to, most.

The affluent consumer is, by and large, engaged with and embracing it all, if slightly more discriminating than most others.

Here, a couple out-of-the-devices scenarios . . .

Money Spent on Experiences

"Last week I spent $1,000.00 to fly out to California, $500.00 a night to stay at a resort to attend a $15,000.00 seminar titled 'Money Isn't Everything.'"

—Bob Orben, TV Comedy Writer and Director of White House Speechwriting during the Gerald Ford Administration

I'll borrow their ad copy:

Today, you rescued the plane, prevented a carjacking, and shot your way out of a crowded subway station—and you never left our resort. Save the world by day. Relax with your favorite cocktail, vintage cigar, and fine cuisine at a true five-star mountain resort by night. A lifestyle typically reserved for secret agents and action heroes is now available to those who dare . . . . Valhalla Shooting Club at Elk Mountain Resort. Ultra-realistic, theme-based, live-fire shooting scenarios put you in control of your destiny with pistol in hand. And when the shooting stops, our resort offers a full complement of activities and luxuries designed to satisfy you and your companion.

Aah, shaken, not stirred. As someone who played with a *Man from U.N.C.L.E.* attaché case in the backyard and grew up on Napoleon Solo, Ilya Kuryakin, James Bond, and the original Avengers, I find the Valhalla adventure appealing. It may or may not be your cup of tea, but some experience—some packaged grand experience or amazing adventure—would be. And there may very well be some such experience you can create within or as extension of your business with enormous appeal to some number of affluent individuals.

One of our longtime GKIC™ Members running jewelry stores in small, Midwest communities once a year takes a dozen or so of his most affluent clients on a trip to the South African diamond mines, where they pick out their own diamonds firsthand to be placed in custom-crafted jewelry. They can also add on an African safari or cruise if they desire. He collects a sizable "experience fee" for putting this trip together and escorting his group. The fees combined are nearly as much as one-fourth of the net profit from one of his stores for the entire year.

Even the rather pedestrian cruise industry has grown up and gone affluent. Take the Four Seasons cruise ship. You do not just grab a cabin at a website, hop on board, and line up for the bon voyage buffet. Instead, you buy a time-share in it, for hundreds of thousands of dollars. The shares sold fast. Other condo cruise ships with penthouse cabins priced into the millions are at sea, with more under hurried construction. People purchasing these floating condos and time-shares aren't doing so purely to take cruises. They are buying into an elite gated community that floats, and they're purchasing a unique experience. One of these ultra-luxury cruise ship residences, *The Magellan*, is described this way:

> The facilities and services of the world's finest resorts
> are part of everyday life aboard *The Magellan*. On-call
> housekeeping staff, a world-class spa, 24-hour concierge

staff, indoor and outdoor pools, six restaurants, a 450-seat theater with Broadway quality entertainment, a casino worthy of Monte Carlo, and an 8,000-square-foot greenhouse with onsite horticulturists are just a few of the conveniences that make living aboard *The Magellan* a unique experience.

Since when are a greenhouse and in-house horticulturist and six restaurants *conveniences?* Since now, for the ultra-affluent. Note this ad is not talking about taking a cruise. *Living aboard.*

Incidentally, time-shares on dry land or afloat are historically notoriously bad investments. Developers frequently flirt with fraud in overselling capacity, amenities deteriorate after units sell out, bankruptcies occur with regularity—even with this new type of high-end, luxury time-share. Overall, resale values rarely even match original purchase prices let alone yield gains. So, shouldn't ultra-affluent individuals know better? Only demonstrates that people are people.

If you are following what most consider the smart money, you've seen it moving to companies, entrepreneurs, and projects creating and providing luxury experiences. As example, two of the world's richest men, Bill Gates and Prince Al-Waleed bin Talal al Saud, partnered in taking the Four Seasons hotel chain private—with its luxury time-share and condo properties and newest addition, cruise ships. Apparently they see big profit potential in this crown jewel company.

Turning to the mass-affluent, the company I admire most in the world, Disney®, continues to diversify, developing and offering new experiences for sale to its customers. Its wedding business, thriving and expanding. Its multigenerational family reunion business, thriving. Its experience resorts like the Animal Kingdom Lodge, booked solid at premium prices. The FastPass® for many, but for some the $290.00 to $315.00-per-hour private

VIP guide with whom you bump all the lines, go backstage, take shortcuts. In the time-share category, the Disney® Vacation Club is rapidly expanding to meet demand. When I took one of my client groups to Disney World® on a research excursion, we had a private lunch with two Imagineers, one of whom developed the group sales presentation used on board Disney® cruise ships to sell the club, who was thoroughly familiar with its growth. He predicted it would increase at least five-fold in less than three years, with new means of marketing and new luxury options. Since then, Disney® has opened the first of a number of planned stores in shopping malls exclusively devoted to selling the Vacation Club time-shares. The company has also gone west, turning 2.5 acres adjacent to the Grand Californian Hotel and Spa® at Disneyland® into 50 Vacation Club villas.

In total, the Vacation Club time-share program is in its 20th year, has more than 350,000 owners, and simply can't add facilities fast enough to meet demand. Current expansion includes the new villas at Disneyland® in California, new Animal Kingdom Villas and the Grand Floridian Resort and Spa® Villas in Florida, and Aulani Resort and Spa® Villas in Hawaii.

Time-shares aren't limited to something you stay and sleep in anymore either. Affluent customers are time-sharing collections of exotic automobiles and portfolios of expensive jewelry, and ultra-affluent clients are time-sharing a "family office," typically comprised of a CPA and life concierge on staff, supervising and coordinating all aspects of clients' lives, from paying bills to planning trips to finding someone to remodel the barn. Instead of owning only one or two exotic cars, you can buy into a time-share and drive dozens. Instead of owning only a few $50,000.00 to $500,000.00 pieces of stunning, one-of-a-kind jewelry, you can draw from a collection of hundreds and never be seen wearing the same piece twice. Instead of using your own Rolodex® to find pool cleaners, find home remodelers, organize trips, buy gifts, and check up on your money managers and investments yourself, you can share a dedicated management team with two or three other families.

Today, the affluent customer can get just about anything he can imagine—and will buy many things he didn't imagine on his own—in the experience category. Oh, if you feel like helicoptering into Valhalla as its next tuxedoed, pistol-wielding, martini-drinking, beautiful-woman-impressing secret agent, you may begin your adventure at www.valhallasecurity/valhallashooting.com.

Money Spent Dining Out

"The best way to have quiche for dinner is to make it up and put it in the oven to bake at about 325 degrees. Meanwhile, get out a large T-bone, grill it, and when it's done eat it. As for the quiche, continue to let it bake, but otherwise ignore it."

—COWBOY PHILOSOPHER TEXAS BIX BENDER, *DON'T SQUAT WITH YER SPURS ON*

We love to eat. We love to eat out.

The shrinkage of the middle-class consumer and the regressed spending of the mass-affluent consumer groups has hit mid-level restaurants hard, between the time I wrote the first edition of this book and the year I'm writing this edition (late 2014).

From 2004 to 2008, U.S. restaurant sales climbed in virtually every category, at every level, topping $180 billion. In those years, 85% of Americans dined out at a minimum of once a month, over 20% paid restaurant tabs at least six times a month, i.e., 1.5 times a week, and nearly 10% ka-chinged ten or more times a month.

From about 2009 to present, the industry segments have experienced very different trajectories.

A late 2013 report in *Nation's Restaurant News* revealed a troublesome, overall trend: People who were dining out multiple times every week and the larger number dining out multiple times every month were not only cutting back to, respectively, once a week or once a month but also were reducing their spending when doing so. Its research forecast a furtherance of the trend. Significantly, while encompassing the entire industry, this reduction in frequency and check size was most concentrated in the middle. The mid-level restaurants have the highest labor cost to sales ratio, tight margins, intense competition, and loss of customers who trade down, and are most directly affected by the shrinking middle class I described in Chapter 1. The enormous boom in mid-level, fast-casual restaurants came to a screeching halt, revealing overbuilding and saturation, resulting in quite a few in Chapter 11 bankruptcies, with many others teetering. I fully expect a Darwinian shakeout to come.

Darden Restaurants is a poster boy for this difficulty. In 2014, it got its Red Lobster® chain sold at a fire sale price, after many months of trying. Its Olive Garden® chain was wounded, limping, and scaring investors—so much so that one of its biggest investors created its own 300-page memorandum of cost-cutting and other recommendations and leaked it to the media. It included a demand that the chain's "endless breadsticks" be ended, or at least tamped down by serving only one breadstick in place of a basket, and waiting for a customer to request another.

The bottom of this food chain is also harmed and hurting. McDonald's® same-store sales year to year and quarter to quarter were down, up to this writing. The category in which McDonalds®, Burger King®, Taco Bell®, KFC®, etc., live has sacrificed price, transaction size, and profit margin just to keep all the doors open and the volume steady. The "$1 Menu," the "$5 Meal," and very aggressive promotional offers have taken control of this category, to their shared detriment.

Upscale, fine-dining chains and independents live on their own island. Some bled a little during the 2008 financial apocalypse, but nowhere near the extent of those in the middle and low groups. This teaches a lot about where you want to position your business, whether a restaurant or not.

As a restaurant moves up, from anybody and everybody, to mass-affluent, to affluent clientele—targeted by its marketing and served by design of its product—price become less and less of a factor in customers' decisions about repeat and even frequent patronage. I listened during a staff meeting at an upscale restaurant as the manager explained, "*We* do not have specials. Denny's® has specials. *We* have chef's features." And that sums it up. While the lure of low price for a lot of bulk or price- or discount-driven specials is very important to the Denny's® customer and is of some importance to the Applebee's® or Outback Steakhouse® customer, it is of near-zero importance to the Fleming's® steakhouse customer.

The same applies to foods delivered to the home. If you compare Omaha Steak's® marketing to Allen Brothers® marketing, you'll see that Omaha, catering to the mass-affluent, relies heavily on sales, special offers, and discounts, while Allen Brothers, selling to the more affluent, relies much less on price-related marketing.

While there appears to be fierce competition in the restaurant industry, it is more about each restaurant finding its market. Certainly the higher up the food chain one moves, pardon the pun, the easier it is to carve out and control a unique segment of the market. And the less competition there is.

Finally, there's a difference between a convenience restaurant and a destination restaurant. Fast-food, low-priced, and mid-priced restaurants marketing to mass-affluent and down tend to live or die by convenience to their customers. For fast-food outlets, location—even side of the street—traffic patterns, and population density are of enormous importance. This makes them vulnerable to shifts in such things, and, although you don't think of McDonald's®, Burger King®, Arby's®, and so on failing, there are surprisingly large numbers of such stores that do close their doors every year, usually having to incur costs of relocation to follow the customers' movements. Better restaurants marketing to mass-affluent and up are only about 50% dependent on convenience and can successfully draw from a bigger radius around their location because customers who like that particular restaurant will drive farther to patronize it. Upscale restaurants and upscale and unique restaurants are destinations, so convenience can be virtually nonexistent and they can still draw maximum crowds every night. Affluent customers are, according to a Food, Beverage and Hospitality Survey of the Affluent, four times more likely than nonaffluent consumers to drive more than 40-minute round-trips to patronize a restaurant of choice.

Reprinted from *No B.S. Marketing to the Affluent Letter.* Diamond Membership. www.GKIC.com

The INTRAV catalogs of tours by first class private jet are magnificently written—"dedicated journey concierges" . . . "redefining travel for the discriminating 21st century traveler." They utilize a private Boeing 757, customized to accommodate 50 travelers—oops, sorry, "elite travelers"—in total comfort. You have your own personalized entertainment programming, in an iPad,® which is yours to keep. (The crass word "bonus" is never said, but this is gift with purchase.) There are several different routings each through several countries, with unique experiences in each place—like attending elephant polo in Jaipur, complemented by cocktails, fireworks, and a military bagpiper band. The fee is $99,950.00 (not $10,000.00) per person, double occupancy required—singles pay a $9,950.00 surcharge. This includes the aforementioned iPad® gift and

$250,000.00 in emergency medical and evacuation (!) insurance. You bypass ordinary security lines and have expedited customs at each airport, fly direct, have an in-flight chef, and maybe most importantly, are traveling with only 25 other couples—absent crying infants or poor people.

CHAPTER 28

Money Spent on Liberty

"There is only one success—to be able to spend
your life in your own way."

—CHRISTOPHER MORLEY, AMERICAN NOVELIST AND JOURNALIST

There are, I think, three kinds of liberty: day-to-day liberty, lifestyle liberty, and mental or emotional liberty. I'd like you to consider each one as something you may be able to deliver through your products, services, or business.

We'll begin with the day to day. The affluent are highly stressed. More than 75% of all affluent business owners and self-employed professionals work 60 to 70 hours a week. The average affluent household with children has each child involved in at least three to five separate, organized activities each week, requiring transportation, supervision, and parental involvement. Families are now spread out over the country, requiring more frequent travel and time away from home and business for personal reasons. Add to this the ever-rising intrusiveness and constant connectedness imposed by technology and the ever-increasing complexity of everyday life thanks to burgeoning choice in every product and service category. Also, the more affluent a person is, the more financial responsibilities, decisions, and seemingly endless paperwork flow he confronts. All added together, it equals high stress, low liberty. By "low liberty," I mean that this person feels as if he has no time for himself, constantly chasing and never catching, always at odds with himself and others, and always disappointing someone. I know these feelings well myself. You might think of us as *desperate* affluents.

On the rare occasions desperate affluents find someone of demonstrated, proven, reliable competence to whom they can transfer some responsibility, they will do so eagerly and pay generously for the relief. These desperate affluents often overpay people by normal or traditional standards but consider the liberty purchased a bargain. I recently had a client tell me he paid his personal assistant $75,000.00 a year, a wage judged by his business partner, CPA, and others as $30,000.00 too much, but because she can be counted on to anticipate his needs, think for herself, and relieve him of having to remember just about everything, he considers it a half-price bargain. Another desperate affluent businesswoman I know has a person who comes to her home twice a week and does the laundry, changes the bedding, goes to the grocer's and restocks the refrigerator, and takes and picks up clothes at the cleaners—for which she pays $500.00 a week. I imagine that works out to something like $50.00 an hour. Too much? Or bargain? What price the liberty to enjoy an evening out or to be able to come home and relax at the end of a high-pressure day instead of having to wash clothes or finding nothing in the fridge suitable for a cobbled-together dinner and having to get back in the car and go out? What price liberty?

In his book *The Art of Selling to the Affluent*, Matt Oechsli writes, "When people are under a lot of stress, they look for relief. They initiate many major purchase decisions to reward themselves for their hard work and as a stress release. The last thing they want is a hassle." He goes further to give these seven drivers of significant buying decisions by the affluent (boldfacing of key words and phrases, mine):

1. They want to be **respected,** even honored, for the level of success they have achieved.
2. They are successful because of the professionalism and **competence** they apply to their work, and they expect no less from others.
3. They will react strongly to any attempts to deceive them, and when (they feel) that happens they take their business elsewhere.
4. They define value **in their own terms.**
5. Instead of striving to keep up with the Joneses, they want to be **different** from the Joneses.
6. They experience enough tension and hassles in their daily work life—they want to be **free** from all that when dealing with people who would like to sell them something (and keep them as customers/clients/patients).
7. They can afford and are **willing to pay** for the best information, the best products, the highest level of **competence,** and the best professional service available.

Next, consider the magnification of this, to lifestyle. The affluent are on a search, a life and lifestyle quest.

They are on

- a quest for respect.
- A quest for competence.
- A quest for integrity.

- A quest for status and value meaningful to them.
- A quest for relief from stress and difficulty and responsibility.
- Most of all, a quest for competence.

They often arrange their lives and the locations in it in ways reflective of this quest.

Many of my clients are impressed by my obsession with "time economics" and time preservation—so much so that one of my most popular books is *No B.S. Time Management for Entrepreneurs*. Our Ohio home was chosen primarily for its eight-minute proximity to the racetrack where I race most of my horses. It is the best available that is close to the track. There's an upscale community 20 minutes away I'd prefer living in, but that would mean 40 minutes, sometimes 80 minutes of commuting on race days—unacceptable. This home is also exactly midway between the Cleveland and Akron airports. Only 15 minutes away from a nice hotel that ably hosts my coaching and client group meetings and highest priced, boutique seminars. Our other home in Virginia is minutes from Dulles Airport, but not in flight paths. A penthouse condo with amenities in its building, and shops and fine dining restaurants just outside its doors, a Hyatt hotel a short walk away. I have a five-minute commute to my spacious basement office where I do most of my work. Fully 90% of all clients come to me. I am far from alone in making these kinds of calculations and choices in order to conserve my most precious and perishable asset: time. Watch how NetJets advertises itself to the affluent; the benefit being sold is time, and largely, preservation of personal time—to get home, to be with family, to more easily get away for vacation—not business efficiency.

They delegate and transfer a lot of responsibility, even though, by nature and experience, they tend to be control freaks. The desperate need for relief from a myriad of overwhelming, stressful responsibilities supersedes their preference for hands-on control of everything. Consequently, many put some or all of their personal wealth under others' management. They hire personal chefs to choose and prepare the foods and meals they eat. They let a clothier choose their wardrobe. A personal shopper choose their gifts for others. On and on. In all these instances they are not just attempting to buy a little time or convenience—they are seeking to buy lifestyle liberty. Not just a reality of minutes freed up or tasks done, but *a sense* of liberation from the mundane and time-consuming.

Which arrives at the third liberty they seek: mental and emotional liberty.

Napoleon Hill, legendary for his book *Think and Grow Rich*, wrote a lesser-known book as his last of many, titled *Grow Rich with Peace of Mind*. That title has a double meaning: that the ultimate aspiration, achievement, and wealth was peace of mind and that you needed peace of mind to be truly rich. In that book, Hill told of finally having to disconnect all his phones, as his celebrity had put him under constant assault from all manner of people with requests for his time, money, and assistance. Donald Trump recently described his life as "one long telephone call." I am at the point Hill found himself, and need a number of barriers to restrict access to me in order to have any peace.

You need to know that the affluent have enormous demands assailing them, and look, above all else, for breathing space. A multimillionaire client recently told me of buying a very expensive "cabin" in a relatively remote area near Jackson Hole, Wyoming, a popular playground of the rich. He showed me a picture of the area around his place, just miles of snow-covered emptiness. He talked of going dogsledding. Mostly, he talked of enjoying the sense of distance and isolation from people and their demands on him.

Beyond this, the affluent are seeking liberty from critical judgment and guilt. This nation attacks its affluent relentlessly, in the media, in politics, in public and private discourse. The affluents' Spidey-sense detects envy, jealousy, resentment, and disapproval emanating from most of the people they interact with and from the public at large. One millionaire told me, "The more successful I get, the more I feel eyes in the dark hungrily watching me." Another said to me, "To my face, they are deferential. Behind my back, they are angry critics who believe themselves infinitely smarter and harder working and more deserving than I." Another described feeling as if the target painted on his chest got bigger and brighter with each passing year. In his outstanding book *Paranoia and Power*, Gene Landrum, the leading authority on the psychology of the rich and powerful, states, "Paranoia is rampant among super achievers." Further, attempts to influence the affluent with guilt for the admittedly growing gap between them and the have-nots is pervasive and unrelenting. It comes from close family members and distant relatives—as comedian and game show host Louis Anderson so painfully showed off in one of the most memorable Oprah shows ever and wrote about in his autobiography. It comes from the endless charities, causes, and others at their doorstep asking for or, in some cases, nearly demanding handouts. It comes from political demagogues, media, and even rich limousine liberals themselves, acting out of guilt. Behind closed doors, this is the frequently discussed, shared angst of the affluent.

How to Make Yourself Magnetic to the Affluent

If you truly understand this *quest of the affluent*, it's not difficult to see what is required of you to make yourself magnetic to them—and to their money.

Not necessarily in any priority order, there are three big things to do.

One, develop, display, and convey a profound position of expertise, good judgment, understanding, professionalism, and competence. Present yourself as the most trustworthy of advisors. The most trusted advisors relied on by the affluent automatically and certainly become very affluent themselves. Almost next to, or only a step behind, every person famous for wealth and power stands an almost equally wealthy—in some cases wealthier—trusted advisor. Think George Ross to Donald Trump. A man whose name I can't recall and is rarely publicly uttered, who has basically run Warren Buffett's business and financial empire for decades. In politics, the Karl Roves and James Carvilles, and politicians' attorneys like William Bennett. There are kings and kingmakers. Millionaires and millionaire-makers.

Two, relieve your affluent clients of time, pressure, anxiety, stress, day-to-day hassle, tasks they'd rather not do or even think about or that should be below their own time's value. Create privilege and luxury-level convenience for them. Make standing in lines, filling out forms, mere mortals' normal burdens go away.

Three, give them acceptance, approval, and applause. They are extremely responsive to those who celebrate their success and respect it as earned. Become known as a supporter and advocate of achievement and affluence. Take philosophical positions that counter the constant criticism they receive from most other quarters.

We will flesh out specific strategies supportive of these three objectives in Book Three.

CHAPTER 29

Connecting with the Affluent
Customer You Want

"It is not enough to conquer; one must know how to seduce."

—Francoise-Marie Arouet Voltaire

Here's the formula:

1. Decide exactly who you want as a customer—notably, deciding on the level of income, net worth, overall affluence, lifestyle and ambitions, aspirations, interests, and attitudes about spending you want him to have.
2. Be sure you have crafted products, services, a business, its positioning—everything—for that consumer.
3. Go to that consumer where he is.

That third point is succinct, but far beyond most business owners' comprehension. Most business owners act as if they are trees with deep roots, at the mercy of whatever fertility or infertility, favorable or unfavorable environment exists and evolves around them. Today, consumers, especially affluent consumers, can be found, identified, effectively communicated with, attracted, and sold to at any distance near or far.

The Power of UN-Obvious Place

At the racehorse auctions I go to, there are a number of sellers of horse business goods and supplies—harnesses, sulkies, wheels, drivers' uniforms and helmets, veterinary supplies. And one pop-up jewelry store. Because, when the guy goes to the auction, he tells his wife: "NO—I am NOT buying ANOTHER horse. I'm just going along to keep the boys company." When he returns home with a rope in one hand attached to another $25,000.00 horse, it's helpful to have a $5,000.00 pair of diamond earrings in the other hand. This is about going to where the right consumer is.

My wealth advisor client advertises in obvious places like *Forbes* and *Investors Business Daily*. But also, and often more productively, in the sports sections of affluent, business-vibrant cities' newspapers and in affluent-aimed magazines like *Cowboys & Indians* and *Private Jet Traveler*. My gun manufacturer client is in the obvious gun magazines and NRA media, but also in motorcycle magazines. The dating service It's Just Lunch, for whom I've done a little work, advertises in airline magazines. This is about going to where the right consumer is.

Be Sure to Circumvent Search

Far more premium-priced goods and services are sold to affluent buyers who were not searching online or by other means for them than are sold to buyers actively engaged in search. Their interest was aroused by direct outreach from the marketer. A copy of my Special Report: *"Why and How to Circumvent Search"* is available at www.NoBSBooks.com.

No Boundaries Anymore

"We're not in Kansas anymore."

—Dorothy, in *The Wizard of Oz*

The U.S. is no longer the leader in wealth creation. The affluent and ultra-affluent in other countries, combined, outnumber roughly 8-to-1 those in the United States, and the fastest growth in new affluents is abroad. Hot spots of wealth growth can be found in Asia, India, South America, elsewhere. A very instructive and fascinating book offering a lot of insight on China is *AGE OF AMBITION: Chasing Fortune, Truth & Faith in the New China* by Evan Osnos.

Many of these foreign markets have rising, even explosively growing middle-class populations. Many have study, ambition, and work ethics that mirror the U.S.'s from post-World War II through the 1980s, now collapsing. The year 2013, for example, was the first in a decade in which the number of entrepreneurial and small-business startups actually declined.

If you have long thought of yourself as a local or U.S. business, it is past time to rethink that, and think global. Many of the great difficulties to marketing and conducting business in faraway places have been erased or minimized. The internet, its media, and e-commerce is a boundaries killer and a major gateway for U.S.-based marketers to the entire globe and to these specific hot spots of rising mass affluent and affluent consumer populations.

At the very least, you must replace local with national. The location of prosperous consumer populations is dynamically changing and re-arranging itself as you read this.

But why would people 1,000 miles away from you pay high prices for what you sell in Boise, Idaho, when there's some of the same stuff within walking distance of their Boston townhouse? Or London townhouse? If you have to ask, you really haven't been paying attention to the changing world around you. Cosmetic surgeons and dentists advertise nationally in airline magazines and affluent, discriminating patients fly to them. My client Ted Oakley, a wealth advisor, has clients in his home cities in Texas, but has more scattered throughout the country, so instead of advertising locally, he advertises nationally. There's certainly a bakery close to everybody, but Fairytale Brownies in Phoenix, Arizona—not celebrated as a gourmet food capital—ships boxes of fudge brownies to people all over the world. Dean & DeLuca® began in 1977 as a little gourmet grocer, in SoHo, in New York. It now markets and ships ultra-premium-priced foods and related items to affluent customers throughout the U.S. and the world. Zappos fast became the world's shoe store. There are neighborhood florists, supermarkets have in-store flower shops, but there is 1-800-Flowers. Darin Garman's investors in Iowa real estate live in Los Angeles, Miami, Toronto, Tokyo.

The more affluent the customer, client, or patient, the less concerned with convenience and the more he is willing

Dan Kennedy's #10
No B.S. Key to the Vault

Redraw your map. Focus more on the ideal
customer than on self-imposed limitations.

to conduct business at a distance, import from afar, or travel to places in order to get exactly what he wants and what he believes to be the best of a category. Personally, I live mostly in Ohio. One of my three wealth managers is in Arizona, most of my real estate investments are in Iowa and managed by the aforementioned Mr. Garman there, my dentist and dental hygienist are in Virginia (and I fly to them by private plane), some of my shirts are tailored and come from England. The affluent buy a great many things without regard for normal and customary boundaries.

You can get a more complete "No Boundaries Report" in the Marketing to the Affluent Resource Section at www.NoBSBooks. com.

We Know Where They Live

"If your ideal customer is a one-legged midget who bowls in a
league on Tuesday nights, has one wife, two kids, three dogs,
and a riding lawn mower, we can get you a list of them
in your ZIP code. It won't be a very big list, but . . ."

—Dan Kennedy, from his famous "Magnetic Marketing" Speech

Finding the affluent consumer ideal for you in your area or pin-pointed like tacks on a map all over the U.S. is no great mystery.

Twenty-two percent of U.S. households have more than 55% of all the earned income. Again: More than half of all the income is concentrated in only one of five households. Surely it must be easier to profit by marketing only to the one in five, while completely excluding and ignoring the four in five. Buying behavior supports such a notion. Based on data from the Mendelsohn Affluent Surveys, we know that the one-in-five group is roughly 200% more likely to own or lease three or more cars per household and 50% more likely to buy at least one new car this year; 200% more likely to own laptops and handhelds;

250% more likely to invest in real estate in addition to their own residence. They own 300% more life insurance. Over one-fourth of them own two residences, thus buying twice as much stuff. They outspend the four-in-five group in virtually every type of product category except camping equipment.

Yet, as obvious as it is that selling to the top 22% while avoiding wasting even a penny or a minute on the remaining 78% has to be the winning strategy, few marketers act this way. Most invest in mass advertising that reaches five in five and hope to be noticed by the one in five. Hope may be a laudatory human emotion, but is a very poor *strategy*. And an unnecessary one. We can do better.

A lot of people ask me about finding the affluent, as if they were all residing in secret, undisclosed locations. Actually, privacy in America and many other places in the world is dead. We not only know where they live but also what they've been buying. Whether they've been naughty or nice.

For starters, there are people who have already gone to a great deal of trouble to spy on them, dig up data on them, monitor their buying behavior, and compile lists of them sorted by their interests and passions, by their level of affluence, by the

Dan Kennedy's #11 No B.S. Key to the Vault

More wealth has been created through the use of mailing lists than any other media.

frequency of their spending in a category, as well as by gender, age, ethnicity, marital status, home ownership, income ZIP code, and a myriad of other divisions. In mailing list lingo, these are called *selects*. The world of mailing lists commercially available for rent is an amazing place. You can pretty much find any kind of group of desired prospects, then drill down closer and closer to your ideal prospects within the group by these selects.

When you pass through the gateway to the mailing list world, you will discover that tens of thousands of mail-order, retail, service, credit card, publishing, and other companies have all their lists of past and present customers, cardholders, and subscribers as well as their prospects or inquiries available for rent. A dirty little secret is that many companies earn substantial sums this way, some eclipsing the net profits from their core businesses, and a comparative few are in business solely to build and rent lists. These are called *response* lists because people have responded to an ad or direct-mail solicitation or have otherwise asked that company for information or made one or more purchases. Another type of list is a *compiled* (nonresponse) list. These are even more widely available and generally less costly to rent. The people on these lists did not, in any way, volunteer to be on them. The list owner accesses one or more sources of public records and information and assembles the list for the express purpose of renting it. Both kinds of lists can be very useful. Both offer different kinds of selects.

For better understanding, we'll work our way through a few hypothetical examples.

Let's assume you own a very upscale French restaurant with a good wine cellar, snooty waiters, and high prices—and you wish to go in search of affluent new customers. This happens to be an easy one, which is why I picked it. There are hundreds of list choices. For example, there is a compiled list of yacht and private plane owners, available by state or county. There are

213,090 prospects on the list. On that list, within a 45-minute driving radius of your restaurant in Beachwood, Ohio, there will be only a small number. Let's assume there are only 200 of them. Those 200 names may be very valuable. We know to create and send them a mailing with planes and boats on the envelope, and maybe a line of copy like "Free Voucher for the Adventure Trip of a Lifetime Enclosed." Inside, we can tell them we know they appreciate the finer things in life, appreciate new experiences, and often fly their own plane or sail their own yacht in search of them. But did they know they could take a trip to one of the finest restaurants in all of France, only a short drive from their own home?

There is also a list available of people in any ZIP codes of your choice, arranged by birthday. As far as we know, everybody has one, once a year. So, in every month, there are quite a few people in reach of your restaurant having a birthday, and most people go out to dinner to celebrate. You can select from that list only married people, or people who own homes in pricey neighborhoods or people with certain incomes. A colleague of mine operates a company that does these "Happy Birthday" mailings for restaurants and consistently gets tremendous response and very good return on investment.

Recommended Resource

For birthday, new mover, and other precision-targeted direct-mail campaigns for your business, contact Dean Killingbeck at New Customers Now: fax (517) 546-2815, phone (517) 548-5522.

But we could get very sophisticated and merge or purge. That means taking only the names appearing on two or more lists. The duplicates. The yacht and plane owners' list giving us only 200 names in our area might thin out to only 10 to 20 birthday names in any given month. But they are the quadruple-perfect prospects. So instead of sending them a birthday card or letter and a coupon for a free birthday dinner, we might send them a beautifully wrapped gift box, a copy of our menu, and a fancy certificate on parchment paper. Doing this, we would spend a lot more per prospect, but we would be spending all our money on ideal prospects.

Let's try another one. You own an upscale but not ultra pricey women's fashion store featuring one-of-a-kind and unusual items. There's a response list available of Peruvian Connection® catalog buyers. The catalog sells knit and woven sweaters and other clothes made from luxury fibers native to the Andes. The women buyers range in age from 35 to 55. Their average household income tops $100,000.00. They're perfect for the clothing store but may also be good for a spa, medical-spa, a cosmetic surgeon or dentist, a gift shop, or even the French restaurant. We won't know unless we test.

Here is the point: If you can describe your ideal affluent customers—whether ultra-affluent, affluent, mass-affluent, young, old, male, female, and so on—you can go into the inventory of available lists and find them, already rounded up for you. In all cases, you can get their physical addresses. In many cases, you can also get their telephone numbers, fax numbers if they are business owners or professionals, and email addresses.

The obvious question is: Why not skip all this and just mail everybody in rich ZIP codes? In some cases, that will produce satisfactory results. But it deprives you of several key ingredients of optimum direct-marketing success, notably precision matching of prospects with offers. Getting down to a smaller number of carefully chosen high-probability prospects allows you to invest your money more wisely, market more efficiently, and craft and present a story about your business as well as an offer that is seen as specifically relevant to the recipient. If you are seeking appointments with affluent investors, you could just mail to the rich ZIP codes. But if mailing the *Investors Business Daily* subscribers in those same ZIP codes, you know you are hitting active stock market investors, and you can tailor your message to them—"Disappointed with Your Results in the Stock Market? What If . . ."

How Much Do We Know?

We know just about everything! One way or another, from one or multiple databases, it is possible for all marketers national in scope and for many only local in reach to obtain and develop a hit list of ideal prospects.

Here are some categories of Leading-Edge Boomers, born between 1946 and 1955, that have been identified and organized into databases by the research company Mature Data Profiles:

SEGMENT	GEOGRAPHY	PROFILE
Gold 'n' Gray	Suburban	Exclusive suburbs. Married, kids in college, many still working part time, consulting. Buy: luxury travel, portfolio management. Retirement nest egg investors.
Credit Commandos	Suburban	Slightly above-average income and heavy credit card users. Empty nesters. Making up for lost time by buying on time.

SEGMENT	GEOGRAPHY	PROFILE
Settled Suburbanites	Suburban	Incomes and home values above average, empty nesters happy to stay where they are—they have the longest average length of residency. Heavy mail-order buyers.
Urban Mix	Urban	Apartment and condo dwellers. Many single. Professionals. Above-average education.
Trailing Boomers, born 1956–1964		
Metro Influentials	Suburban	Highest income and home value, into stocks and other investments, luxury travel, fine wines. Are about living out their dreams.
And Seniors, born 1945 or earlier		
Rich Retirees	Urban (Concentrated in Northeast cities.)	Well-educated, well-off. Small households. Eclectic interests indulged, from cooking to theater to travel. Big mail-order buyers, not surfing internet.
Boomerang Bohemians	Suburban	Free-wheeling RVers, travel, bounce between homes and kids' homes. Use email, shop online.

I've listed only 7 of 34 breakout categories encompassing 130 million names, addresses, and so on, which can also be pulled apart by exact age, gender, geography, mail-order response, marital status, net worth, occupation, even whether they wear corrective lenses! A list compiled from this data could also be overlayered against a specific company's list of subscribers or buyers. In short, you can drill down with incredible specificity to identify and reach out only to people perfectly, precisely, and multi data-point matched with your current customer, ideal customer, or product or service offer. And you should.

Recommended Resource

Now, I'm going to suggest you do yourself a great favor. The person to learn all about mailing lists, selection of lists, access to lists, and profitable use of lists from is Craig Simpson. Craig's book, to which I contributed, *The Direct-Mail Solution*, is a practical crash course. Beyond that, you can find other helpful resources at www. simpson-direct.com. And if you decide to communicate with Craig directly, you'll find his contact information at that site as well.

Think of the power of combining precision-targeted lists of affluent buyers ideally matched with your business with a marketing system as described in the other chapters here!

A Sample Affluent List—and What We Know about It

Magellan's is a leading catalog and mail-order company selling travel-related products, including luggage, in-flight comfort products, health and safety items, books and DVDs, dual-time wristwatches, men's and women's apparel, and items specifically for globe-trotters, like adaptor plugs and translators. The company's catalogs can be seen and obtained at www.Magellans.com.

Their customers are mass-affluent and affluent, with an average household income of $75,000.00. Average age 55-plus, 59% female. If renting its lists, you can select by age brackets, gender, and geography as well as purchase activity. For example, as of this writing, there were 265,600 customers who had purchased at least once within the past 12 months; broken out, 51,000 of those had purchased apparel.

Direct-marketing companies that repeatedly rent and mail to segments of this list include obvious ones, like Omaha Steaks®, Orvis®, Grand European Tours®, and *Condé Nast Traveler*, as well as less obvious ones, like *The Wall Street Journal* and AARP. These users suggest that any marketer of the obvious—travel, gourmet foods, wine—as well as marketers of financial publications, financial services, investments, and anything related to upscale retirement living could potentially use this list. Had I such a business or a client in such a business, I would definitely investigate further.

Sources: www.CatalogSuccess.com/infocenter and www.BelardiOstroyALC.com.

Where Should You Drill for Oil?

Years ago, I got to know a "professional psychic" I met at the bar, after his show in the lounge at the Playboy Club in Phoenix, Arizona. He had a home worth more than a million dollars perched high on Camelback Mountain, drove a Rolls-Royce, and seemed wealthier than might be expected for an entertainer working such small venues. He told me he used his performances only to "drill for oil." By that he meant making himself visible and approachable to a few wealthy patrons who chose to employ him privately for advice on a variety of matters, at substantial fees. He said he named his approach "drilling for oil" in honor of one of his first patrons, a very rich Texas widow who had inherited her late husband's oil business. She hired the psychic to walk her vast oil fields and choose the next five places to drill new wells and paid him an ongoing royalty on the production of any successful wells. He bore none of the costs of the dry holes. And, as he said, "How psychic must you be to pick one winner out of five—in an oil field!"

BOOK THREE

How Can I Get Them to
Give Me Their Money?

Reshaping Your Business, Products,
Services, Prices, Advertising,
Marketing, and Sales Practices:
Specific Strategies for
Attracting the Affluent

CHAPTER 30

Affluent Consumer Entrapment

"Creativity is overrated. Most business success comes from doing boring, diligent work, from developing a system that produces consistent results and sticking to it."

—RAY KROC

You need a direct-marketing system.

In this book I lack space and time to belabor these points as I do in other works of mine, but here are two vital facts: One, all wealth derived from business is based on systems. Two, most businesses have some sort of operations system but lack the more valuable marketing system. To be successful attracting and marketing to the affluent, you will need to spend more per prospective customer, client, or patient (reasonable in light of their greater value), so you cannot afford to let any of them slip through your fingers. Further, they judge your competence and trustworthiness from the outset, so how organized you are in your marketing influences their willingness to do business with you. For these and other reasons, you need a direct-marketing system.

What is such a thing? As its name implies, it *directly* reaches out to, connects with, and brings the desired prospective customer, client, or patient to you.

All systems use bait to lure the desired creature into the trap. I'll switch to more elegant language in a few minutes, but for starters, tolerate my being deliberately coarse and simplistic with a basic example, Consider the company Fisher Investments. By my standards and my clients' standards, it has a primitive and simplistic system, but it will do as the basic example, and if you stop to think about it, you are probably aware of the company. It is a multiproduct investment and money-under-management firm aiming at mass-affluent and affluent (but not ultra-affluent) investors. You've probably seen TV commercials, magazine ads, *USA Today* ads, or *The Wall Street Journal* ads, or possibly received direct-mail solicitations. All that advertising does is offer bait to lure you into the trap. The bait is one or more free reports, like *The 9 Mistakes Affluent Investors Make*, a free audio CD, a free DVD, or a package of all that information. The titles and promises of what you will discover from these things are the real bait. You will discover lies your current broker, banker, financial planners are telling you, taxes you are paying unnecessarily, safe but high-yield investments you don't know about. You will get this from a highly credible and authoritative source. That's the bait. Whom is that bait for? Relatively new mass-affluents with little knowledge or confidence about investing. People aware they should be investing their money but who do not know what to do or whom to trust. Affluent people frustrated with stock market ups and downs or losses.

My comments mean no judgment, pro or con, about Fisher Investments as an investment firm. I have no firsthand knowledge and no opinion. I am only making observations in my area of expertise—marketing—and using Fisher as an example.

Fisher's bait lures those particular creatures into the trap. By design, there are a lot of creatures it does not lure.

The trap is a place where the creature's name, address, email address, fax number, and phone number are captured and, of utmost importance, permission to use this information is secured.

Dan Kennedy's #12, No B.S. Key to the Vault

The most valuable asset is a list of high-value customers and prospective customers who invite and welcome communication from you.

Additional information may also be asked for and captured by a trap, such as age or occupation or income, so as to assign the captured creature to a different subtrap to be shown and fed slightly different sales messages appropriate to him. From there, a follow-up process begins. In Fisher's case, it is simplistic; the package sent is more an excuse for immediate and direct follow-up by telephone agents than anything else. We can do better and be more sophisticated, as I'll show you. Still, what Fisher does is apparently effective and successful for that company. A website is the ideal trap medium, as it allows us to automate this entire process, even to the point of the customer doing his own data entry work for us. But a recorded message and voice mail, a call taken by a live human, a reply form or card returned by fax or mail can all serve as traps as well.

Before going further, there is one very important point to be made. Fisher Investments, targeting mass-affluent and affluent investors in order to then offer professional money management services, does exactly the same things as, for example, TempurPedic® does to cast a much broader net and then sell mattresses, or the lowest of low-end "burial insurance for just 50 cents a day" companies advertising on TV do to target the very nonaffluent and then sell a term insurance policy. Regardless of what they are selling or to whom they are selling, virtually all direct marketers do the same thing: They use bait to lure desired creatures into a trap. The only changes are to the bait. You need the right bait for the desired creature. There is no creature that can't be lured into a trap with the right bait. Let me say it again: There is NO creature that can't be lured into a trap. With the RIGHT bait.

Now, we'll get more sophisticated and use more elegant language, with which you may feel more comfortable!

Our direct-marketing system, just like the previous examples, will extend an invitation designed for a specific audience via a variety of means and media. You might use any or all of these to extend your invitation:

- Print advertising, in newspapers, magazines, newsletters, or other publications
- Banner advertising at others' websites
- Buying traffic for your website with Google™ AdWords® or other means
- Using publicity to get articles about you placed in different publications and places
- Direct mail to rented or compiled mailing lists
- Email to opt-in lists
- Radio or TV advertising

And I could list a hundred more options.

Regardless of means or media, in every place, the same invitation is extended. It is kept simple and clean. It is NOT an attempt to sell your products or services at all. It is an invitation for the recipient to request and be provided something of relevance, interest, and value to him, free of charge. The more appealing and specifically relevant the item offered, the better the response.

This is Step 1, usually called LEAD GENERATION by direct marketers.

The individuals accepting your invitation arrive at your "place," and enter your foyer. And only the foyer. They are not permitted to roam the mansion as they please. The foyer is a nice place, be it website, recorded message, live human on the phone, something like an exhibit booth at a consumer or business exposition, or even your store, showroom, or office. But in many cases, it's a website or the handling of an incoming call. There, they sign the guest book. That means they provide the information you want, in exchange for receiving the appealing information or gifts you offered them in your invitation. Think of the foyer as nicely appointed, with the guest book on a big, gold podium, with a spotlight shining on it. But nothing else is there. It is premature to display product, describe services, talk price, or do anything else but get the guest book filled out.

At a website foyer, there may be what's called in internet lingo a *double-squeeze page*. It's actually two guest books. First, the person is asked only for his email address, thus reducing the request to one item. In exchange, he may get an email newsletter, ebook, or something else electronically delivered. When he provides his email address, a door opens and a butler appears with yet a second guest book. In other words, a fresh landing page materializes, now asking for full physical address, possibly fax, possibly phone, and possibly additional questionnaire-type information. In exchange, the person will then be sent offline a package of information, materials, and gifts, likely including a book and/or an audio CD and/or a DVD. This strategy winds up creating two different lists for follow-up: 1) the timid and likely only curious or mildly interested people willing to provide only an email address and 2) the more compliant, likely more interested, and likely better prospects willing to provide all their information. And depending on what information they are provided, they may be further divided. We'll get there.

Now that they have signed the guest book or guest books, one of two things may occur immediately. One, they may be thanked, promised that the information they asked for will arrive in a few days, and politely ushered out. Or, two, they may be given the option of entering a very short corridor that provides access to only one or two rooms. Again, not free run of the whole mansion. There might be a nice little reading room, where they can read their ebook. Or a little theater where they can watch a short film, possibly of happy customers giving their testimonials. There is usually no direct, instant path into a showroom or salesman's office where selling them is immediately attempted, although there are exceptions to this, including on the internet.

Step 2, then, is CAPTURE IN THE TRAP.

What I have described so far has many virtues. It alters your advertising from being product or service directed to being customer directed. It automates everything, so you or staff members are not engaged in unproductive, repetitive manual labor. It gives the prospect a nonthreatening, satisfying experience devoid of sales pressure. It provides you with a very valuable asset, a database of people who've stepped forward, raised their hands, and identified themselves as interested prospects. Finally, if you wish, it allows you to run smaller, simpler ads, keeping the front-end costs low and investing most of your resources only in interested prospects.

If this is new and unfamiliar to you, I can only urge you to stop and carefully re-read it, as there are ways it can go awry. And I encourage you to go to traps offered by sophisticated direct marketers and experience their entire systems for yourself. The best—and cheapest—way to learn this methodology is by playing prospect with companies doing lead-generation advertising.

Next, a series of proactive follow-up steps occur, from you, the marketer, to the prospective customer, client, patient, or investor.

We have prospects who have signed the guest book. We may treat them all the same and assign them all to the same Follow-Up Communications Program. Or we may divide them in some way, assigning different ones to different Follow-Up Communications Programs. Regardless, they will all get a series or sequence of multimedia follow-up communications, all designed to persuade them to take one next step. In rare cases, that step might be making a purchase. In many, it will be scheduling some sort of appointment; coming to your place of business or inviting you or your sales representative to their office or home; attending a seminar, webinar, or teleseminar; completing and returning an application. Whatever. Everything moves the prospects toward this one next step. Typically, there will be a deadline for taking that step, with rewards for doing so and penalties for not doing so. A sample series of follow-up contacts might look like this:

Day 1 after having signed guest book	Send requested book, brochure, and DVD. Send email acknowledging request and telling them package is on its way.
Days 2–10	Daily email, a lesson in a course on wise buying/investing/using the sort of thing being sold . . . tips plus reminder of offer.

Day 4	A letter with a booklet of customer testimonials . . . encouraging them to review everything sent.
Days 5, 7, 9	Three jumbo postcards, each focusing on a different benefit.
Day 10	"Only 5 days left" letter with encouragement to go to a website and view ten-minute special presentation.
Days 12, 13, 14	"Countdown to deadline" emails.
Day 15	Representative places outbound call.
Day 16	Email extending deadline and inviting then to 30-minute webinar and group question-and-answer session.
Day 19	"Last chance" letter with CD or DVD of the webinar.
Day 21	Representative calls again.
Day 25	"Offer withdrawn notice" letter.
Months 2–5	General email newsletter, once a week.
Month 6	New series of letters or postcards extending original invitation and inviting them to re-raise hand and start process over with free information.

Step 3, then, is follow-up.

What I've just laid out is still somewhat simplistic, compared with the systems my businesses and many of my clients' businesses use. These systems may divide up the prospects to begin with and send different communications to 2, 4, or 20 groups. Those not responding to the entire system may be moved at its end to the start of another one, leading to the sale of a lower-priced or higher-priced or otherwise altered version of the product or service or an entirely different product or service.

The follow-up is where the giant opportunity is because most businesses do little or no follow-up whatsoever. Response develops through follow-up. Whatever the response from a single attempt, it tends to as much as double with the second and third follow-up attempts, and double again with the fourth through whatever follow-up steps. So, if you got a 1% response from mailing out a package of information to a group of prospects, you would likely get another 1% or better from the second and third follow-up steps combined, and yet another 1% or better from the subsequent follow-up steps combined. If you begin with 1,000 prospects, that's ten sales if you contact them only once or 30 or more with comprehensive follow-up. If you sell a $1,000.00 item, you're choosing between obtaining $10,000.00 or $30,000.00 or more from the same group of prospects.

When marketing to the affluent, this math changes, favoring follow-up even more. While many prospect groups' yield might be flat: 1%+1%+1%, an especially affluent prospect group's yield might be tiered: one-fourth of 1%+2%+5%. My theory about this is that it takes more communication and more time to directly create trust with affluent customers. Because their value is greater, the added investment of more steps in follow-up is easily justifiable and usually a bigger economic win.

Once somebody understands the virtues of this kind of system, does he hurry to develop his and get it working for his business? Candidly, no.

Problems and Solutions

There are three chief reasons that, frankly, the vast majority of marketers shown this systematic approach fail to develop it for their own businesses. My book *No B.S. Direct Marketing for Non-Direct Marketing Businesses* (Second Edition) includes many inspiring and amazing case histories from people in a variety of nondirect-marketing businesses who have done the work necessary to transform their businesses this way, and I urge you to read it. And they are representative of experiences and results typical among all the GKIC™ Members who follow this path. But I'll be the first to tell you they are rare birds. Here's why.

- *Problem 1.* It's work to get it built, tested, and working for you successfully. Sadly and stupidly, most people would rather spend every day of their entire lives chopping wood manually with a dull axe, complaining all the while, than turn off the TV and put in a few extra hours a night for a few months building an axe-sharpening device or, better yet, an electric or gas-powered wood-cutting machine.

- *Problem 2.* It's complicated. Most people desperately want a magic pill, not a diet regimen incorporating food choices, portion control, nutritional supplementation, and exercise. That, incidentally, is why 99% of the fat folk stay fat. In business, it's the same thing. There's rarely a single, simple magic pill-like solution to any problem or exploitation of any opportunity. There's even virtue in possessing a complicated process, as most competitors will be too lazy and simple-minded to copy it, even if it is successful and shown to them.

- *Problem 3.* Specific to marketing to the affluent—the higher up in affluence you go, the more protected are the prospects. Gatekeepers screen the communications you try to get to them. There are obstacles in your way. It is not necessarily easy to reach out to them and attract them. Also specific to the affluent—the higher up in affluence you go, the less responsive to advertising and more responsive to peer recommendations and referrals people are.

Now, for what it's worth, the solutions . . .

For Problem 1, work. What we are talking about here is nothing less than the transformation of your business from random acts of marketing that produce erratic and unpredictable results to a machine that runs dependably and efficiently, day in and day out, much of it automatically. Ownership of such a machine is a wonderful thing. But you can't expect to build such an enormously valuable thing for yourself with nominal effort or investment. You will need to, first, thoroughly understand it, and then experiment with specific application to your business.

For Problem 2, embrace the complexity! It's a source of power. But, to be fair, the actual mechanics of managing the prospects (databases) and the multistep, multimedia follow-up with color-coded file folders and Post-It® notes or ordinary contact management software can be messy. There is one software system that has been built from the ground up to manage, automate, implement, and track exactly these kinds of marketing systems—and only one. It is called InfusionSoft, and I

Recommended Resource

Infusion Software is the only all-in-one database, contact, customer relationship management program designed to support any business' implementation of a Kennedy-style direct marketing system. Information at: www. Infusionsoft.com/Kennedy.

urge you to investigate it. Free demonstrations are available (see Recommended Resource box). In interest of full disclosure, I am a stockholder in and advisor to the company.

Problem 3 requires two things. One, appearing in the places where your affluent prospects pay the most attention. This will lead to different media choices than, say, your regular daily newspaper, mass-circulation magazines, or run-of-day TV or radio advertising. Two, direct mail to carefully selected lists using more elaborate pieces and delivery means than ordinary mail. In business-to-business environments, you may need specific strategies for the professional gatekeepers. The good news is, there tends to be less clutter in their mailboxes because the majority of marketers give up. You should not be deterred by this difficulty; it is in proportion to the value of the customer or client to be obtained. And make no mistake: The affluent customer or client can be drawn to the trap with clever direct marketing. The investment advisor currently managing my retirement funds started the process of securing me as a client with a direct-mail piece including a large roll of duct tape inside a plastic bag, delivered via Federal Express.

A maid service solicits homeowners in an exceptionally affluent neighborhood by delivering DVD players preloaded with a 20-minute DVD of its clients' testimonials, filmed in the clients' luxury homes. It reported to me a 30% response rate from this campaign. This approach not only delivered media that could not easily be ignored or casually tossed in the trash but also addressed the fact that affluent customers rely more on referrals than on advertising, by delivering simulated referrals— clients like them, possibly known to them, speaking to them on the DVD from their own homes. Such social proof from true peers can successfully bridge the gap between advertising and the affluent client's preference for peer recommendations. This company has now moved this into a marketing system like I've described in this chapter, driving affluent homeowners into its website trap to request the DVD, or view it instantly there, and download free reports about care of antique furniture, stain removal from Oriental rugs, and similar topics.

If you are one of the rare birds who commits to development and implementation of this kind of direct-marketing system, you'll soon be sending me similar success reports.

FIGURE **30.1:** No B.S. Direct-Marketing System

Advertising	Online Traffic	Direct-Mail	Publicity	Misc.

LEAD GENERATION

Step One

Single Funnel

TRAP

Web Site	Inbound Call

Capture Leads – Information – Permission

Step Two

Multi-Step Multi-Media

FOLLOW-UP

Step Three

Mail	E-Mail	Telephone	Tele-Seminars	Webinars	In Person	Other

CHAPTER 31

How to Use the Power of the
Internet to Market
to the Affluent

By Lindsay Dicks with J.W. Dicks and Nick Nanton

A wise man once told me, "People buy People." That man was my father, and I think I was 15 when I first heard that phrase. He had learned it from my grandfather many years ago when he first learned about personal branding himself. That philosophy has now become a daily part of my life. What I didn't know then was *the reason* that "people buy people" and, taking it a step further, why people buy from those that they "know, like, and trust." At an early age, my father was teaching me a very valuable lesson, one I didn't fully appreciate until years later in business.

The fact that people buy from people that they know, like, and trust becomes highly valuable when you are marketing your product (or service) because price is no longer the reason the consumer makes the purchase.

This fact becomes even more valuable applied to the affluent market who buy on personal choice, not price. Their personal choice is largely defined by their relationship to the person (or brand), thus understanding how to sell to the affluent allows you to sell at higher prices—and make more money!

The Online Marketing Game

More and more we are living in a skeptical society that has MASSIVE amounts of information at its fingertips. Be it computer, tablet, or smartphone, consumers are able to find answers to their questions within seconds. My mother is a great example of this—ask her a question she doesn't know the answer to and she promptly whips out her iPhone and "Googles" the answer. While I was growing up, she would have looked it up in the encyclopedia, from which she always came back with an answer, but it took much more time to research what she was looking for.

A fall 2013 report done by the Shullman Research Center says, "80% of affluent consumers prefer to do research online."

Today, it takes seconds to find any answer you are looking for, and it only takes seconds for the consumer to make a snap judgment that you are or aren't that answer.

A study done by Jakob Nielsen of the Nielsen Norman Group in 2011 says, "Users often leave web pages in 10 to 20 seconds, but pages with a clear value proposition can hold people's attention for much longer."

It is important to remember the internet was made for the consumer. If people get to your website, it is because they searched for something or they are looking for you specifically to find out more information. But one way or another, THEY are searching. Thus, if you look at every person who comes to your website as a someone who is raising his hand, then the question becomes "How do I give them what they are searching for?"

Within your marketing, you **MUST** answer these three questions:

1. Who are you?
2. Are you trustworthy?
3. Can you help me with my problem?

Keys to Marketing to the Affluent Online in Ways that Answer these Questions

Develop a Marketing Website

Your website should be a place of vast (current) information. But first and foremost, it should represent who you are and what you do. So often I see a website that is more like a static brochure than a dynamic, personality-driven, multimedia website that answers those three important questions. These specific types of websites we call Marketing Websites.™

To be a Marketing Website™ you must have these ten things:

1. *Personality*. Personality isn't just about adding a photo to your website, although it's a great start. It's about putting YOU into your business online.

   Most affluent buyers are not in the hunt for in-depth technical product knowledge; they are in search of the go-to experts who they can trust to make the best decisions and advise them on the best solutions.

   Adding personality into your website through photos, video, and your writing is about building that relationship with consumers and solidifying their belief that you are the person who is going to make their life easier.

2. *Credibility*. Credibility is one of the leading factors in becoming trustworthy. And when dealing with the affluent market you cannot have a website that displays you as a "sleazy salesman."

What makes you a credible expert? Have you been seen in the media? Are you involved in trade associations within your niche? The BBB? Are you a bestselling author? All of these factors play a vital role in showcasing your credibility.

One of the best ways to establish immediate credibility is through the use of recognizable logos. Displayed correctly, these logos from media appearances or trade associations can bring immediate awareness and validation. Simply displaying "Been in business for over 25 years!" can also bring credibility to your business.

3. *Testimonials.* Testimonials are a powerful third-party verifier and help make you credible through social proof. Wikipedia defines social proof as "a psychological phenomenon where people assume the actions of others in an attempt to reflect correct behavior for a given situation."

In essence, "monkey see, monkey do," but as Wikipedia goes on to say, "This effect is prominent in ambiguous social situations where people are unable to determine the appropriate mode of behavior, and is driven by the assumption that surrounding people possess more knowledge about the situation."

The best types of testimonials are ones that not only use text to convey their message but also the person's photo or video.

4. *Lead capture with auto responders.* Remember, when people come to your website they have searched for something to get there. When they do get to your website, you need to capitalize on their visit by capturing their information so you can continue to stay in touch with them. If you rely just on your phone number on your website, then you are relying on only one way for the consumer to contact you—to call. There are a number of reasons that they may

not be ready to do this. By providing other ways to get information, you open up your funnel for leads.

5. *Keywords and targeted meta data.* Without getting extremely technical—knowing your keyword(s) and putting them into your meta data (specific pieces of code that tell search engines like Google what your site is about) is VITAL to get your website ranked in the search engines.

   If you are unfamiliar with what your keywords are, Google offers a free keyword tool that will help you discover the keyword(s) that people are searching for and the amount of competition for those keywords. Go here for more information: www.google.com/sktool/. Ideally you want to look for the keyword(s) with high traffic and low competition.

6. *WordPress.* If your website isn't on WordPress, get it there! There are a number of great reasons to use WordPress, but first and foremost, by nature it is great for search engine optimization (SEO) because it is built with clean code that makes it easy for search engines to spider and index your website. WordPress also offers endless plugins that can enhance just about every aspect of your website.

   Here are a few of my favorites:
   - W3 Total Cache: http://wordpress.org/plugins/w3-total-cache/
   - Google® XML Sitemaps: http://wordpress.org/plugins/google-sitemap-generator/
   - All in One SEO Pack: http://wordpress.org/plugins/all-in-one-seo-pack/
   - Booking Calendar: http://wordpress.org/plugins/booking/
   - Broken Link Checker: http://wordpress.org/plugins/broken-link-checker/
   - The Events Calendar: http://wordpress.org/plugins/the-events-calendar/

- AddThis: http://wordpress.org/plugins/addthis/
- Members: http://wordpress.org/plugins/members/

7. *Current, relevant content.* Current, relevant content is important for two reasons. First, it gives the search engines a reason to continually come back to your website crawling for more content and information to be indexed into the search engines. If you do not have updated content on your website, you give the search engines no reason to come back to your website.

   Second, if people come to your website and it's outdated, the first question that then runs through their head is "Are you outdated?" Developing a keyword-rich blog can be one of the best ways to continually add current relevant content. Effective blogs are ones that have content that acknowledge a problem that's currently being faced in your industry, mentioning how you have been able to take care of that problem for your clients, and then providing a mini CTA (call to action).

8. *CTA (call to action).* Unfortunately, it's not enough to have great content. Good content with no action is going to be just as unsuccessful as a website with no content. CTAs should be used throughout your website to take visitors through a predetermined path. By using CTAs on your homepage, you can connect with visitors' pain points and lead them to an interior page that will solve their problem.

   CTAs should also be used on interior pages to get visitors to take specific action. These types of CTAs should be connected to a lead capture device such as a free consultation or special report. If a person has just read an entire page of copy on your website about a particular service, there is no better time to ask, "Ready to take the first step in becoming financially free? Download the FREE Special

Report '10 Keys to Creating the Life You've Always Wanted Now!' "

Remember, it's about building the relationship—so if visitors are not ready to pick up the phone and call you, capturing their information is crucial so that you can continually market to them and stay in the forefront of their mind. Even if they are not ready to make a decision that day, creating a relationship with them so that you are their "friend in the business" is vital.

9. *RSS feeds and social bookmarking icons*. Both RSS feeds and social bookmarking icons allow further engagement with your website.

    RSS stands for "really simple syndication." This form of syndication allows consumers to receive your information without giving away any of theirs. They can simply sign up for the feed and every time you add a new piece of content to your website, they will get it in their inbox.

    Social bookmarking allows users to save links to web pages that they like. The value in social bookmarking is that unlike a private bookmark within your own computer and browser, social bookmarks are public and tagged by keywords, so they can be a great tool for others to promote the content on your website, increasing traffic.

10. *Social media icons*. Social media icons allow the user to connect with you socially if *they* choose. Will everyone want to visit your Facebook page? No, but for the consumer who likes to get his/her information through social media, it should be an option for them.

    Another great way to connect your website to your social media is through products like Twitter Cards. Twitter Cards *take your tweets one step further by adding a rich snippet of content. By adding a few lines of HTML to your websites anytime someone sends out a link to it (for example, they tweet a blog post or retweet one of yours)*, a "card" will be added to the tweet that's visible to all of their followers. For example, this "card" could be an image, a video, or a preview of a new product. For more information about Twitter Cards go to: https://dev.twitter.com/cards.

Creating a "Wow" Experience

The affluent consumer wants to feel special. When people sign up on your website, do you simply send them an automated thank-you email? Or do you send them a personalized message through video thanking them for their decision?

The WOW experience is about going above and beyond what everyone else is doing. It is a personal touch that helps to build on your relationship.

Five examples on how to create an online WOW experience are:

1. Send each new lead a personal message through Facebook to connect.
2. Use O-to-O marketing (online-to-offline or vice versa) and send a personalized thank-you card through https://sendoutcards.com/.
3. Send birthday and anniversary cards and video messages.
4. Develop a smartphone app exclusive for customers to receive inside information and tips.
5. Have online chat services so visitors can get their questions answered in real time.

O-to-O Marketing

The use of offline-to-online (or vice versa) marketing can be a very effective way to market to the affluent consumer. For example, send sales letters through the mail that then direct consumers to a PURL (personalized URL). The key to O-to-O marketing is that you keep the message consistent throughout so that when you do take the consumer from the sales letter to the specific landing page, the landing page message is congruent with the reason it got her there.

Get Social and Online Reviews

Online marketing is about developing a web presence greater than your website. The biggest misconception about social media is that you are going to tweet something and get an immediate ROI back. Not to say that it *won't* happen, but if you are a financial planner, for example, the chances that someone sees a tweet and immediately buys from that link are slim.

However, social media is a third-party verifier of who you are and what you do and is extremely powerful when it comes to your Digital DNA™.

SEO (search engine optimization), as defined by Wikipedia is "the process of improving the ranking of a website on web search engines." Simply put, it's making sure that when someone searches for something, you are what they find.

The "typical SEO" that you will hear discussed is when someone searches for a service or pain point. For example, when someone searches "Financial Planner North Carolina" or "IRS Help Oklahoma," you hope that your website ranks number one or at the very least shows up on that first page of Google. This type of search is what we call a keyword search.

However, what often is not discussed is the second type of search, a referral search. This search can be done for a number of different reasons; for example, someone has received your business card, heard you speak, heard you on the radio or TV, or has a friend/family member give a referral to you. One way or the other, they are searching for YOU (or your company) directly. The results of this search are what we call your Digital DNA™.

Digital DNA™ is where the power of social media becomes so valuable. When someone searches for something, Google will return ten answers to the search query. Where are you in these search results? If done correctly, when someone searches for you, you want all ten search results to be about you. Within the search results, the consumer should see your website, blogs, articles, press releases, videos, photos, etc., all validating who you are and what you do. By doing this, you minimize the chances of this consumer being distracted and going anywhere else other than where you want them to go.

Another factor in your Digital DNA™ can be online reviews. Review websites like Yelp® and Google® Reviews are increasingly important, especially for local businesses. In June 2013 BrightLocal released its Local Consumer Review Survey that says, "85% of consumers say that they read online reviews for local businesses." The survey goes on to say, "79% of consumers trust online reviews as much as a personal recommendation" and that "Facebook and Twitter are also growing strongly as recommendation channels."

Overall, social media can play a key role in not only your Digital DNA™ but also in how consumers connect with you. **Here are just a few additional ways to get social:**

- Facebook ads
- Facebook-sponsored posts
- LinkedIn ads
- LinkedIn groups
- Use hashtags to connect your content to current popular topics and questions.
- Join in the current conversation by writing social media content around major news events.
- Use Facebook Like Gates to force Facebook users who have not already liked your page to do so before they can

see content. Here is a great easy-to-use WordPress Plugin: https://wordpress.org/plugins/like-gate/.

- Share other people's content that you find valuable and useful. Pocket (https://getpocket.com/) is a great resource to save information you find until you're ready to use it.
- Use images with your posts.

Going Mobile

More than six in ten affluents own smartphones. Many are seemingly attached at the hip, so having your website easily accessible via smartphone (or tablet) is a must. Today, your website must be mobile responsive, meaning the elements of your site accommodate different screen sizes. Trim down the content, keep it simple, and make buttons/links larger. WPtouch is a great WordPress plugin that makes your website mobile responsive with just a little bit of customization (to download the plugin, go to: https://wordpress.org/plugins/wptouch/).

Affluent consumers, like all consumers, are increasingly spending time on the internet accessing a wide range of information from news to entertainment to how to solve XYZ problem. According to Ipsos Media and I-Prospect, quoted in *Research Alert*, November 2013, affluents spend an average of 41.6 hours online per week, up from 37.4 hours in 2012. The key is to be everywhere they are online, including social media. Engagement and being personal is crucial to developing a long-term relationship with these buyers.

CHAPTER 32

Developing an Affluent-Attracting Platform

By Greg Rollett with Dicks+Nanton Celebrity Branding Agency

Although it's a foregone conclusion that the affluent have money, it does not necessarily make them more sophisticated about what to do with their money and who to trust with it.

Case in point: a 27-year-old financial advisor who went looking for affluent investors in Honolulu. Prior to making her case to the affluent, she had never handled more than $10,000.00 in a brokerage account.

Yet using specific media channels, she, predatorily, quickly began to make her case to targeted investors in the area. After establishing trust through her media platforms, she began generating interest for a hedge fund that had high expectations. A few weeks later she had raised $2.5 million for this fund.

The fund didn't exist. Well, unless you consider taking lavish trips to Miami, London, and other parts of the world a thriving hedge fund. She was later busted by the SEC, arrested, and turned over to the sharks. This is just one small incident of many where the affluent are elegantly robbed.

Now, we absolutely do not condone this kind of thing and find it extremely sad. But there are some very good lessons here that are worth looking at. Instead of focusing on the illegal fund, I want to focus on how she was able to convince these investors to pour money into something that didn't exist.

It takes on the same theme as many parts of this book. *The affluent buy based more on who than on what.* THAT is the real lesson I want you to take from this story.

That "who" takes a place in their life and slowly begins to build rapport, likability, and then trust. Once trust is established, the checkbook starts to open itself.

To the affluent, this trustworthy individual is comparable to a celebrity. Someone who is valued and deemed important. Someone who continually shows up in their life in a favorable way, from all directions.

The Path Toward Becoming the Trusted Celebrity Advisor

In order to establish yourself in this trusted advisor role and become that celebrity in the minds of your targeted affluent group of prospects, you must create and leverage a media platform that has proven to build trust.

It is not a place to regurgitate facts, to deliver another Top 10 list or sell your wares as any other salesperson would do.

It is a place to integrate personality. To inject emotion. To build and tell your legend.

This media needs to come from many angles to give you the appearance of being seen everywhere. Major media and celebrity icons know this.

The Secrets Oprah and Seacrest Know about Building Multichannel Platforms that Are Out in the Open for All to See

It's why Oprah controls you on TV, on the web, and with her own magazine. Notice that she has her own magazine and didn't rely on publicists or PR agents to get her cover articles. She put herself on the cover of a magazine she controlled and has continued to put herself on the cover each and every month since April 2000.

Knowing the value of projecting to your market who you are seen with, Oprah has only shared the cover of her own magazine twice—once with Michelle Obama and once with Ellen DeGeneres.

Working in multiple channels and formats is no stranger to possibly the hardest working man in Hollywood, Ryan Seacrest. He toils five days a week, four hours per day on the radio to 150 markets, has a weekend gig hosting the Top 40 Countdown Show, hosts *American Idol* on Fox, and produces hit reality shows like *The Kardashians.* Then he adds in specials like New Year's Rocking Eve and contributions to *The Today Show,* the Olympics, and more.

This is a guy that knows how to be seen—and be seen in all the right places for his market.

Which begs the question, what can you do to be seen in all the right places for the affluent prospects you desire in your market?

The answer is to create a media platform that puts you at the center of their universe, showing up at every direction.

But not just showing up. Showing up as an ambassador. As a resource. As someone who understands their needs, shows up exactly when a problem arises, and is seen with people in the places that matter to them.

This means you cannot show up only online. It also means you cannot only show up in the paper or the yellow pages or at the gala in your country club.

What is needed is the creation of a platform—a deliberate media strategy based on the creation of your own media that is directly dropped right into the laps of the affluent targets.

In his book, *Platform*, Michael Hyatt says, *"Without a platform—something that enables you to get seen and heard—you don't have a chance. Having an awesome product, an outstanding service, or a compelling cause is no longer enough. A platform is your tribe. People who share your passion want to hear from like-minded people. A platform enables you to cut through the noise and deliver your message or product right into the heart of your best prospects."*

The simplest, quickest, and still most effective piece of media to put into your affluent-attracting platform is your print newsletter.

Why Old Faithful Is Still Number One

Your newsletter is your direct connection to your market. It is your sounding board. It is your version of Oprah's magazine. And it should be treated as such and not just something you send out because you heard Dan Kennedy tell you to send it out.

Your newsletter should be deliberate. It should be strategic. Engaging. Personal and emotional.

In an issue of the *CXM Letter*, one of the newsletters I publish for my clients and prospects, you might hear me talking about my days as a rapper in a rock band, my thirst for mud runs like the Spartan Race or the Warrior Dash, my kids Colten and Ryder, the success of my clients, and the inner workings of campaigns that are successful.

All of this builds a relationship between me and my readers, strengthening my bond with them. And as every month seems to get better than the last, my trust and goodwill increase with them as well.

As it should yours. Every piece should be calculated to do these things. If a section of your newsletter is not indoctrinating your market, strengthening your relationship with the readers, showcasing your importance through where you are seen and who you are seen with (think affluent magnets), and connecting you to something that creates meaning for them—dump it.

Your newsletter is also a place to cement your opinions of authority. Look, no one is paying you, especially at the top of the pyramid, for wishy-washy answers.

You wouldn't want your doctor second-guessing the prescription he is writing you, nor a financial advisor who flip-flops on where you should put your money.

"Let's see, we could do an IRA, or maybe an annuity would work, or better yet, let's try a mutual fund."

The top of the pyramid pays for absolutes. Or at least the appearance of absolutes. When you hire Dan Kennedy as a copywriter, you are paying for an absolute marketing campaign that will provide results.

When my mentor Jack Dicks was observing one of my presentations delivering Q&A to the audience, I was caught giving what he considered the "political answer." I was telling them that different marketing works for different circumstances and you need to test this and then test that.

While that is technically correct, the audience wants an absolute. They want the one thing that will give their brain the endorphin rush it needs to satisfy the open loop.

The affluent are the same way. The financial advisor from Hawaii mentioned at the beginning of this chapter, gave her affluent clients an absolute. An absolute fund to invest in. She didn't give them options. And once her platform allowed her to have that conversation, they were already geared towards putting their money into that absolute.

Formulate your own set of absolutes and talk about them often in your print newsletter, in interviews, in blog posts, in your products, and anywhere else you can insert them.

Expanding Your Affluent-Attracting Platform

Once you've mastered newsletters, you can begin to explore other mediums to develop your affluent-attracting platform. When looking at our celebrity examples, a next step would be to introduce radio and TV. There is an inherent trust in what we hear on the radio and what we see on TV. It is considered gospel.

We work with numerous financial advisors who continue to use radio as an avenue to attract high-net-worth investors, either at drive time or during the morning hours of the weekend. The listeners of these shows are seduced by the allure of working with the guy on radio. Many times these financial advisors were placed on the same stations as talk radio staples such as Glenn Beck, Rush Limbaugh, Sean Hannity, and others. There are also options for endorsements from these figureheads. This creates an opportunity to be seen on and with celebrity figures who have generated trust within their market.

And it's not just financial advisors who can leverage radio. I am the host of the *Rollett Report* on our Orlando Clear Channel Station, 102.5FM and 540AM. I talk about marketing to small-business owners and entrepreneurs, encouraging calls from those willing to spend $2,000.00 or more per month on a marketing agency.

Once a call takes place, they are then put into our media platform of newsletters, emails, direct mail, shock and awe, videos, transcripts of past radio shows, and more. This creates a sense of being everywhere, now that they have shown interest in working with me.

And the phone rings seven to ten times every single week.

Can't get on the radio? Then get on iTunes®. It is not radio, but Apple® does attract the affluent. As of June 2013, Apple® had sold more than 600 million iOS devices. And every single one of them provides access to podcasts directly on the device from the customer's account. Also understand that every iTunes® account is connected to a credit card, giving you direct access to the users' buying power.

Even though podcasting is not radio, the top-rated podcasts continue to be affluent-loving content. From multiple NPR shows to Freakonomics Radio, TED Talks, *The Wall Street Journal*, Meet the Press, and more.

Again, this platform allows you to put yourself in company with these and many other popular media brands that are increasing every day, from the likes of Joel Olsteen to Rachel Maddow, Dave Ramsey to Tim Ferriss.

It can be done by a 27-year-old rookie in Hawaii swindling money from affluent investors, and it's been done by Madoff and others for centuries. The great thing is you actually have something that can help your market. It is now your responsibility to create a platform to tell the world about it.

CHAPTER 33

You Need to Choose
Your Words Carefully

"Some things a king never has to say: 'Can I play too?' . . .
'Hey guys, wait for me.' . . . 'I never seem to get laid.'"

—GEORGE CARLIN

I n marketing or selling to the affluent, language matters more than in most other selling situations.

The affluent tend to be better educated, with better
vocabularies than the general public. Beyond that, they are more
language sensitive. By that I mean they are consciously and
unconsciously judging the people speaking to them or the media
communications directed at them for appropriateness. *Is this a
person of my station?* is the question.

Sydney Barrows, who offers a terrific telecoaching program
for business owners and doctors in all kinds of professional
practices on SalesDesign®, is exceptionally intuitive and skilled
at script that communicates class and secures trust. In her first
business, she discovered that asking, "And how will you want

to take care of this?" rather than "How would you like to pay for this?" made a measurable difference in selling to an affluent clientele. Most businesses have opportunities to substantially increase sales purely through choosing and using more sophisticated, better-crafted language—when answering the phone and greeting customers, clients, or patients, during the actual sales presentation, and in advertising and marketing materials.

Recommended Resource

SALES LANGUAGE is critical. Mark Twain said the difference between any word and just the right word is the difference between lightning bugs and lightning. You can fine-tune your own sales language, develop ultra-effective scripts, and convert ordinary selling into performance art—all dealt with in depth in Sydney Barrows' short-term telecoaching program. Information at: www.SydneyBarrows.com.

By far, one of the most interesting uses and values of precisely chosen language is what I call *romancing the stone*, giving rather ordinary products the kind of elite cachet that creates differentiation, competitive edge, and support for premium pricing out of thin air.

I would like you to read three different product descriptions from a J. Peterman catalog and see what common strategies—and odd strategies—are in play. We'll discuss them after you read them.

Sample 1

Gatsby was amazing. He even managed to see to it that the book about him was regarded as a novel, fiction, as though he didn't exist. Even Fitzgerald, by the time he was through writing it, believed he'd made the whole thing up. There were those who knew the truth all along, of course; knew everything except where all that money came from. (Even by today's standards, when millions mean nothing, only billions matter, Gatsby was incomprehensibly rich.) Gatsby walked into rooms wearing a shirt with no collar. Even a little thing like that made people talk. And probably will still make them talk. The Gatsby shirt, of course, has no collar. Only a simple collar band. The placket is simpler also: narrower. (Gatsby had them made in France, originally.) The cotton we have used in our uncompromising replica of Gatsby's shirt is so luminous, in and of itself, that even a person who notices nothing will notice something. Gatsby, of course, could afford stacks of these shirts; rooms of them. Never mind. All that matters is that you have one, just one. A piece of how things were.

Sample 2

Fame isn't gradual; one moment you're comfortably obscure; the next you can't buy a cantaloupe without navigating through a thicket of fans and well-wishers. Without consulting you, people will choose a photograph; it will appear in all the documentaries, all the newspaper articles, all the books written by or about you. It will become more than you. Forever. Churchill understood. He decided what he wanted that image to portray ten years before that famous "spontaneous" photo was snapped. What image do you want to leave for posterity? The Irish Tweed Vest . . . .

Sample 3

New York Subway strike of the late '70s. Bank presidents start wearing sneakers to work. JFK goes hatless at his inauguration. Good-bye, hats. Steve McQueen, Sean Connery, Bill Holden discard ties in favor of turtlenecks. Some of it is progress. Now, marooned for a week in Paris or Osaka, this turtleneck sweater will keep you or me well dressed. Relaxed, but just a little dressy. (Both at the same time.) 55% silk, 45% cashmere. Pretty seductive stuff. Warm, but not heavy, not bulky. Beautifully detailed and finished. Sleek 7" high ribbed turtleneck. Set in sleeves. Good with blazers, old tweedy jackets, slacks, jeans. People expect to see a Walther PPK strapped over it, so you don't even need to bother.

The Gatsby shirt sells for $89.00. There are 104 words before the product is referred to! This violates every known rule of mail-order catalog or direct-response copywriting. One of the reasons for such a violation—nearly universal throughout every Peterman catalog—is the *who* he is selling to: affluent consumers with above-average educations, who wish to perceive themselves as sophisticates, as well as, of course, to a great degree, his own "Peterman cultists," as explained in his own words at the end of this chapter (see pages 326 to 342). What is even more important to see here is what he is actually selling—and it is not a shirt. Here is that same block of copy again, with boldfaced type to make what is really being sold leap out at you, rather than gently permeate the subconscious, as was intended by delivering it wrapped in the story.

Gatsby was amazing. He even managed to see to it that the book about him was regarded as a novel, fiction, as though he didn't exist. Even Fitzgerald, by the time he was through writing it, believed he'd made the whole thing up. There were those who knew the truth all along, of course; knew everything except where all that money came from. (Even by today's standards, when millions mean nothing, only billions matter, Gatsby was incomprehensibly rich.) Gatsby walked into rooms wearing a shirt with no collar. Even a little thing like that **made people talk.** And probably **will still make them talk**. The Gatsby shirt, of course, has no collar. Only a simple collar band. The placket is simpler also: narrower. (Gatsby had them made in France, originally.) The cotton we have used in our uncompromising replica of Gatsby's shirt is so luminous, in and of itself, that **even a person who notices nothing will notice something.** Gatsby, of course, could afford stacks of these shirts; rooms of them. Never mind. All that matters is that you have one, just one. A piece of how things were.

An aspiration is being sold here, not a product. The overall aspiration is to be like Gatsby. To be different, iconic, and interesting, even a bit mysterious. The more specific aspiration is to be noticed and talked about. And in case you hadn't noticed, affluent people like being noticed, and most go about that deliberately, whether very consciously or unconsciously.

This copy also uses language that would usually be dumbed down for advertising purposes. These high-brow words are strategically chosen and used to convey a sense of superiority to the buyer. By involvement in dialogue at this level, the reader is being recognized as a more sophisticated, intellectual individual. To say it in a very unclassy way, its meaning is: *You're a classy fellow and we know it, and this is for the classes, not the masses. They won't even appreciate its description.* With that in mind, I've bold-faced some more key words:

> Gatsby was amazing. He even managed to see to it that the book about him was regarded as a novel, fiction, as though he didn't exist. Even Fitzgerald, by the time he was through writing it, believed he'd made the whole thing up. There were those who knew the truth all along, of course; knew everything except where all that money came from. (Even by today's standards, when millions mean nothing, only billions matter, Gatsby was **incomprehensibly** rich.) Gatsby walked into rooms wearing a shirt with no collar. Even a little thing like that made people talk. And probably will still make them talk. The Gatsby shirt, of course, has no collar.

Only a simple collar band. The placket is simpler also: narrower. (Gatsby had them made in **France**, originally.) The cotton we have used in our **uncompromising** replica of Gatsby's shirt is so **luminous**, in and of itself, that even a person who notices nothing will notice something. Gatsby, of course, could afford stacks of these shirts; rooms of them. Never mind. All that matters is that you have one, just one. A piece of how things were.

Finally, the end—**all that matters is that you have one, just one**—defies selling logic. The first impulse of most marketers is to encourage buying one of each of the four available colors, probably with a buy three, get one free offer. I confess it instantly occurred to me when I read the catalog page. Instead, this line dares to discourage buying more than one. In doing so, an air of exclusivity is conferred on the product, as might ordinarily be attached to a unique piece of jewelry, a classic car, or some collectible.

Sample 2 sells a rather odd tweed vest for $199.00. Or does it? The entire scenario described here speaks to two aspirations of the affluent: importance and legacy. The thought of having fans and well-wishers and photos snapped of you is a very appealing fantasy for a great many people. I know it for fact; I have that experience, and I am constantly asked what it is like. Further, the idea of being the author of a book has strong importance and legacy appeal. In fact, my Platinum Members Bill and Steve Harrison, who conduct the Publicity Summit, publish *Book Marketing Up-Date,* and provide a range of services to authors, very effectively use a story about people coming in large numbers from far away to a person's funeral because they were influenced by his book. Again, as a much-published author, I can assure you, every successful person believes he has a profoundly interesting and important story to tell, a book within. All this to sell a vest! This *is* how your thinking about whatever you sell and do must change if you are to be effective with affluent clientele and rise to the top price or fee levels in your business category.

As an aside, this copy reveals something about the age of the Peterman customers. The references to documentaries and to Churchill will be meaningful to those 50 and over, most meaningful to those 60 and over, and pretty much a disconnect for anyone under 40. For those in the last category, documentaries or news reels were shown in the movie theaters before every movie throughout the World War II era, and were very popular in early TV. Winston Churchill is, of course, famous, but you probably don't know about the photo referred to unless you are of a certain age.

Sample 3 sells a turtleneck sweater for $250.00, or $185.00 on sale. We can certainly find nice turtleneck sweaters for half that price in many stores and catalogs. But we can't find *copy* like this anywhere else!

First, there is aspirational identification. Here I've boldfaced the key references:

> New York Subway strike of the late '70s. Bank presidents start wearing sneakers to work. **JFK** goes hatless at his inauguration. Good-bye, hats. **Steve McQueen, Sean Connery, Bill Holden** discard ties in favor of turtlenecks. Some of it is progress. Now, marooned for a week in Paris or Osaka, this turtleneck sweater will keep you or me well dressed. Relaxed, but just a little dressy. (Both at the same time.) 55% silk, 45% cashmere. Pretty seductive stuff. Warm, but not heavy, not bulky. Beautifully detailed and finished. Sleek 7" high ribbed turtleneck. Set in sleeves. Good with blazers, old tweedy jackets, slacks, jeans. People expect to see a **Walther PPK** strapped over it, so you don't even need to bother.

As noted earlier, you need to be of a certain age. If you are, not only are the five iconic figures (the fifth is James Bond—not named, but we know his gun of choice) familiar to you, but they instantly conjure mental pictures, maybe even mental movies. They are the men women swooned over but men admired, not resented. Countless products and services are bought by consumers because of the "I Want to Be Like ____" factor, and even the most affluent consumers respond to such appeals.

This copy also puts us into mental movies:

New York Subway strike of the late '70s. Bank presidents start wearing sneakers to work. JFK goes hatless at his inauguration. Good-bye, hats. Steve McQueen, Sean Connery, Bill Holden discard ties in favor of turtlenecks. Some of it is progress. Now, **marooned for a week in Paris** or Osaka, this turtleneck sweater will keep you or me well dressed. Relaxed, but just a little dressy. (Both at the same time.) 55% silk, 45% cashmere. Pretty **seductive** stuff. Warm, but not heavy, not bulky. Beautifully detailed and finished. Sleek 7" high ribbed turtleneck. Set in sleeves. Good with blazers, old tweedy jackets, slacks, jeans. **People expect to see a Walther PPK strapped over it, so you don't even need to bother.**

The reader can visualize himself in his turtleneck, at a Paris café . . . then catching the attention of a beautiful and mysterious woman. As a stand-in for James Bond, a dashing, romantic, fascinating figure. And who *doesn't* want *that*?

The temptation will be to presume none of this applies to you, because you do not sell shirts and sweaters; you are a dentist or financial planner or you own a landscaping company or even manufacture safety devices sold to and installed in food-processing plants. Resist this temptation! Commitment to talking about what you do or sell in factual, logical, straightforward, and thus dull and uninteresting language leaves you vulnerable to commoditization and price-based competition and bars you from ever becoming a subject of fascination among a target audience of affluent clients. Being boring and ordinary is a choice, not something forced on you by your particular business.

This also goes far beyond your advertising. As a professional direct-response copywriter routinely commanding project fees for ads, direct-mail campaigns, websites, and the like upwards of $100,000.00 plus royalties, I have enormous appreciation and admiration for copy like the Peterman catalog examples dissected here. I spend many hours of every week surrounded by thesaurui, swipe files, even novels, agonizing in search of precisely the perfect word or phrase or story to get a persuasive point across in print. But to confine this to print misses a greater opportunity and a more critical need.

Out of the Mouths of . . .

This approach does NOT apply just to words put into print. It applies equally to what you and your salespeople say verbally. Here, frankly, a toxic waste dump of sloppiness has occurred in most businesses. What comes out of the mouths of most people about their products and services is, bluntly, trash and slop. It is thoughtless. Uncrafted. Inconsistent. When captured via recording and transcribed and reviewed in print, it is humiliating. The affluent consumer is as repulsed by this as if the sales professional reeked of garlic, alcohol, sweat, and uncontrolled gas.

I am consistently appalled at what I hear professionals, business owners, and sales professionals saying.

This gets to a philosophical decision. I and the aforementioned Sydney Barrows share a view of selling as performance art. As such it is to be planned, scripted, physically choreographed, rehearsed, and ultimately performed. Most sales professionals unfortunately view the presentation as something that they should just be able to *do*.

This also gets to sales management and management decisions, if you employ salespeople or nonsalespeople who still

have sales job functions, such as front-desk staff in a professional office. The question is whether you are going to tolerate
sloppy, inconsistent, ineffective communication or you are going
to design the most effective language and choreography possible and insist on its implementation. To help you make this
important decision correctly, and act on it successfully, I suggest
reading my book *No B.S. Guide to Ruthless Management of People
and Profits*.

The Catalog That Started a Cult

by John Peterman

"Two eggs over easy, crisp bacon, hold the grits." Sarah, my usual
waitress at the Saratoga, knew my breakfast order by heart. This
morning, though, in November 1990, she brought something extra
on the tray: a newspaper with an article circled.

"Special of the day, John," she said.

I took a closer look. It was a piece by Tom Peters, the best-known
business thinker of our time, writing on a subject close to me:

I wish the J. Peterman Co. of Lexington, Ky., would win the
1991 Malcolm Baldrige National Quality Award. Their Winter
1990 catalog, "Owner's Manual No. 8," just arrived; as usual,
I dropped what I was doing and sat down to read it.

No photos, just hand-drawn illustrations. And wonderful,
whimsical text . . . . The J. Peterman catalog is fun. The products and presentation are "world-class quality" writ large. A
few thousand more J. Petermans and we could kiss our economic woes goodbye.

The Catalog That Started a Cult, continued

I didn't need sugar in my coffee after that.

A fairly steady rain of other articles soon began to appear, like one by Holly Brubach, in *The New York Times Sunday Magazine*, that made me check my hat size:

> The stuff of J. Peterman's catalogue copy—the acute powers of observation, the delight in the smallest details of everyday life, and the urge to record them—is the stuff of literature and it sets J. Peterman apart from his fellow mail-order entrepreneurs: He is a merchant poet.

The fact is, I never had myself confused with the charming fellow that people sensed was there, just out of reach, behind the words on our catalog pages; he was the product of more than one mind. But my memories and convictions went into him. I was delighted, once, to come across a certain small detail of life from long ago—a pair of fawn-colored leather spats. I had no intention of reproducing the spats for sale; instead, we ran a drawing of them with copy entitled "Circa 1906," to express something of what I felt the company stood for:

> They are old. They are useless. But they are beautiful.

> I bought them at a vintage clothing sale—not to sell, but as a reminder of how well stuff used to be made: pearl buttons 1/8" thick, leather seams with 14 stitches per inch.

> They also remind me of more recent things, which (amazingly) we've given up with hardly a murmur of protest.

> Peaches worth eating and doctors who make house calls. Real starch in shirt collars. Bakelite. Books sewn in signatures. Strike-anywhere matches. Soapbox orators. Car

The Catalog That Started a Cult, continued

engines you can tune yourself. Meaningful S.A.T. scores. Lüchow's, foghorns, taffeta dresses, and sparklers on July 4th.

Isn't it time to take some kind of stand here?

I'm saving all I can. I hope you are too.

I guess that is as close to poetry as you'll find in a mail-order catalog.

■   ■   ■

A recent friend of mine told me that years ago, late at night on Nantucket, she and her housemates used to sit in their waterfront rental, listening to the waves break on Tom Nevers beach, drinking Barolo, and reading from the Owner's Manual. "Steff was getting married that summer," she said. "I needed a dress to wear to the wedding, and she needed something to wear to a cocktail party in her honor. We started reading our catalogs out loud as we were looking through them, and soon, the others were in on the act. We'd start with the copy that was there, then make up our own finishes. Or we'd 'introduce' one product to another—'The tall, thin, brooding man in the J. Peterman Shirt meets the woman wearing the Flip-Up Sunglasses at Café de Flore, 1 A.M. sharp; secret documents are exchanged.'

"Knowing about the catalog was sort of an inside thing," she said. "It was like being a member of a club, and you felt more a part of it with each issue."

People loved to read the Owner's Manual even if they never actually bought anything. When we'd take them off the mailing list, eventually, they'd write letters pleading with us to put them back on again. Some customers confided that they bought an item

The Catalog That Started a Cult, continued

once a year or so to make sure that they didn't miss a mailing. Fortunately, others bought a lot more.

(As the catalogs kept coming out, getting thicker and thicker, direct-marketing experts became converts, too; they called us "the anti-catalog," and meant it as a compliment.)

Many people related to the catalog in a very personal way, almost as if it were a letter written by a good friend who can take you out of yourself, out of your routine—or remind you of who you really are. We told stories, gave candid opinions and confidential advice. We often spoke in an intimate one-on-one way, as in this copy for our Women's Tuxedo Shirt:

> The question, really, is how did you get by this long without it? No wonder you've been a little sulky; I know I'm not the only one who's noticed it.

In return, readers weren't shy about letting us know when we pleased or displeased them. We once took a matching tweed jacket and pants that had a wonderful, gentleman-in-the-country quality and named them the "E. Digby Baltzell Memorial Tweeds," in tribute to the dapper sociologist who wrote *The Protestant Establishment* and invented the acronym "WASP":

> "You must meet the WASP man," hostesses would say. A dashing figure at the Germantown Cricket Club, around the quad at Penn. Invariably wore candy-striped shirt and bow ties with his tweeds, although he'd defend, in principle, your right to do otherwise.

A former student wrote in, outraged: How dare we exploit the great man for our tawdry commercial purposes? But Mrs. Baltzell

The Catalog That Started a Cult, continued

wrote to us, too. She thoroughly enjoyed the copy. The suit was just like the ones her late husband favored. There was going to be a symposium in his honor, and all his old colleagues would be wearing the Memorial Tweeds.

The Owner's Manual was filled with references to Alexander the Great, the Russian Navy, Kanchanaburi, Tolstoi and Vita Sackville-West, Ludwig Wittgenstein and chaos theory, Georgia O'Keeffe, "Bear" Bryant, Gable and Harlow, and Wendy Hiller, some of them pretty obscure. "Thanks for bringing back memories of my rum-running days," someone would tell us. Or, "Where can I get that P.D. Ouspensky book you referred to?" When we made errors, occasionally, vigilant readers were quick to respond. "Churchill was elected in April, but he didn't move to 10 Downing until October." "You can't 'clubhaul a ketch.'"

Several times, scrupulous college professors wrote in for an OK to use our material in their literature classes. Well, why not? We offered everything from fresh aphorisms ("A shirt is the pedestal upon which a human face stands to present its case") to whole novels condensed into a few paragraphs, like this copy for our WWII Canadian Air Force Duffelbag:

A farmer's son, growing up in Alberta, Canada, sees a lot of sky.

It sets him dreaming.

At 16 he's flying a crop duster.

At 23 he's an RCAF volunteer in the Battle of Britain. Bader's 242 Squadron. A Hawker Hurricane of his own.

Scrambling twice a day to intercept German ME 109s soon convinces him that he is not, in fact, immortal. But there are compensations.

The Catalog That Started a Cult, continued

At the pub in Duxford, the wings on his uniform have a persuasive effect on the local solicitor's daughter. (Other envious soldiers are now referring to fighter pilots as "The Brylcreem Boys.")

No question of marriage. Not until he's demobbed. And that will happen in '43, thanks to fragments of a 7.92mm slug encountered over France.

He will limp a bit walking down the aisle.

She will think he never looked more handsome.

It wasn't only the writing that was admired. Collectors asked (and still do) to buy Bob Hagel's artwork. People who know about these things say Hagel has a line that can't be confused with that of any other artist; it gets to the essence of things in an energetic, unhesitating way that's never merely pretty to look at.

Some customers even wanted to collect me. I received quite a few mash notes from ladies all over the world inviting me to dinner, if ever I were in their neighborhood. One California woman applied for a position with the company as a massage therapist; she enclosed a nude photo of herself leaning against a fine specimen of an elm tree.

Little did she know that Audrey, my wife, was in charge of the mailroom, and opened all my mail before I got it.

■ ■ ■

The rapport that customers had with the company showed in another remarkable way: They often turned to us as a kind of Society for Historic Preservation, sending in things they were afraid

The Catalog That Started a Cult, continued

might disappear from the face of the Earth unless we reproduced them—an authentic old Norfolk jacket, a 1928 Air Corps briefcase, a great-great grandmother's blouse.

Our earliest "customer-sourced" item was The Counterfeit Mailbag. A retired mailman from Houston sent us the mailbag that had served him for 30 years, thick leather with a large rounded flap in front, a style discontinued by the cost accountants. Some details were missing, so I got another from a former letter carrier in Lexington and found a manufacturer; the bag went on to become as much a perennial as the J. Peterman Shirt:

> The secret thoughts of an entire nation were carried in leath-
> er bags exactly like this one . . . I borrowed an original from
> a friend, a retired mailman who, like thousands before him,
> was kind enough to test it out, for years, on the tree-lined
> streets of small towns everywhere. Before you were born.

A few years later, we had a surge in consignments of WWII military uniforms and equipment, like Army shirts with buttoning neck flaps to protect against possible mustard-gas attacks; we put together a collection and ran a piece entitled "We Were Soldiers Once, and Young":

> I think the 50th Anniversary of D-Day sparked it.

> Veterans around the country got up from the 6:30 news to
> rummage through closets and battered trunks, emerging
> with wonderful WWII gear, a lot of which they forwarded to
> us: "Can you do something with this?"

> Here are three of the items. Faithful reproductions of shirts in
> which they trained, fought, grumbled, flirted with Red Cross
> doughnut girls, and when you come down to it, saved the world.

The Catalog That Started a Cult, continued

That one didn't produce any big sellers, but I felt I owed it to Uncle Joe.

■ ■ ■

The J. Peterman Company was looking good from the outside during the early 1990s, and it looked good to us on the inside, too. Revenues grew from $19.8 million in 1990 to $45 million in 1992. Profitability was up. We moved to bigger offices in an industrial park on Palumbo Drive. They were palatial compared with Midland Avenue; there was even a tree in front.

It felt like the sky was the limit.

We had done a lot of in-house training up until that point—my assistant Paula Collins, for example, developed into one of the best merchants in the business. I kept that policy, but I also realized that we had to have seasoned, professional help with our increasingly complex finances and our growing need for new products. In April 1990 I hired John Rice as our CFO and head of operations, and in October I brought Tom Holzfeind on board as our first vice president of merchandising.

John was at Haband, the mail-order giant run by Duke Habernickel, "The Prince of Polyester," which sells a million pairs of pants a month. He hadn't been looking for a job. I won him over because we were a more exciting place to be, and, on a pragmatic level, we were offering options. He had always wanted to work someplace where he could be more than just an employee, he told me. John hit the ground running, spending his first two weeks at Commercialware, our software provider in Boston, nailing down our new fulfillment system. We were soon taking orders, shipping product, and getting paid like clockwork.

The Catalog That Started a Cult, continued

Tom came from the ritzier Horchow catalog operation, where he worked directly with the legendary Roger Horchow as head of merchandising; he now runs the Smithsonian Catalogue. Tom grasped the Peterman concept right away. His taste was impeccable. He knew what it takes to put a catalog together. He'd developed good agent contacts on his travels overseas. And he was secure in himself, with none of the confrontational attitude that is all too common in the world of retail, merchandising, and catalogs. That made him an excellent teacher who played a major role in developing our merchants.

On the creative side of the business, Don seemed reluctant to share responsibility for writing the catalog—he could create a perfect world there, where he had absolute control—but he was having a tough time turning out dozens of new pieces for each edition by himself. He tried a number of big-name copywriters, without much success, before enlisting Bill McCullam, who became the senior writer for the company until we closed our doors. Bill had been a creative director on BMW and Waterford Crystal, among other upscale advertising accounts, and had started in direct marketing; some of his direct-response print ads and TV commercials had run profitably for over ten years. Later, he was joined by a select group of other writers including Amy Bloom, author of the novel *Love Invents Us* and a National Book Award finalist.

■ ■ ■

One day in 1992, I realized as I was walking through the halls that I didn't recognize all my employees anymore. I was hiring managers and interviewing prospective merchants, but there were a lot more souls coming on board than that—John Rice was hiring,

The Catalog That Started a Cult, continued

Audrey (reporting to John) was bringing in customer-service reps, the warehouse manager was staffing up, etc.

I didn't like not knowing the people who were working for me, and, more important, I didn't like them not having a firsthand sense of who I was. So I started to hold regular Friday breakfasts, a practice that lasted until 1997. My assistant would pick eight employees from around the company at random, all levels, all departments. We'd meet in my office and sit around my old Philippine mahogany poker table for a get-acquainted meal and conversation. This was not a bagels-and-orange-juice buffet. Waiters served scrambled eggs and Potatoes O'Brien and fresh fruit on real china. We used a House-of-Commons coffeepot and silverware. I'd ask questions to get to know everyone, and they'd ask questions, too—hesitantly, at first, but as the event became an established fixture, more freely. We'd cover a topic, from kids and restaurants to what we were selling, how the business was doing, what their ambitions were. We eventually held lunches, as well, because having to show up at 7:30 A.M. could put a strain on commuters.

Morale was excellent in the early 1990s. Turnover was very low. We were goal-oriented, not method-bound. People had freedom to solve problems the way they thought best. They could work their way up to responsible positions at a much earlier age than elsewhere, and legitimately feel identified with the company's success. There were lots of celebrations, too, brought off with skill by Audrey—company picnics, Christmas dances, Halloween costume parties. I've heard rumors of a photograph showing me in a Roman toga, with a tilted laurel wreath on my head, standing next to John Rice decked out as Dame Edna, but no blackmail demands have been made yet.

The Catalog That Started a Cult, continued

One other thing: We trusted each other. Employees were often surprised at that, having come from companies where regimentation was the rule. I recall Robert Bolson, who'd been a dispatcher at the Lexington Police Department. He started as our head nighttime service rep when we were still on Midland Avenue and stayed with us until the end, ultimately becoming a writer. When Audrey gave him the keys to lock up on his first night, he looked at her in astonishment and smiled. "I'm going to like it here," he said.

■ ■ ■

The catalog seemed to have an insatiable appetite for new products now. Tom, Paula, Don, and I were frequenting antique shows, small clothing shops from SoHo to Ghirardelli Square, and beginning to travel to Europe. We only wanted things that were unique or hard to find elsewhere.

We were way ahead of the curve on many items, and I'd say we launched the curve in some cases, like the collarless shirt and other period clothing. During Operation Desert Storm, we were the only place where civilians could obtain the same high-tech sunglasses issued to Stealth-bomber pilots in the Persian Gulf. We were also the first catalog to carry those chunky, comfortable walking shoes made by a certain French company called Mephisto. We bought our Mephistos from the person in charge of their U.S. distribution; it was one of the few times we purchased from a sales rep—they usually want to sell to as many outlets as they can, which guarantees the item won't be special—but the Mephisto man was just starting to figure out the territory, and his product really was wonderful:

The Catalog That Started a Cult, continued

Weeding my way through the jungle of "biomechanically perfect" and "orthopedically engineered" and "air-injected" run-
ning-jumping-springing-catapulting shoes out there, I believe
I have found the ultimate walking shoe. (Walking, after all, is
what most of us do most of the time.)

I met Martin Micheali, the owner of Mephisto, on my first
European buying trip. Don and I took the train from Paris to
Sarrebourg, where the Mephisto factory is. The Sarrebourg station
has a large cobblestone square in front, and cars have to park on
the other side. Only one car was there, with a gent I assumed to
be Martin standing next to it. As we walked across the cobble-
stones to join him, he seemed to be appraising my gait. He held
out his hand; "Peterman?" "Yes," I replied. "Hmm, I thought you'd
be taller."

On the London leg of that first trip we stayed at Blakes Hotel,
which became my standard for hotels and for customer service in
general. Blakes is a small place in South Kensington, set in a row
of 19th-century townhouses, and identified by a discreet brass
wall plaque; it's favored by film and music types who value their
privacy. I went up the front steps, through the large doors, across
an intimate lobby that glowed like an Old Master painting (mirrors,
dark burnished leather, mellow wood, baskets of oranges). "Ah,
Mr. Peterman, we've been expecting you; you're checked in." No
questions, no forms to fill out; I presented my credit card at the
reception desk and that was it. From then on the entire staff did
everything they could to make us feel like personal guests.

We spent a week "working" London, from Savile Row to
Portobello Road to Jermyn Street, discovering hunting coats and

The Catalog That Started a Cult, continued

Victorian carpet bags and a glorious bone-handled badger shaving brush which we sold with copy that captured the feeling of our expeditions:

> Jermyn St., and nearby Old Bond St., are exactly what you (if you were an Englishman) might dream about if you unexpectedly found yourself pinned beneath an avalanche of boulders at the bottom of the Min Gorge in China.
>
> Waiting to be rescued, your mind might turn to the cool hushed perfection of all the tiny elegant shops along certain London streets, shops where clerks read your mind, anticipate your wishes, bringing forth soothing potions, perfectly fitted shoes, impeccable linen suits, cartridge belts, shooting gloves, rare oriental carpets, cucumber sandwiches, leather-bound first editions, coin-silver snuff boxes . . .
>
> Dreaming of these things, no doubt, has kept many an Englishman sane.

We did most of our getting about in those black London taxis built roomy enough to accommodate a gent in a top hat. The drivers always knew exactly where we were going; to qualify for a license, they spend at least two years traveling around the city on motorbikes acquiring "The Knowledge"—memorizing over 16,000 streets, landmarks, stores, restaurants, and other destinations in a 113-square-mile area. (Curious fact: The part of the human brain dedicated to spatial relationships grows significantly larger in London cabbies.) In the evenings we'd stroll the hushed back alleys of Kensington; if there'd been no cars, we could have been in 1900 or even 1850—but there were cars. Classic Bentleys,

The Catalog That Started a Cult, continued

Jaguars, an occasional Vauxhall, even a 1920 Pierce-Arrow parked casually, its owner unafraid of crime.

All that magnificent machinery set me thinking. We were planning to visit Chartwell, Churchill's home; why hire a car with a driver, when we might rent something special on our own? So I told the desk clerk at Blakes that we'd like a Morgan roadster for a few days. "We'll get right on that, Mr. Peterman." Within two hours, the phone rang in my room. "Mr. Peterman, we've had the staff check every Morgan dealer and car-rental agency in London and we're unable to find a Morgan. The manager's brother owns a Morgan, though, and the manager is contacting him to see if it's available now."

As it turned out, the chap was out of the country. We never did get the car. But the effort that went into trying to fulfill my request was remarkable. Most hotels would have made a few calls and abandoned the search. Not Blakes.

■ ■ ■

The Owner's Manual had a simple guarantee printed on the inside cover: "Absolute Satisfaction. Period." My Blakes experience made me determined to live up to that guarantee. One time, Audrey marched into my office with a small army of customer-service reps, holding a pair of boots at arm's length. A customer had worn them out doing farm work, and he felt they should have lasted longer. He'd mailed them back to us for replacement, still covered with cow manure. The reps looked at me imploringly. These were dress boots, not intended for heavy-duty use. The man had gotten his money's worth. They were only defending the company's best interests.

The Catalog That Started a Cult, continued

It was a Big Moment. "We either have absolute satisfaction or we don't," I said. "Ninety-nine-point-nine percent of our customers are honest. This man probably does feel the boots didn't hold up. If we send him another pair, he'll tell his friends about our great service. They'll become customers, too. That's the kind of company we want to be. That's the kind we're going to be."

We sent him new boots for free.

■ ■ ■

People who achieve fame are usually brighter and more adventurous than average, whatever their public image. So I wasn't surprised when the catalog became an "inside thing" early on with celebrities—Nicole Kidman, Clint Eastwood, Tom Brokaw, Paul Newman and Joanne Woodward, Kim Basinger, Tom Hanks, Mia Farrow, Bill Murray, Angela Lansbury, and Sidney Pollack, among others. Once, as I was walking through our customer-service area with a venture capitalist, we happened to overhear a conversation. The VC's eyes widened. "Is that *the* Frank Sinatra on the phone?" he asked. I looked at the service rep's computer screen. "Well, his middle name is Albert."

We had a rule that any customer who wanted to talk to me should be put right through if I were available. I took an order that way from Kelly McGillis, who bought fireman's coats for herself and Jodie Foster. I felt shy about asking her bust size; being an actress, she wasn't a bit shy at all. I ended up as a sort of personal shopper for quite a few well-known people. One was Bill Simon, former secretary of the treasury. I used to spend time on the phone with him each November as he planned his holiday shopping. He liked to get my take on what different products were really like, whom they

The Catalog That Started a Cult, continued

might suit, should he get this or that to furnish the house on his ranch? He didn't place orders with me; his secretary would call one of our service reps later. One time, though, he did ask me if he could get a discount on a big order. "Bill," I said, "when you were secretary of the treasury, did I get a discount?"

■　■　■

Oprah Winfrey was one of our major fans, and when her producer called and asked if I would be on a show about catalog shopping, I didn't see how I could turn down such an excellent customer's request.

The drill was much as it had been when I was a plant doctor on *Good Morning America*. They sent me the airplane ticket, I flew to Chicago, was met by a limousine, taken to a good hotel, then whisked to Oprah's studio early next morning. They put me to work in the makeup room this time—I'd been asked to bring lots of possible items for models to wear, and I made up outfits on the spot to suit their looks. There was a fellow in charge of wardrobe who had his own ideas on how to dress the models, but because we were presenting Peterman, and I was Peterman, they ended up dressed the way I wanted.

I met Oprah when I joined her onstage. The program was in progress; they were at a commercial break. I walked on, shook her hand, and said, "I'm John Peterman." She smiled warmly.

"No, you're J. Peterman . . . 'J.' is more mysterious." She turned to face the audience and the camera light blinked on.

Mostly, I just sat back and enjoyed the show. Oprah was a dynamo of enthusiasm. She swept here and there, picking up item after

The Catalog That Started a Cult, continued

item, holding them out, putting them on, saying how the Owner's Manual was her favorite catalog, how she loved the copy, loved this dress, loved that coat, owned three of those shirts. She tried on several hats, turning around, asking the audience, "Isn't this great?" She put on the Shepheard's Hotel bathrobe and confided that it was the softest, most luscious robe and that she wore hers every morning.

The show ran just after Thanksgiving, and at the end of my segment they flashed our 800 number on the screen. Our incoming lines started to sizzle. The show aired first on the East Coast, and the volume of calls mounted in waves as it went on in successive time zones. Everyone in the company was manning the phones, scribbling orders on scraps of paper because our computer system was overtaxed. We managed to take about 25,000 calls in an atmosphere of pandemonium . . . then sudden silence.

Hurricane Oprah had crashed the Lexington, Kentucky, phone system.

Chapter from the book *Peterman Rides Again: Adventures Continue with the Real J. Peterman through Life and the Catalog Business* by John Peterman. Used with permission from John Peterman.

You Need to Choose Your
Prices Carefully

"If you can actually count your money, you
are not really a rich man."

—J. Paul Getty

O
ne of the most interesting lines of copy I've seen
aimed at the affluent is "Reassuringly Expensive."

Price Strategy is critical in successfully marketing
to the affluent. In the first edition of this book, I devoted three
chapters just to the subject of price, but even that was woefully
inadequate, given the many opportunities to be had with a
thorough understanding of Price Strategy. Subsequently, I
wrote an entire book on the subject, *No B.S. Price Strategy*, with
a terrific co-author, Jason Marrs, a superhero of sorts: The Man
Who Competes At Premium Prices With Free! So, I have put the
three chapters about price from the first edition of this book up
at www.NoBSBooks.com as a downloadable document. They're
yours for the taking. I strongly recommend you get and study the

complete book, *No B.S. Price Strategy*. It is a perfect companion to this one.

Before leaving the subject, I will make six important points:

First, most marketers, service providers, merchants, and professionals horribly underestimate the amount of Price Elasticity that exists in their category of goods or services. That misunderstanding inflicts a myriad of evils. For one thing, it leaves a lot of money on the table unnecessarily, to no good end. Second, it sometimes raises skepticism or doubt in the minds of affluent customers who are not so eager for "a steal" that they don't worry over a seemingly too-low price. Third, it creates timidity and weakness without cause.

Second, when selling to customers more affluent than themselves, many marketers erroneously impose their own value judgments and price sensitivity on others who think very differently than they do. I frequently hear "Well, *I* would never pay so much for *that!*" from clients objecting to the price strategies I recommend for them—and from skeptical clients stunned when they see how easily I raised their prices and profits without losing or repelling customers.

Third, price is a complex matter containing many opportunities. Sometimes an income boost is as simple as just raising prices. All that was needed was courage. More often, though, there are less bald and overt ways to boost income by increasing average transaction size and average, overall customer value. This is why you need the complete course in Price Strategy in the *No B.S. Price Strategy* book.

Fourth, with affluent consumers, who you are selling to and who you are (perceived to be) to them has more to do with acceptance of prices than does what you are selling. Greg Rollett mentioned this in his chapter. This is a very difficult reality to grasp, then profit from because most marketers are product-centric and stuck there by deeply ingrained habit of thought.

Fifth, how you sell—process—has as much or more to do with price acceptance than does what you are selling.

These fourth and fifth points can both be seen in the case history included in the final section of this book, about Jones and Co. Styling Opticians.

Finally, sixth, where you sell—place—has as much or more to do with price acceptance than does what you are selling. There is a different expectation of price and different sensitivity to price if standing in the meat section looking at steaks in Walmart, at grass-fed beef steaks in an upscale supermarket, in a butcher shop, or in a catalog requested from a company like La Cense Beef (www.LaCenseBeef.com).

In short, price does not exist in a vacuum. It exists in context. You can control that context. Price Strategy does not operate separately either. It commingles with the context you create and control.

Price, Profit, Power

Survival of the fittest in exceptionally competitive market conditions or in difficult economic environments as well as maximum prosperity and greatest growth in good conditions reflects power—or weakness.

There are many important kinds of business power. For example, the power to outspend competitors in acquiring new customers, even to the point of killing competitors off entirely, without going broke yourself. The power to use virtually every media, not just a few, with such frequency and perseverance that you are omnipresent and known to one and all as the leader. The power to so favorably impress, inspire, and richly satisfy a customer he wouldn't leave you for love nor money, and can't help but spread your legend to the world. All such power is directly related to and dependent on one thing . . . .

Profit

The lower your profit margins, profit per transaction, and profit per customer factors are, the less power you have. And maximum profitability comes from one thing . . .

Price

Poor price strategies yield poor profits, which produce weakness and fragility.

Fortunately, marketing to the affluent is a great empowerment for premium prices and excellent profits—but not automatically.

CHAPTER 35

Every Marketer to the Affluent Should Be in the Information Business

"We all like to buy something from an expert—somebody we like, respect and trust. The buyer thinks—'I don't understand any of this technical stuff, but hey, if he understands it, the product must be super!'"

—Joseph Sugarman, Direct-Marketing Genius behind many successes, including Blue-Blockers®, and author of *Advertising Secrets of the Written Word*

The more affluent the customer and the more significant the purchase or its price, the more likely perceived expert status will play into the decision. As the stakes rise, the affluent consumer looks for a bona fide expert for assistance. This may mean the cleaning of Oriental rugs or leather upholstery or the management of a windfall of several million dollars obtained from the sale of a business. By positioning and presenting yourself as an expert in your field, you gain competitive differentiation and advantage, create support for charging premium prices and fees, make yourself more attractive to the affluent customer and lay the groundwork for media acceptance and publicity. It is, in short, well worth doing!

There are several intertwined paths to expert status. All but one are open to anyone, anywhere, at any time. The one that is not is academic qualification and bestowed or earned credentials. Fortunately, these are of the least importance in influencing customers and clients. So if it is too late for you to pursue your MBA from Stanford or you chafe at the patience, hoop-jumping, butt-kissing, and other silliness required to get some association, committee, or made-up body of authority to confer upon you a certification, relax. The other paths have more power and are immediately accessible.

For nine consecutive years, I was a featured speaker on the number-one public seminar tour in America, sharing the platform with former U.S. Presidents, Lady Margaret Thatcher, Mikhail Gorbachev, and countless business leaders, and, more importantly, for about 20 years I made more money per year as a professional speaker than 99.9% of my peers in the profession's association. I never obtained one of its several professional designations, got none of its alphabet soup letters to place after my name. Lacking these "credentials" had zero effect. For nearly 30 years I've been a highly paid advisor to brand-name corporations and their CEOs as well as entrepreneurs the world over, and, in the most recent tax year concluded, paid taxes on more than $2 million in personal income from my consulting activities. I have a high school education. I never served any sort of formal or informal apprenticeship in my field of advertising. I belong to no consultants association, have no professional certifications or credentials. If I should need an MBA for some odd reason, there are thousands of people with MBAs who can be rented quite inexpensively. My clientele has never once cared about or questioned any of this. The world has accepted me—and will accept you—based on my self-developed presentation. Period. Should you wish to be embraced as an expert or even as *the Expert* in your field, be it dog whispering or interior decorating or travel to Morocco or investing in municipal bonds, in your community, nationally, or globally, there is one simple thing far, far, far more important than any sort of credentials you may or may not have: decision.

The affluent, incidentally, are even more likely to accept you as you present and credential yourself than other socio-economic groups, because so many of them have achieved their status through self-determination rather than academic or other qualification, certification, or appointment. They got there more by guile and grit than gift or credentials. There is a never-acknowledged secret handshake, an understanding between all us emperors with no clothes. As disturbing as all this is to people who have painstakingly piled up degrees and framed diplomas and alphabet soup designations after their names yet make far less money than we do, often while working for us, it is reality.

So, to the three paths to expert status:

Path 1: Publication
Path 2: Promotion
Path 3: Publicity

Path 1: Get Published or Publish Yourself

You can take a traditional path, by becoming a "real" author and having a book published by a "real" publisher. For purposes of promoting yourself as an expert to a selected affluent group, there's little advantage to that over self-publishing. The faster path is publishing your own books, white papers, and newsletters. The principle at play is: If it looks like a duck, walks like a duck, quacks like a duck, it'll be accepted as a duck. If your self-published book looks like a bookstore book, it'll be just as useful to you as one published by a real New York publisher. People attach a lot of mystery to all of this it doesn't deserve. Printing is printing.

As an author of 22 books published by real publishing houses plus countless books and other information products and newsletters of my own, I can assure you that you are automatically granted a certain amount of expert status purely and solely as a result of having authored a book. As the classic advertising maxim goes, perception is reality, and people's perception of authors is favorable. I believe, at barest minimum, you need a book you've authored and a newsletter you publish consistently, preferably monthly, that presents you as a knowledgeable expert.

Path 2: Promote Yourself as Author and Expert

Now you have something to promote other than your products and services, for instant elevation from merchant to expert, which also provides natural competitive differentiation. Over the years, I've switched many clients from promoting their businesses to promoting books about their expertise. And, while your affluent prospect might throw out your junk mail about real estate investing unread, he may not be so quick to discard his monthly copy of the *Bay Area Investors' Real Estate Trends Letter*.

Path 3: Publicity

Being the author-expert is the door key to the media. Your local newspaper may not be eager to give free advertising to your nursery, but it may be eager to write a feature story about the local author of *101 Secrets of Green Thumb Gardening: How Anyone Can Amaze Their Friends and Neighbors with a Beautiful Backyard.* Your local talk radio host may not be eager to give you free advertising for your financial planning practice, but he may welcome you as a guest to discuss your book *10 Dumb Mistakes Very Smart People Make about Money.*

You may even find, as you employ these strategies for promotion of your business, that you'd be interested in making a second business out of it. Countless numbers of my clients and

Glazer-Kennedy Insider's Circle™ Members have found their way to multimillion-dollar business opportunities as well as interesting and fun activities, prestige and prominence, and personal growth along this evolutionary path. This is such a common occurrence in our world that we host an annual conference, the Info-Summit™, just for information marketers. If this interests you, I recommend another book from this publisher, *The Official Get Rich Guide to Information Marketing: Build a Million Dollar Business within 12 Months,* to which I contributed. You can also get more insight into this field at www. info-marketing.org.

Is an Expert an Expert If No One Knows?

Here is a phone conversation recounted by Dr. Thomas Stanley, one of the foremost authorities on millionaires and author of the bestselling book *The Millionaire Next Door*:

> DR. STANLEY: Who is your main adviser?
>
> DECAMILLIONAIRE: A securities broker in California.
>
> DR. STANLEY: But didn't you tell me you're a resident of New York? Did you once live in California?
>
> DECAMILLIONAIRE: I'm a New York native—never lived in California.
>
> DR. STANLEY: Then tell me how you became a client of a stockbroker in California.
>
> DECAMILLIONAIRE: I read his articles on investment strategy. I called him on the phone. He is quite famous.

Is an Expert an Expert, continued

Once we know where the fish are and who they are, we can make ourselves more attractive to them. How can we condition them to recognize us and to develop favorable images of us? The top producers in the insurance industry as well as related areas are often endorsed by the business media within their market territory. These top producers write articles about the insurance and financial problems of their target market. They appear on TV programs that feature business topics and experts. They conduct seminars that attract not only prospective customers but also key influencers such as accountants and other trusted advisers. You too must develop an appreciation for the benefits of being perceived primarily as an expert rather than as purely a marketer (of insurance). Publicizing your expertise via highly credible channels of communication will enable you to reap handsome rewards.

The person that most people, including me, consider the best professional fisherman on Lake Lanier, one of Georgia's most popular lakes, is Bill Vanderford. When I think of fishing on Lake Lanier and catching the big fish, I think about Mr. Vanderford's guide service. He is considered the top expert . . . . In addition, no one knows more about how to market his services than Bill.

Bill teaches a continuing education course at a local college on how to fish Lake Lanier. When the Atlanta or Georgia media want to do a story on Georgia fishing, they interview Bill. Bill is the author of Everything You Ever Wanted To Know About Fishing Lake Lanier.

What Bill has done is to stake out his claim to the Lake Lanier market.

Is an Expert an Expert, continued

Prospects are likely to feel more confident about hiring a fishing guide who has written a book on fishing. This is especially important if the prospect is an executive who hopes to entertain clients.

Abridged from a chapter in *Marketing to the Affluent* by Dr. Thomas Stanley.

BOOK FOUR

Field Trips, Demonstrations,
and a Case History

Book 4 Preface: You Have to See It to Believe It

I have often said that the instructions for assembling a kid's bicycle are important, but without the picture of what it's supposed to look like on the box, you can get into a lot of trouble or, looking at all the pieces spread out on the floor and a 48-step instruction booklet, feel an overwhelming sense of hopelessness and despair!

So, I want you to see everything I and my co-authors have presented implemented, in use, successfully, in actual businesses. What it looks like, not just instructions.

One of the great GKIC® Members, Conor Heaney, generously provided a complete case history chapter about his business— with samples of key marketing tools. That chapter follows. His videos can be seen and other information accessed at: www.jonesand.co/video.

In addition, I suggest you take field trips to the following websites and explore these businesses' marketing to the affluent:

www.Historic-Restorations.com

Its owner, Danielle Keperling, has won a Marketer of Year Award from GKIC, and has been featured in the *No B.S. Marketing to the Affluent Letter*. Her business is entirely for affluent clients in a niche area of interest. She does a terrific job with her marketing, using information marketing, and with price strategy.

www.TuscanGardensSeniorLiving.com

Tuscan Gardens is a new business in development in which I have a financial interest. It is a unique concept entry into the luxury assisted-living field, a very promising business category. From 2009 to 2025, demand for senior housing will outstrip supply, with seniors age 75+ going from 19 million to 44 million. Between 2021 and 2025, the 75+ population will grow 23%. This suggests a literal tidal wave of seniors requiring special considerations in housing. Tuscan Gardens is niche-targeted at the exceptionally affluent senior, providing stand-alone residential villas in a secure, service-rich setting, clustered in small communities of 60 units or less.

www.GardnersMattressandMore.com

Surrounded by lower-priced competitors, Gardner's successfully sells mattresses at 4 to 12 times average prices, selling specialty, luxury mattresses to affluent customers. We own a mattress purchased from it for the kingly sum of $35,000.00. It should sleep *for* me. The company is a highly skilled user of information marketing that creates informed customers predetermined to purchase from them, with expert positioning, and by erasing price resistance. Its store "Dream Room," inspired by suggestions from Sydney Barrows (mentioned elsewhere in this book), is a perfect differentiation device for selling to the affluent.

www.KennedysBarberClub.com

To be clear, while it bears the same name as my own, and I am an investor in Kennedy's All-American Barber Club, I am not involved in its management, operations, or even directly in its product, price, and marketing strategies—although all that is inspired by me and demonstrates the strategies presented here. Importantly, you'll see that the shops use a membership model and monthly membership dues in place of fee for service. A similar approach is at the core of the extremely successful Iron Tribe Fitness business, featured in my book co-authored with its founders, *No B.S. Guide to Brand-Building by Direct Response*.

www.Highpoint.edu

My friend of many years, Nido Qubein, as its President has done a phenomenal, awe-inspiring, widely reported on job of transforming a small downscale college into an explosively growing, vibrant, robust, somewhat Disney®-fied showplace of academic excellence, creativity, and *luxury*.

www.GKIC.com

While GKIC™ (formerly: Glazer-Kennedy Insider's Circle) is not *strictly* for the affluent, the growing Membership comprised of small business operators, midsized company owners, entrepreneurs, private practice owners, and sales professionals throughout the U.S. and dozens of other countries certainly attracts successful, affluent individuals—and helps create them! Many of our resources cater to high income earners, and within GKIC™ events and training programs like "The 7-Figure Income Academy" are mainstays. You will see differential and tiered pricing, tiered status, an ascension ladder, and premium pricing at work.

CHAPTER 36

How an Optician Repositioned His Business to Attract the Affluent

By Conor Heaney

I t was 2010. I was 30 years old, and I'd just bought my second optical practice. The first one was ticking along nicely, and I felt ready for a challenge. So I bought a fixer-upper. An established practice that was dangerously close to closing its doors.

This was a business that went bankrupt in the late '90s, had four different owners in ten years, and was notoriously difficult to make profitable. But unlike the previous owners, I have been able to make it a success. I had something they did not. A guide. And it now sits proudly on my bookshelf, dog-eared and tattered *but used*.

I picked up the first edition of the *No B.S. Marketing to the Affluent* book in early 2010 just a few months after taking ownership of my new practice. There I was, at the beginning of a huge project to transform a failing business that I thought had potential as a high-end optical boutique, and then a copy of Dan Kennedy's *No B.S. Marketing to the Affluent* lands on my desk. I couldn't have asked for a better guide and manual to re-invent this business. It was the perfect opportunity for "testing" on a grand scale. And that's the story I'd like to share with you here.

I'm Conor Heaney. I'm an optometrist, and I own an optical practice in Manchester in the U.K. Let me give you a quick rundown of how we turned a business around from the brink of bankruptcy to dizzy heights of success and achievement.

But first, let me show you a few results that came from taking a business and repositioning it to appeal to the affluent:

- The practice had 50% growth in the first two years. And it has grown every year since. We're achieving an additional 17% growth this year again.
- Our average sale value is over five times the industry average. Here in the U.K. the average amount spent on a pair of glasses is about £150. Our average is over £750, and clients routinely spend £2000 to £3000+ on their "eyewear."
- More than 80% of prospects that have an "Eyewear Style Consultation" purchase eyewear from us on the same day.

The Reason Why Most Opticians Struggle

Most optical practices are having an identity crisis. They simply don't know what they are anymore. They create a confused and mixed-up identity of a medical-professional-fashion business. A Frankenstein. A business fashioned out of different parts that don't go together very well. They fail to differentiate themselves in the eyes of the modern customer. They lack a clear USP (unique selling proposition). They try to appeal to everyone, and as a result, they don't strongly appeal to anyone.

Most opticians see themselves as a clinical or medical professional. But they exist in a retail environment. Most practices take a loss on the eye examination in the hope that the person will buy glasses. That has always been the case. Now there is online competition selling glasses at cheap prices. Many customers go to an optician for an eye examination and take their prescription information and go elsewhere to buy glasses. They shop around for more stylish glasses (which is a big trend), or they go online to buy cheap glasses at a fraction of the price. So it's a difficult time to be an optician.

I believe that we are actually a retail business. We no longer have the luxury of assuming customers will come to us, have an eye examination, and buy glasses from us just because we're their opticians. Customers don't behave that way anymore. They now have far more choices when it comes to buying glasses. It is no longer seen as a purely functional purchase. People now see their eyewear as statement. For many it is something they enjoy wearing. We have many eyewear aficionados as clients.

I once read about a shoe designer who said every morning she dressed from her shoes up. She'd pick the shoes and work the rest of her outfit around them. Well, we have clients that get dressed from their eyewear down. And they want the same feelings when purchasing new eyewear that they get when they make any other luxury purchase in any other category.

A New Sales Process That Eliminates the Headaches of Retail

We are a retail business that has developed a successful process that eliminates what all retailers hate: haphazard browsing, price comparison, time wasters, and being used as a "showroom" before buying online.

If you're in retail you'll know what I'm talking about. The internet has trained some customers to behave badly and expect something for nothing. It has trained them to devalue everything that you do. You become a commodity in their eyes.

And, yes, they're happy to waste your time, use your store as a showroom for trying things on, and take your product specifications to search online.

I noticed an increasing trend in this kind of customer behavior in my first business. And it was one of the reasons I set out to design a business that cut out all of that.

One low point sticks in my memory from around 2008. I was helping a prospect one day who walked in. He was looking for some new glasses for his wedding day, and he had never been happy with how he looked in glasses. So he was searching for something different. Something special. And I pulled out all the stops. I introduced him to a new world of eyewear. An hour later he had found a frame that he had fallen in love with. All he needed to do was to come back with his fiancée to make his final decision. And out he went feeling on top of the world, excited he had found something he would feel great wearing. He was full of praise for what I did and for how amazing the products were that I introduced him to.

The very next day I got a text message from a friend who owned an optician store in another part of the country. He wanted to know if we had the exact frame in stock that I had shown the prospect the day before. He said he had a guy who called and wanted to buy it. And the day after that I received another call from a different optician who I knew asking about the same frame. This was a rare frame, so it didn't take much detective work to discover that the guy, who was singing my praises for guiding him to the perfect frame, was now taking the information and shopping around. But to rub salt in the wound, I was being hassled by other opticians to see if they could get the frame from me at wholesale prices so they could undercut me and make an easy sale to this guy. All this wasted time and hassle because we had no process to stop it. It was madness. That was one of the turning points for me to re-engineer my sales process.

In the new practice we decided to tackle the problem head-on. I decided to eliminate "browsing." So we took the bold move of removing stock from display. No longer could anyone just walk in and try frames on and browse around and use us as a showroom. And I don't mean that we put the frames in locked displays or behind glass. No. We *removed* the frames from display. We made the practice look more like an upscale hotel than an optician. There were no frames in sight apart from a feature display, a display that wouldn't look out of place in a modern art gallery.

The environment looked great. But it kind of confused customers. The mantra we heard from anyone who walked in was, "Um, where are all the glasses?" But at least it became easy to engage in conversation with customers. Suddenly they couldn't say, "I'm just looking!" We replaced "just looking" and "browsing" with a unique Eyewear Style Consultation.

A Unique Eyewear Style Consultation

I had two things I wanted to achieve with the Eyewear Style Consultation. I wanted to eliminate all the hassles of retail and regain control of the sales process. And I wanted to position this consultation in a way that differentiated us and gave us the position of "expert." Something that is very attractive to affluent clients.

We made it an appointment-based service. "By appointment" emphasized the professional expertise positioning *and* allowed us to control the sales process. It appeals to affluent clientele who are used to making appointments because their time is important. They like that they can schedule a time, come in, and see the expert. And it also means we can give a higher level of service by being better prepared, knowing who is coming in and when. It adds real value to what we do. And the perception it creates is useful if you want to sell a high-ticket item.

We went a step further too and made the Eyewear Style Consultation a core part of our business and one of our USPs. It is the perfect solution to a significant problem in our target market.

From experience we know that the main problems our target customer has are:

- They don't know what glasses suit them and their face shape. That is, they don't really know what they're doing when it comes to choosing eyewear.
- They're bored with the same mainstream products they find in most opticians. They are looking for something different and stylish. They see themselves as an individual.
- They have had a bad experience elsewhere, so they are looking for an expert. They may have a complex prescription or significant vision problems that weren't handled well by the last optician. Or they may just have high standards and want the best.

We position our Eyewear Style Consultation as the solution to each of these problems. We didn't just make this up. We strategically created a positioning as *the* solution to their problem. Our solution is perfect for affluent clients because:

1. Their time is important, so they don't want to spend one weekend, never mind two or three weekends, shopping around on a grueling search for eyewear.
2. They value expertise. They want to see an expert. That is how they operate.
3. They expect the highest level of service. We are the perfect fit *for them.*

Almost any business could do this. Figure out the biggest and most common problems your customers experience when it comes to your "thing." Then offer some form of consultation where you address all those issues. In your marketing, talk about the problems. Show the client that you understand them. And position yourself as the expert. Position your consultation as the solution to their problems. Remember, often the biggest pain customers complain about is that the shopping process for your "thing" is confusing, unpleasant, inconvenient, time consuming, and frustrating. If you can transform their experience, you're on to a winner.

There Must Be Sales Choreography

In retail there has been a recent trend for uniquely designed, stylish interiors. Shops and boutiques have truly created an amazing environment. And here in the U.K. we have our fair share of "trendy" opticians. But environment alone is not enough.

The shopping environment is only the stage. It's extremely important. It sets the scene, it creates a certain atmosphere, and it projects a message. It sets the customer's expectations. But what matters a whole lot more is the performance that takes place on that stage. It is useful to think of your customer experience as a performance. Or a piece of theatre. Are the actors skilled and practiced at their performance? How well do they use their stage and their props? Do they know lines? Do they deliver them confidently? Is the script actually engaging? Do they know how to win over their audience?

It's not just about the building and environment that you create. It's also about the people and the processes. This is stagecraft. This is sales choreography. Without it, all you have is a building. Yes, it might be a very nice building, an impressive environment. But it is just a building. It is the people inside the building that bring it alive and use it to create an experience. And the way people create a memorable experience is through choreography and practice.

Crafting Effective Sales Scripts

We crafted effective sales scripts for every key stage of our sales process. But let me walk you through an early stage of our process: the initial conversation we have with "browsers" who walk in "cold" expecting to just look at glasses. After we removed the stock from display, these early minutes in the sale process became critical.

First, everyone thought I was crazy to remove the stock from display. When a customer walks into a store, they expect to be able to browse. When you take away that option, it put the salesperson under a bit of pressure.

When there is product on display, it buys a little time to build rapport and to engage the customer. And a shop full of products is a more comfortable environment because the customer's attention is usually focused on the product rather than on the salesperson. But when we took away the products, suddenly the salesperson was the "main event" from the moment the prospect walked in. They were 100% in the limelight. They had nowhere to hide. They would either sink or swim in a matter of minutes.

So we tested and developed effective scripts to engage the clients, put them as ease, start a discovery process, and lead them down the road to an Eyewear Style Consultation.

We started with basic scripts. A few questions that we wanted to ask. A few helpful statements we wanted to make about what we do. A few short stories we could tell. And we role-played all that regularly. We'd take the most common things browsers would say, and we'd practice responding to their statements and questions in an effective way.

But we discovered that scripts need to go hand in hand with sales choreography. And sales choreography became a huge part of this early stage in our sales process. How the prospect physically moved through the practice. How we directed their attention and kept them engaged. How we put them at ease and helped them open up.

We'd position our frame drawers in a location that would draw people all the way into the practice. We'd open a secret drawer while we were speaking with them to reveal a large collection of exquisite and unique eyewear. That would entice them. We'd select one or two frames and ask if they'd like to try it on. We'd position mirrors on tables as a way of getting people to sit down. We'd get people to go from standing to sitting at a table by casually saying "Let me get a few frames together for you while you have a look at that one. Try it on. There is a mirror there. Just have a seat." We'd keep them seated and engaged by another member of staff bringing them a tea or coffee. We'd build their anticipation by presenting frames on leather-padded trays much like a jeweler might present an expensive piece of jewelry. And before we'd present the frame to them to try on we'd describe the quality, the individuality, the exclusivity of these types of products and why what we're showing them is different from the mass-produced products they'll find at most opticians.

By this stage the browser is caught up in "an experience." An unexpected experience. And then while they're "ooh-ing" and "ahh-ing" over a few stylish frames, we're more interested in gathering information about them. At this stage they're warmed up and much more open with us. So we're *casually* having a conversation about them, their requirements, their problems, what they'd ideally like, what they've done in the past, their budget, timescale, how and when they'll make a decision, whether they'll want to come back with their partner, etc. We're exploring needs and qualifying them in a comfortable, relaxed, helpful way.

We are not in any way giving a sales presentation. Really we're just giving them an overview of the styles and letting them try on a few frames as a way of keeping them engaged while we "interview" them. We're the ones asking the questions. And then once we have some information and if they are a good fit for us, then we'll "sell" a free Eyewear Style Consultation. We explain how we work, why we do things this way, and how it might be a good solution to the problems they just shared with us. Then we schedule an appointment for their consultation later that day or for another day depending on time and what we feel is most effective based on their buying criteria that we identified.

And that is how we go from a cold browsing experience where we have little control, to a consultation, by appointment, where we have control, expert positioning, information we can use to influence and persuade, pre-established rapport, and a pre-qualified prospect.

And it results in a sale over 80% of the time. It also saves time by weeding out time wasters, and anyone who isn't a good fit for what we do, within a few minutes.

In addition to this kind of sales choreography, we also use many "props" that help us create the desired kind of experience. The great thing about props is that even if it is something small, it can be "focused in on," pointed out, or talked about so it becomes a memorable part of the experience.

Here's a taste of some of our props: fresh flowers in every room, real tea served in a stylish china cup and saucer, a selection of 19 flavors of teas, a Nespresso coffee machine that serves a proper cappuccino or latte, freshly served Pimm's with fruit in the summer, mulled wine in the winter, a selection of handmade Belgian chocolates, coffee table books with inspiring photography of a lifestyle clients aspire to (e.g., *The Conde Naste Travel Book*, *The Sartorialist*), jazz music, and on and on.

Everything Matters!

Everything in the practice has been thought out in advance. We have considered the message it sends out and whether it fits in with the perception we are trying to create for our clients as every detail plays a part in conveying our message. We look at everything through our client's eyes. Everything has an appealing design and style; from the pens we use, to how we dress, to the chairs and furniture. Everything matters.

More Money With Less Work

Now it takes a bit of effort and investment to put on a show like this and to create this kind of customer experience. So if you go to all this trouble, you kind of want to get paid! We "get paid" by focusing on premium pricing. Premium pricing allows you to work less and make more. In fact, if I had to pick just one strategy, premium pricing would be it.

Without this piece of the puzzle I would probably have failed like the previous owners of this business. When I took on the project of buying this practice, we changed a lot of things at once, the effect of which was the bottom third of existing customers magically disappeared. All of a sudden we were seeing fewer, but of much higher quality, clients who would spend a lot more money with us. And then a constant stream of these ideal clients started showing up at our door. The lower-end clients simply stopped coming in.

We had fewer clients, but the clients we had were much more profitable than the ones we got rid of. We were able to devote our full attention to doing the best job we could for our ideal clients because we weren't busy running around serving a mass of low-quality clients who aren't profitable for us. And it was a lot more enjoyable and fulfilling work.

How Much Is an "Expensive" Frame?

In my first practice the average frame price was £250. The majority of our frames were between £200 and £300. And a small percentage of frames were above £300. As a result, my staff and I thought that anything over £300 was an expensive frame. The £300 was the point at which we'd get a little nervous because it was "expensive."

I remember the day I started in my second practice. The very first thing we did was completely change the stock. And we purposely bought stock to position us as high-end. Well, overnight my perception of what an expensive frame was changed. Why? Because most of the frames on the shelves were between £300 to £400. And there were frames over the £400 mark as well. Suddenly a £300 frame felt like a bargain.

But here's the thing, the customer's perception of what was expensive changed, too. Suddenly they felt that up to £400 was normal because most of the frames were that price.

The Law of Contrast

There is a principle in human perception, the contrast principle, that affects the way we see the difference between two things that are presented one after another. The contrast principle is well established in the field of psychophysics and applies to all sorts of perceptions.

If a customer looks at a £400 product and then a £300 product, the £400 product seems expensive to them, and the £300 product seems "not expensive." But if instead, they look at the £300 product first, followed by a £200 product, the same £300 product that would have seemed "not expensive" in the first scenario now seems "expensive." This is the law of contrast at work.

You can control what your customers, and your staff, perceive as expensive by the stock that you carry and the pricing that you use. If you want to sell more £400 products but the majority of your products are less than £300, then customers and staff will struggle because the £400 will be perceived as expensive by most customers and most staff.

The way to do it is to have the majority of products at the price point you want to be selling at. Take £400 for example. Then get rid of your lower-end products. Or at least get them off display. Hide them away, and get them out only if you really need to. And also start selling £600 and £800 products as well. These make your £400 products seem "not expensive." This is the contrast principle. You'll be amazed how it works.

How an £895 Frame Was Perceived as "Not Expensive"

Mike is a great client. A successful businessman, in his late 40s, with a large head, so he finds it difficult to find glasses that fit him. But he likes his eyewear. We give him a call whenever we get something in that we think would be up his street. And he came in recently to look at a few frames from a new line. And as expected he liked them. The frames were at the more expensive end of the spectrum, ranging from £700 to £1500. He ended up buying a frame that was £895. He said he was happy that he liked the £895 frame and not the expensive ones! The law of contrast and how the products were presented meant that the £895 frame was seen as not expensive.

Avoid Price Comparison

When we raised prices, we also took steps to avoid price comparison. We work with niche eyewear brands that are exclusive, individual, not worn by the masses, and not so easy to find (hence avoiding price shopping). But more important than this, we attract clients who are not concerned with price shopping. And we have created a process (the Eyewear Style Consultation) that practically makes it impossible to price compare.

How We Attract Properly Prepared Prospects

Prospects *apply* online for a free Eyewear Style Consultation. They submit their information and fill in a form with their motivations for applying. They tell us what problems they are having and what they want help with. Our "Client Experience Co-ordinator" calls them to qualify them and book them in for an Eyewear Style Consultation if we're a good fit.

When we first launched the free consultation offer, we had a very low conversion rate from these people who were coming in for the free consultation. They were price sensitive, shopping around, planning to buy online, etc. All the same old problems we were trying to avoid. Staff would get frustrated about feeling obliged to give these people the free consultation they were promised even though they knew it was a waste of time.

That was our initial feedback from trying this. At that stage all the prospect had to do was complete the application form and book their appointment. So we quickly added the extra step of the phone call to qualify or disqualify them. We framed it like this: "A short phone call is required before we can schedule your Eyewear Style Consultation. Once we receive your application, we will call you to explain how the eyewear styling process works, what information to bring, and what to expect. This call will take five to ten minutes." And that extra step totally transformed the results so that we now convert over 80% of the consultations.

The phone call is done in a relaxed, friendly, conversational manner. Even when we disqualify a prospect (because of budget or some other reason), it is done in a helpful way and the prospect generally seems happy that we have been open and honest with them and explained why we are not a good fit for what they want. We have saved them the time and hassle and potential embarrassment of coming in for an hourlong consultation only to find out the price is out of reach for them at the last minute. It's also extremely useful on the phone call to have the information that they gave us on their application form about their "problem." That is where these calls begin. We follow the problem—agitate—solution formula.

The latest thing that we are testing is changing our offer from "free consultation" to "'free book." I've written a book for consumers called *The Definitive Guide to Choosing Glasses That Make You Look Good*. (See Figure 36.1 on page 374.) The plan is to delay the sale by offering the book as the first step to educate and prepare the prospect and then drive them to a free consultation after a series of followups by email and real mail.

The other reasons I had for writing this book were many. We are already using it as a tool for referrals by giving clients copies when they collect their new glasses. It obviously adds to our expert positioning and will make it easier to get PR coverage for the practice. And I'm also going to use it as the offer we promote to attract new clients from direct mail as well as advertisements.

A book is a great way to build a relationship with a customer before they ever step foot in your business. And when they do come in, they are predetermined to buy from you. The book does a lot of the work and makes everyone else's job easier.

Showing Up Differently

The building I am sitting in as I write this used to be home to the Bank of England. It's an old and impressive building. And it has a prestigious address. It was the focal point for the city's financial and professional community and the commercial heart of the whole region. The banking hall itself is an architectural masterpiece and a Grade 1 listed building. It is a luxurious and grand environment.

Dan Kennedy talks about "showing up differently," and that is really what this building does for us. (See Figures 36.2 and 36.3)

FIGURE 36.1

The Definitive Guide To Choosing Glasses That Make You Look Good

The 6 Common Eyewear Buying Mistakes & How To Avoid Them

Conor Heaney

BSc Hons MC Optom - Jones And Co. Styling Opticians

FIGURE **36.2**

FIGURE **36.3**

We don't look like an optician is *supposed* to look. And it works very well for us. Rather than relying on location and passing footfall, we have created a "destination practice." We incorporate the uniqueness and character of the building into the experience we create for clients. It becomes a part of the story we tell.

The building is a really obvious example, but the principle of showing up differently is at work in everything we do. Even down to the language we use. We sell "eyewear" not glasses. We have an eyewear "gallery," not a glasses store. People don't look at glasses, they have an "Eyewear Style Consultation."

Make Your Business about Something

Make your business about something. Make it stand for something. Design it in a way that taps into people's emotions and values.

At Jones And Co. Styling Opticians I made the business about something more than the core deliverables. I made it about style, individuality, exclusivity, expertise, personal service, and relationships.

For example, we create exclusive events where we fly in the world's finest eyewear designers to showcase their collections for our clients (including eyewear in the £10,000-plus range crafted from precious metals and personalized with diamonds).

And our clients tell stories *about* us. Stories about the events. About the building. About the drinks we serve. About the Eyewear Style Consultation. About the way we source our exclusive frames. About our expertise.

What I'm most proud of is creating an exclusive and aspirational business that is expertly balanced with "real" relationships. In my experience most affluent consumers enjoy dealing with real people and being treated as a real person. They don't want to be seen as a walking wallet. We talk colloquially with clients. Just because they desire the finer things in life doesn't mean they want stiff, posh, snooty, impersonal service. Yes, the service standards are world class—but they are delivered in a "real" way.

Make Your Business for Someone

We designed the practice to be *for* successful people who see themselves as individuals. *For* people who value style, service, and expertise. We are *for* people who want to look good and feel good in eyewear.

Inherent in your USP must be a deep understanding of your ideal customer and how you make their life better. So my business is 100% focused on a very particular type of customer. We understand them and know them better than most people know their closest friend. We have a deep understanding of them, and that allows us to create a business that appeals to them. We build real relationships with them. We know who they really are. And they know who we are and what we stand for. We believe in the same things. We fit. We know what their values, hopes, dreams, fears, pains, and desires are.

We produce a successful monthly print newsletter for our clients called *"Jones And Co. LIFE."* (See Figure 36.4 on page 378.) Not a day goes by in the practice without clients mentioning the newsletter, commenting on a particular story and sharing their own version of that story, or just saying that they enjoy receiving it.

The newsletter is one of the ways we *show* our clients that we understand them and that we are like them. I put a lot of personality into the newsletter. I share stories from my life that are relevant, and I try to strike a cord with the client who is reading it. I want them nodding their head in agreement. I want them thinking, "That's so true. I feel the same way. These Jones

FIGURE 36.4

JONES LIFE
AND CO.

Volume 1, Issue 7   by Conor Heaney

Feeling Guilty

I'm concerned people might start to think I'm some kind of slave driver.

In fact my mum will be appalled when she reads this.

I grew up as one of 4 brothers with only 1 sister. So for the boys in our house, we were always taught that girls are different from boys. And we should be nice to them and look after them. "You only have one little sister" was a common reminder from my parents in case we forgot. (Even though my sister Megan was a tom-boy and better at football than the rest of us combined).

I was raised to always walk on the outside of the pavement to protect any female I'm accompanying. I'm not sure if that was to protect them from splashes if a car drives through a puddle, or to actually take the impact first if a car veers on to the footpath. No matter what the reasoning, to this day I physically can't walk on the inside of the pavement. I always move Catherine or the kids to the inside. Old-fashioned.

However I'm not sure on the etiquette of letting young ladies do the heavy lifting of putting out A-board signs. And it is something I am currently battling with feelings of guilt over.

You see, every morning at a few minutes before 9 o'clock, 2 or 3 stylishly dressed, young, professional women emerge from number 82 King Street, each laden down with a chrome pole and base. These poles must weigh 30 kilos. The thing is heavy. After 2 or 3 trips to take everything out,

www.jonesand.co   82 King Street, Manchester M2 4WQ   t: 0161 834 7798   ①

And Co. people are just like me." It has to be an entertaining read, but what I'm really doing is showing them that my belief system is the same as their belief system in certain, important areas. And that builds trust and stronger relationships.

An unintended bonus from this print monthly newsletter has been that I have a stronger relationship with many more clients than before, even though I now work less and less in the practice, and I see very few clients. But when I am in the practice, I am bombarded with praise and personal conversations from clients who feel they know me even if I have never actually met them. It's a great strategy for getting free from working "in" the business while still keeping a strong relationship with your clients. They still feel that connection with you even if you are not there, and it also gives them a route to give feedback direct to you, if you choose.

Constant Testing

If I said we got here in one fell swoop, I'd be lying. This wasn't easy. There were a few bumps in the road. Obstacles we didn't foresee until they were upon us. But it was all part of the learning and testing process. It also meant when we found a solution, we understood why it worked and also knew five other ways NOT to do it.

Expect a Few Bumps in the Road

The first Eyewear Style Consultation didn't work. The first funnel attracted mainly time wasters and people that were not a good fit for us.

Removing stock from display met with lots of resistance from would-be browsers until we figured out effective scripts to lead them along with our sales process. This motivated us to create effective scripts and fast!

In our attempt to be exclusive, the language we used early on in our marketing was a bit too pretentious. I know there are subtle differences in the U.K. market compared to the U.S. market, and it took us a little while to find our sweet spot.

Generally, every step of the way involved initial resistance, poor results, tweaking it until it was effective, followed by success. But without those first few clumsy, awkward attempts at each new thing, we would never have discovered the successful way to do it.

The lesson here is that nothing happens with any idea until you try it. Then you get feedback. And by then you're already moving, so it's easier to adjust and tweak and change direction until you make it work.

CONOR HEANEY is a practicing optometrist and director of Jones And Co. Styling Opticians. His practice has one of the highest average sale values in his industry—more than five times the industry average. He has refined a unique approach to retail in his optical practice. See the practice at www.jonesand.co. For business owners in retail or optics, you can discover more at www.conorheaney.com/DanKennedy.

About the
Author

DAN S. KENNEDY is a multimillionaire serial entrepreneur, strategic marketing and direct-marketing advisor, and one of the highest-paid direct-response copywriters in America, working in all media. To communicate directly with Mr. Kennedy about his availability for speaking engagements, consulting, or copywriting, fax to (602) 269-3113 or write to Kennedy Inner Circle Inc., 15433 N. Tatum Blvd. #104, Phoenix, Arizona 85032. Mr. Kennedy famously does not use email or other online communication.

Other Books by the Author

In the No B.S. series, published by Entrepreneur Press
  No B.S. Price Strategy

No B.S. Guide to Brand-Building by Direct Response

No B.S. Guide to Marketing to Boomers & Seniors

No B.S. Trust-Based Marketing

No B.S. Direct Marketing to NON-Direct Marketing Businesses

No B.S. Ruthless Management of People and Profits, Second Edition

No B.S. Grassroots Marketing

No B.S. Business Success in the New Economy

No B.S. Sales Success in the New Economy

No B.S. Wealth Attraction in the New Economy

No B.S. Time Management for Entrepreneurs, Second Edition

Other Books by Dan Kennedy

The Ultimate Marketing Plan, 4th Edition—20th Anniversary Edition (Adams Media)

The Ultimate Sales Letter, 4th Edition—20th Anniversary Edition (Adams Media)

Making Them Believe: The 21 Principles and Lost Secrets of Dr. J.R. Brinkley-Style Marketing (GKIC/MJ)

Make 'Em Laugh & Take Their Money (GKIC/MJ)

My Unfinished Business Autobiographical Essays (Advantage)

The New Psycho-Cybernetics with Dr. Maxwell Maltz (Prentice-Hall)

Other Books, Contributed to by Dan Kennedy

Uncensored Sales Strategies by Sydney Barrows with Dan Kennedy (EP)

Marketing Miracles: Odd, Unusual, Breakthrough Strategies That Build Great Businesses (CelebrityPress)

Stand Apart: The World's Leading Experts Reveal Their Secrets to Help Your Business Stand Out from the Crowd to Achieve Ultimate Success (CelebrityPress)

Book the Business: How to Make Big Money with Your Book without Even Selling a Single Copy by Adam Witty & Dan Kennedy (Advantage)

The Official Get Rich Guide to Information Marketing: Build a Million Dollar Buisness Within 12 Months by Robert Skrob (IMA/EP.www.info-marketing.org)

Book Information at: www.NoBSBooks.com

Newsletters Published by GKIC.com

No B.S. Marketing Letter

No B.S. Marketing to the Affluent Letter

Marketing Gold Letter

Diamond Marketing Letter

No B.S. INFO-Marketing Letter

Other Newsletters

Look Over Dan's Shoulder Copywriting Letter (Lillo Publishing. 330-922-9833)

Marketing Your Services for Freelancers (Lillo Publishing/ American Writers & Artists)

Index